THE POETRY OF

DEREK WALCOTT

1948–2013

THE POETRY OF

DEREK WALCOTT

1948–2013

Derek Walcott

SELECTED BY GLYN MAXWELL

FARRAR, STRAUS AND GIROUX

NEW YORK

FARRAR, STRAUS AND GIROUX
18 West 18th Street, New York 10011

The first line of "Sea Grapes" has been modified by the author.

Library of Congress Cataloging-in-Publication Data
Walcott, Derek.
  [Poems. Selections]
  The Poetry of Derek Walcott 1948–2013 / Derek Walcott ; [selected by
the poet Glyn Maxwell]. — First edition.
      pages   cm
  Includes index.
  ISBN 978-0-374-12561-5 (hardcover)
  I. Maxwell, Glyn, 1962–   II. Title.

PR9272.9.W3 A6 2014
811'.54—dc23
                                                    2013034997

Designed by Gretchen Achilles

Farrar, Straus and Giroux books may be purchased for educational, business, or promotional use. For
information on bulk purchases, please contact the Macmillan Corporate and Premium Sales Department at
1-800-221-7945, extension 5442, or write to specialmarkets@macmillan.com.

www.fsgbooks.com
www.twitter.com/fsgbooks • www.facebook.com/fsgbooks

1   3   5   7   9   10   8   6   4   2

The editor would like to thank Maria Cristina Fumagalli, Leanne Haynes,
and Caryl Phillips for their assistance.

To Elizabeth, Anna, and Peter

CONTENTS

Owing to limitations of space, the epic poem *Omeros* (1990) has not been included in this collection, but it is available from FSG (ISBN: 978-0-374-52350-3).

25 Poems

(1949)

The fishermen rowing homeward in the dusk,
Do not consider the stillness through which they move.
So I since feelings drown, should no more ask
What twilight and safety your strong hands gave.
And the night, urger of the old lies
Winked at by stars that sentry the humped hills,
Should hear no words of faring forth, for time knows
That bitter and sly sea, and love raises walls.

Yet others, who now watch my progress outward
To a sea which is crueler than any word
Of love, may see in me the calm my voyage makes,
Parting new water in the antique hoax.
And the secure from thinking may climb safe to liners,
Hearing small rumors of paddlers drowned near stars.

IN MY EIGHTEENTH YEAR

for Warwick Walcott

Having measured the years today by the calendar
That tells your seventeenth death, I stayed until
It was the honest time to remember
How the house has lived with and without you well.
And I do not chide death's hand,
Nor can I hurl death taunts or tantrums
Because the washing faiths my father walked are no more light,
And all the gulls that were tall as his dreams
Are one with his light rotting in the sand.

Nor can I hurl taunts or tantrums.
Or blast with syllables the yellow grave
Under the crooked tree where all Lazarus is history.
But greater than most is death's gift, that can
Behind the bright dust that was the skeleton,
(Who drank the wine and believed the blessed bread)
Can make us see the forgotten price of man
Shine from the perverse beauty of the dead.

We started from places that saw no gay carracks wrecked
And where our green solitudes did not look deciduous;
And afternoons after schools, well our aunt Sorrow came,
Disciplined, erect,

To teach us writing. Outside boyhoods chased their leather
Football along the level glare of playing fields, and
Sweated and cursed amiably, while we sat, with slow tears
Shaping the heart's weather.

It is too early or too late, to ask if we were gifted
With this pain that saw all, yet was no man's remedy,
Blessed or cursed with vision that saw growth's long confusion
That time has not lifted?

We learned to hate from too much rumor, friends and masters,
The bully who jeered because we could not swim at nine,
And the blond child, the one with too much money; then liked
These eccentric wasters

Of time, who could not see like us their deep affliction;
Of whom we envy now industrious idleness, their
Ability to forget or postpone death as an
Inevitable fiction.

And love came, cracked the hearts it joined just as love ought,
Was our tallest delight and our deepest affliction,
Taught us more than philosophy did that we wanted
Freedom from, not of, thought.

Where you rot under the strict gray industry
Of cities of fog and winter fevers, I
Send this to remind you of personal islands
For which Gauguins sicken, and to explain
How I have grown to know your passionate
Talent and this wild love of landscape.

It is April and already no doubt for you
As the journals report, the prologues of spring
Appear behind the rails of city parks,
Or the late springtime must be publishing
Pink apologies along the black wet branch
To men in overcoats, who will conceal
The lines of songs leaping behind their pipes.

And you must find it difficult to imagine
This April as a season where the tide burns
Black; leaves crack into ashes from the drought;
A dull red burning like heart's desolation.
The roads are white with dust and the leaves
Of the trees have a nervous spinsterish quiet.
And walking under the trees today I saw
The canoes that are marked with comic names
Daylight, St. Mary Magdalene, Gay Girl.

Made me think of your chief scenes for painting
And days of instruction at the soft villa
When we watched your serious experience, learning.
And you must understand how I am lost
To see my gifts rotting under this season
You who defined with an imperious palette
The several postures of this virginal island

You understand how I am lost to have
Your brush's zeal and not to be explicit.

But the grace we avoid, that gave us vision,
Discloses around curves an architecture whose
Sunday logic we can take or refuse,
And leaves to the simple soul its own decision
After landscapes, palms, cathedrals or the hermit-thrush
And wins my love now and gives it a silence
That would inform the blind world of its flesh.

After that hot gospeler had leveled all but the churched sky,
I wrote the tale by tallow of a city's death by fire.
Under a candle's eye that smoked in tears, I
Wanted to tell in more than wax of faiths that were snapped like wire.

All day I walked abroad among the rubbled tales,
Shocked at each wall that stood on the street like a liar,
Loud was the bird-rocked sky, and all the clouds were bales
Torn open by looting and white in spite of the fire;

By the smoking sea, where Christ walked, I asked why
Should a man wax tears when his wooden world fails.

In town leaves were paper, but the hills were a flock of faiths
To a boy who walked all day, each leaf was a green breath

Rebuilding a love I thought was dead as nails,
Blessing the death and the baptism by fire.

As John to Patmos, among the rocks and the blue live air, hounded
His heart to peace, as here surrounded
By the strewn silver on waves, the wood's crude hair, the rounded
Breasts of the milky bays, palms, flocks, and the green and dead

Leaves, the sun's brass coin on my cheek, where
Canoes brace the sun's strength, as John in that bleak air,
So am I welcomed richer by these blue scapes Greek there,
So I will voyage no more from home, may I speak here.

This island is heaven away from the dustblown blood of cities,
See the curve of bay, watch the straggling flower, pretty is
The winged sound of trees, the sparse powdered sky when lit is
The night. For beauty has surrounded
These black children, and freed them of homeless ditties.

As John to Patmos, among each love-leaping air,
O slave, soldier, worker under red trees sleeping, hear
What I swear now, as John did,
To praise lovelong the living and the brown dead.

I with legs crossed along the daylight watch
The variegated fists of clouds that gather over
The uncouth features of this my prone island.

Meanwhile the steamers that disturb our lost horizons prove
Us lost.
Found only
In tourist booklets, behind ardent binoculars;
Found in the pale reflection of eyes
That know cities, and think us here happy.

Time creeps over the patient who are too long patient.
So I, who have made one choice,
Discover that my boyhood has gone over.

And my life, too early of course for the profound cigarette,
The turned doorhandle, the knife turning
In the bowels of the hours, must not be made public
Until I have learnt to suffer
In accurate iambics.

I go of course through all the isolated acts,
Make a holiday of situations;
Straighten my tie and fix important jaws,
And note the living images
Of flesh that saunter through the eye.

Until from all I turn to think how
In the middle of the journey through my life
O how I came upon you, my
Reluctant leopard of the slow eyes.

Epitaph
for the Young:
XII Cantos

(1949)

Voyaging,
     In the first strong wind, gathering purpose,
We observed the wreckage drifting at morning,
Signifying
     Land, and flotsam of other purposes,
And then the sun,
   White birds, blue wave arched with porpoise,
To the left
      A rim of fragile islands, virginal,
      Noise of leaves in sails, purple underside of gulls,
      Fishpots and canoes,
Other existence sharpening the senses.

Talk less of solitudes, corners of lonely talent,
Behind the meek applause and mental skirmishes
Solitudes are sucked like sails and dreams will drown.
The ghosts vanish, stars fall like eyes,
And only sour legends of the sea and oily winds remain
To sprawl my boyhood on a dung of words.
When I see children walk a light of mildness,
Wearing in their flesh the hope I was,
I cry to time of the hoax of martyrdoms,
I would warn, fearing
To break old enchantments. A heart cracked early
Never heals.
O wrong river, salt as tears.
The years bring honors, prefect, wise at school,
Solemn investigation of inch-high corruptions;
Responsibility comes long before
The first shaving set.

Islands curved like the fling of a stone to sea,
Beach white at morning, a cloudless sky,
The first island unhaunted, quiet.
We put into a bay with a wide beach eager to land,
There was

                No tenant sound of bird in the dry season,
                No awful ruin, broken temples in the clearing,
                Or sudden departure from camp, fire still smoking,
                No wailing bird or marauder,
                No cracked crucifix, only

The doomed lushness of a green mind
Beginning to nurse its death with images, ambitions,
Unwilling to exile the fine anxiety.
The gifted, seeking out gnarled holes of solitude,
Separate in crowds, lonely and laughing,
Transfer their hate of self to love of objects,
Early are nursed by nature to the hermitage,
Instinctive always with migratory companions,
Nursing neurosis like a potted plant.
Younger, painting meant honesty to us,
Sexless as statue we felt her passionate mouth
Bury us in desire for freedom. Rebellion
Is the death I suffer from; that hope
I fished like dreams at noon, prevents and stores me up
And will not let me live like animal.

Not with excesses, but thoughtless and satisfied,
While like an arrowing pylon by hardening talent
Shot to the clouds, the boy I was is weakening.
I hear the power I possess knock at my roots,
And see the tower of myself whose height attracts
Destruction, begin a crazy crack and waltz of ruin.

In that villa, overlooking the town
We did not learn much, but we were secure

On Saturdays, in the smell of oil and paint.
With the dry leaves rustling outside like the sea,
Like wind in sails, leaves scraping along the roof like rats.
Outside
The hill looked on a neutral summer,
The low peninsula, the smooth invitation of the bay,
The rocks warm, dotting the slope,
The sheep punctual and pastoral crossed the hillside grass,
And then at evening again the broad light dying
From the exiling sea.
In a seclusion that only tempted thought,
All actions inform retreat is safest.
Supine or pained, thought troubles us, sirs,
When I am twisted in bed like yesterday's paper.

FROM

Poems

(1957)

Time is the guide that brings all to a crux,
Who hangs his map will move
Out of the mere geology of books,
To see his valley's palm wrinkled with loves.

These sleep like islands, and I watch sleep lick
Their arms' flung promontories, remove
With individual erasure all their love
Of muscle. Now towards the sea there, I look

Where rippling signatures of water break
Over the sighing dormitories of
The drowned whom soft winds move,
Here these inquiet mouths like rivers speak.

Or from these boys, who in the uncertain luck
Of sleep, expect to live,
The breath curls from their separated lips like
Mists of time that over valleys grieve.

O child as guiltless as the grass,
From that green country of your eyes,
I cannot tell you how you pass
Into this country, where the skies
Are ominous all afternoon;
Into the cold and adult lies
Around a naked guiltless past;
Into this country where the leaves
Drop in incalculable waste
Of what was young and therefore dies;
Into this country where the light,
Being kind and murderous to the trees
Will not teach itself how to last
But bleeds again into the night
Then breaks into a pox of stars.
O boy, whose breath, however slight
Shakes my grown tree of veins to toss
And bury innocence in leaves,
And shatters an enchanted glass,
And cuts the mooring of a kite.
O boy, my nephew, wasting these
As the day spends its coins of light,
Ghost of my growing, sleep, while night
Locks up in dark the light that kills,
Till time, a thief at your barred eyes
Pries open bright interstices.

He walked a bridge where
Gulls' wings brush wires and sound
A harp of steel in air,
Above the river's running wound.
Natural and architectural despair.
Life was a package in his restless hand,
Traffic of barges below, while wind
Rumpled his hair like an affectionate teacher.

Liberty offered God a match.
Dusk smoked. There was no cure,
The bridge, like grief whined in the air
Marrying banks with a swift signature.
The bums spat, cursed, scratched.
O distant Mexico, Quetzalcoatl
Not, by gum, Wrigley's and Spearmint, and spitting jaws
O the red desert with nomadic laws.

Bye, bye to Brooklyn,
The bay's lace collar of puritan America
And bye, bye, the steel thin
Bridges over barges, the wharf's hysteria,
The canyons of stone.
The whirlpool smiled—"Knowledge is death alone."

The sea was only ritual, he had
Already seen complexity go mad
In the asylum, metaphor. He stood
From Brooklyn, on the brink
Of being, a straw doll blown
From Manhattan to Mexico to sink
Into that sea where vast deliriums drown.

Behind the stained water of the lucent panes, they
Bend their white monotony of prayers,

Their lips turn pages of their meditation,
Selling identity for coins of faith.

A life devoted to whispers. Are they
Secure from doubt, do work and prayers

Postpone the heretic, Thought, the anemic meditation,
Chapped hands and a prayer's palm is all their faith.

Does that one in gardens, cultivating rows of prayers
To the Little Flower, remember Wales or Mayo? They

Are expressionless as gowns, their laughter
Faith makes hysteria, deepening meditation.

Early to rise and hard to die, does the bell's cracked faith
Weary or win, do the young nun's prayers

Offend the wrinkled sister who clucks at meditation
As interrupting cooking? O how assured are they?

Admirable sacrifice, since they are human, that they
Young in direction, bend sapling strong to faith,

Faith. A worn carpet under an old nun's feet, and prayers
A novice's candle nervous with meditation.

The peanut barrows whistle, and the ladies with perfumes
And prophylactics included in the expenses
Hiss in a minor key, the desperate think of rooms
      With white utensils.

Walking near parks, where the trees, wearing white socks
Shake over the illicit liaison under the leaves,
Silent on the heraldic sky, the statue grieves
      That the locks

Have still to be tested, and stores shut up their eyes
At the beggars and hoodlums, when the skin breaks
From the city and the owls, and maggots and lice,
      Strike alight the old hates.

THE WRATH OF GOD flames like a neon sign on railings, they
Scatter their cargo of sleepless fleas,
The nightclubs wink like sin, and money hushes
      Heals all disease.

By lanternlight the pocomania of the Second Coming when
De Lawd say Him going tyake us by the hand, or in antiphony
A calypso wafts from the pubs, and Ulysses again
      Postpones Penelope.

The theaters are wounded with midnight, and the lymph
Of the innocent and guilty pour from their sides,
The housewife, the young lovers, the soldier, the nymph-
      Omaniac in their tides.

And always to the alone, the stone villas with the prosaic
Essay on façades, wink out their yellow welcomes, one by one,

And down dog-forsaken boulevards, the Arab mosaic
      Of stars, the Morse of doom,

Point some to a wife warm bed, or the arms of lice
Kneeling to the shout in the street, and sleep's equation
Lays the black down with the white, and death at half the price
      Suggests her house.

FROM

*In a
Green Night*

(1948–60)

A wind is ruffling the tawny pelt
Of Africa. Kikuyu, quick as flies
Batten upon the bloodstreams of the veldt.
Corpses are scattered through a paradise.
But still the worm, colonel of carrion, cries:
"Waste no compassion on these separate dead"
Statistics justify and scholars seize
The salients of colonial policy.
What is that to the white child hacked in bed?
To savages, expendable as Jews?

Threshed out by beaters, the long rushes break
In a white dust of ibises whose cries
Have wheeled since civilization's dawn
From the parched river or beast-teeming plain;
The violence of beast on beast is read
As natural law, but upright man
Seeks his divinity with inflicting pain.
Delirious as these worried beasts, his wars
Dance to the tightened carcass of a drum,
While he calls courage still, that native dread
Of the white peace contracted by the dead.

Again brutish necessity wipes its hands
Upon the napkin of a dirty cause, again
A waste of our compassion, as with Spain.
The gorilla wrestles with the superman.

I who am poisoned with the blood of both,
Where shall I turn, divided to the vein?
I who have cursed
The drunken officer of British rule, how choose

Between this Africa and the English tongue I love?
Betray them both, or give back what they give?
How can I face such slaughter and be cool?
How can I turn from Africa and live?

RUINS OF A GREAT HOUSE

though our longest sun sets at right declensions and makes but winter arches, it
cannot be long before we lie down in darkness, and have our light in ashes . . .

BROWNE, *Urn Burial*

Stones only, the *disjecta membra* of this Great House,
Whose mothlike girls are mixed with candledust,
Remain to file the lizard's dragonish claws;
The mouths of those gate cherubs streaked with stain.
Axle and coachwheel silted under the muck
Of cattle droppings.

         Three crows flap for the trees,
And settle, creaking the eucalyptus boughs.
A smell of dead limes quickens in the nose
The leprosy of Empire.

        "Farewell, green fields"
        "Farewell, ye happy groves!"

Marble as Greece, like Faulkner's South in stone,
Deciduous beauty prospered and is gone;
But where the lawn breaks in a rash of trees
A spade below dead leaves will ring the bone
Of some dead animal or human thing
Fallen from evil days, from evil times.

It seems that the original crops were limes
Grown in the silt that clogs the river's skirt;
The imperious rakes are gone, their bright girls gone,
The river flows, obliterating hurt.

I climbed a wall with the grill ironwork
Of exiled craftsmen, protecting that great house
From guilt, perhaps, but not from the worm's rent,
Nor from the padded cavalry of the mouse.
And when a wind shook in the limes I heard
What Kipling heard; the death of a great empire, the abuse
Of ignorance by Bible and by sword.

A green lawn, broken by low walls of stone
Dipped to the rivulet, and pacing, I thought next
Of men like Hawkins, Walter Raleigh, Drake,
Ancestral murderers and poets, more perplexed
In memory now by every ulcerous crime.
The world's green age then was a rotting lime
Whose stench became the charnel galleon's text.
The rot remains with us, the men are gone.
But, as dead ash is lifted in a wind,
That fans the blackening ember of the mind,
My eyes burned from the ashen prose of Donne.

Ablaze with rage, I thought
Some slave is rotting in this manorial lake,
And still the coal of my compassion fought:
That Albion too, was once
A colony like ours, "a piece of the continent, a part of the main"
Nook-shotten, rook o'er blown, deranged
By foaming channels, and the vain expense
Of bitter faction.

   All in compassion ends
So differently from what the heart arranged:
"as well as if a manor of thy friend's . . ."

CHAPTER I

la rivière dorée . . .

The marl white road, the Dorée rushing cool
Through gorges of green cedars, like the sound
Of infant voices from the Mission School,
Like leaves like dim seas in the mind; ici, Choiseul.
The stone cathedral echoes like a well,
Or as a sunken sea-cave, carved, in sand.
Touring its Via Dolorosa I tried to keep
That chill flesh from my memory when I found
A Sancta Teresa in her nest of light;
The skirts of fluttered bronze, the uplifted hand,
The cherub, shaft upraised, parting her breast.
Teach our philosophy the strength to reach
Above the navel; black bodies, wet with light,
Rolled in the spray as I strolled up the beach.

CHAPTER II

"Qu'un sang impur . . ."

Cosimo de Chrétien controlled a boardinghouse.
His maman managed him. No. 13.
Rue St. Louis. It had a court, with rails,
A perroquet, a curio-shop where you
Saw black dolls and an old French barquentine
Anchored in glass. Upstairs, the family sword,
The rusting ikon of a withered race,
Like the first angel's kept its pride of place,
Reminding the bald count to keep his word
Never to bring the lineage to disgrace.

Devouring Time, which blunts the Lion's claws,
Kept Cosimo, count of curios, fairly chaste,
For Mama's sake, for hair oil, and for whist;
Peering from balconies for his tragic twist.

CHAPTER III

la belle qui fut . . .

Miss Rossignol lived in the lazaretto
For Roman Catholic crones; she had white skin,
And underneath it, fine, old-fashioned bones;
She flew like bats to vespers every twilight,
The living Magdalen of Donatello;
And tipsy as a bottle when she stalked
On stilted legs to fetch the morning milk,
In a black shawl harnessed by rusty brooches.
My mother warned us how that flesh knew silk
Coursing a green estate in gilded coaches.
While Miss Rossignol, in the cathedral loft
Sang to her one dead child, a tattered saint
Whose pride had paupered beauty to this witch
Who was so fine once, whose hands were so soft.

CHAPTER IV

"Dance of death"

Outside I said, "He's a damned epileptic
Your boy, El Greco! Goya, he don't lie."
Doc laughed: "Let's join the real epileptics."
Two of the girls looked good. The Indian said
That rain affects the trade. In the queer light
We all looked green. The beer and all looked green.
One draped an arm around me like a wreath.

The next talked politics. "Our mother earth"
I said. "The great republic in whose womb
The dead outvote the quick." "Y'all too obscene"
The Indian laughed. "Y'all college boys ain't worth
The trouble." We entered the bare room.
In the rain, walking home, was worried, but Doc said:
"Don't worry, kid, the wages of sin is birth."

CHAPTER V

"moeurs anciennes"

The fête took place one morning in the heights
For the approval of some anthropologist.
The priests objected to such savage rites
In a Catholic country; but there was a twist
As one of the fathers was himself a student
Of black customs; it was quite ironic.
They lead sheep to the rivulet with a drum,
Dancing with absolutely natural grace
Remembered from the dark past whence we come.
The whole thing was more like a bloody picnic.
Bottles of white rum and a brawling booth.
They tie the lamb up, then chop off the head,
And ritualists take turns drinking the blood.
Great stuff, old boy; sacrifice, moments of truth.

CHAPTER VI

Poopa, da' was a fête! I mean it had
Free rum free whiskey and some fellars beating
Pan from one of them band in Trinidad
And everywhere you turn was people eating
And drinking and don't name me but I think

They catch his wife with two tests up the beach
While he drunk quoting Shelley with "Each
Generation has its *angst*, but we has none"
And wouldn't let a comma in edgewise.
(Black writer chap, one of them Oxbridge guys.)
And it was round this part once that the heart
Of a young child was torn from it alive
By two practitioners of native art,
But that was long before this jump and jive.

CHAPTER VII

lotus eater . . .

"Maingot," the fishermen called that pool blocked by
Increasing filth that piled between ocean
And jungle, with a sighing grove
Of dry bamboo, its roots freckled with light
Like feathers fallen from a migratory sky.
Beyond that, the village. Through urine-stunted trees
A mud path wriggled like a snake in flight.
Franklin gripped the bridge-stanchions with a hand
Trembling with fever. Each spring, memories
Of his own country where he could not die
Assaulted him. He watched the malarial light
Shiver the canes. In the tea-colored pool, tadpoles
Seemed happy in their element. Poor, black souls.
He shook himself. Must breed, drink, rot with motion.

CHAPTER VIII

In the Hotel Miranda, 10 Grass St., who fought
The Falangists en la guerra civil, at the hour
Of bleeding light and beads of crimson dew,

This exile, with the wry face of a Jew
Lets dust powder his pamphlets; crook't
Fingers clutch a journal to his shirt.
The eye is glacial; mountainous, the hook'd
Nose down which an ant, *caballo*, rides. Besides
As pious fleas explore a seam of dirt
The sunwashed body, past the age of sweat
Sprawls like a hero, curiously inert.
Near him a dish of olives has turned sour.
Above the children's street cries, a girl plays
A marching song not often sung these days.

CHAPTER IX

"le loupgarou"

A curious tale that threaded through the town
Through graying women sewing under eaves,
Was how his greed had brought old Le Brun down,
Greeted by slowly shutting jalousies
When he approached them in white-linen suit,
Pink glasses, cork hat, and tap-tapping cane,
A dying man licensed to sell sick fruit,
Ruined by fiends with whom he'd made a bargain.
It seems one night, these Christian witches said,
He changed himself to an Alsatian hound,
A slavering lycanthrope hot on a scent,
But his own watchman dealt the thing a wound
Which howled and lugged its entrails, trailing wet
With blood back to its doorstep, almost dead.

CHAPTER X

"adieu foulard . . ."

I watched the island narrowing the fine
Writing of foam around the precipices then
The roads as small and casual as twine
Thrown on its mountains; I watched till the plane
Turned to the final north and turned above
The open channel with the gray sea between
The fishermen's islets until all that I love
Folded in cloud; I watched the shallow green
That broke in places where there would be reef,
The silver glinting on the fuselage, each mile
Dividing us and all fidelity strained
Till space would snap it. Then, after a while
I thought of nothing, nothing, I prayed, would change;
When we set down at Seawell it had rained.

Imprisoned in these wires of rain, I watch
This village stricken with a single street,
Each weathered shack leans on a wooden crutch,
Contented as a cripple in defeat.
Five years ago even poverty seemed sweet,
So azure and indifferent was this air,
So murmurous of oblivion the sea,
That any human action seemed a waste
The place seemed born for being buried there.
                    The surf explodes
In scissor-birds hunting the usual fish,
The rain is muddying unpaved inland roads,
So personal grief melts in the general wish.

The hospital is quiet in the rain.
A naked boy drives pigs into the bush.
The coast shudders with every surge. The beach
Admits a beaten heron. Filth and foam.
There in a belt of emerald light, a sail
Plunges and lifts between the crests of reef,
The hills are smoking in the vaporous light,
The rain seeps slowly to the core of grief.
It could not change its sorrows and be home.

It cannot change, though you become a man
Who would exchange compassion for a drink,
Now you are brought to where manhood began
Its separation from "the wounds that make you think."
And as this rain puddles the sand, it sinks
Old sorrows in the gutter of the mind,
Where is that passionate hatred that would help

The black, the despairing, the poor, by speech alone?
The fury shakes like wet leaves in the wind,
The rain beats on a brain hardened to stone.

For there is a time in the tide of the heart, when
Arrived at its anchor of suffering, a grave
Or a bed, despairing in action, we ask
O God, where is our home? For no one will save
The world from itself, though he walk among men.
On such shores where the foam
Murmurs oblivion of action, though they raise
No cry like herons stoned by the rain.

The passionate exiles believe it, but the heart
Is circled by sorrows, by its horror
And bitter devotion to home.
And the romantic nonsense ends at the bowsprit, shearing
But never arriving beyond the reef-shore foam,
Or the rain cuts us off from heaven's hearing.

Why blame the faith you have lost? Heaven remains
Where it is, in the hearts of these people,
In the womb of their church, though the rain's
Shroud is drawn across its steeple.
You are less than they are, for your truth
Consists of a general passion, a personal need,
Like that ribbed wreck, abandoned since your youth,
Washed over by the sour waves of greed.

The white rain draws its net along the coast,
A weak sun streaks the villages and beaches
And roads where laughing laborers come from shelter,
On heights where charcoal burners heap their days.
Yet in you it still seeps, blurring each boast

Your craft has made, obscuring words and features,
Nor have you changed from all of the known ways
To leave the mind's dark cave, the most
Accursed of God's self-pitying creatures.

De shepherd shrieves in Egyptian light,
The Abyssinian sweat has poured
From armpits and the graves of sight,
The black sheep of their blacker Lord.

De sisters shout and lift the floods
Of skirts where bark n' balm take root,
De bredren rattle withered gourds
Whose seeds are the forbidden fruit.

Remorse of poverty, love of God
Leap as one fire; prepare the feast,
Limp now is each divining rod,
Forgotten love, the double beast.

Above the banner and the crowd
The Lamb bleeds on the Coptic cross,
De Judah Lion roars to shroud
The sexual fires of Pentecost.

In jubilation of The Host,
The goatskin greets the bamboo fife
Have mercy on those furious lost
Whose life is praising death in life.

Now the blind beast butts on the wall,
Bodily delirium is death,
Now the worm curls upright to crawl
Between the crevices of breath.

Lower the wick, and fold the eye!
Anoint the shriveled limb with oil!
The waters of the moon are dry,
Derision of the body, toil.

Till Armageddon stains the fields,
And Babylon is yonder green,
Till the dirt-holy roller feels
The obscene breeding the unseen.

Till those black forms be angels white,
And Zion fills each eye.
High overhead the crow of night
Patrols eternity.

PARANG

Man, I suck me tooth when I hear
How dem croptime fiddlers lie,
And de wailing, kiss-me-arse flutes
That bring water to me eye!
O, when I t'ink how from young
I wasted time at de fêtes,
I could bawl in a red-eyed rage
For desire turned to regret,
Not knowing the truth that I sang
At parang and la comette.
Boy, every damned tune them tune
Of love that will last forever
Is the wax and the wane of the moon
Since Adam catch body-fever.

I old, so the young crop won't
Have these claws to reap their waist,
But I know "do more" from "don't"
Since the grave cry out "Make haste!"
This banjo world have one string
And all man does dance to that tune:
That love is a place in the bush
With music grieving from far,
As you look past her shoulder and see
Like her one tear afterwards
The falling of a fixed star.
Young men does bring love to disgrace
With remorseful, regretful words,
When flesh upon flesh was the tune
Since the first cloud raise up to disclose
The breast of the naked moon.

A CAREFUL PASSION

Hosanna, I build me house, Lawd,
De rain come wash it 'way.

Jamaican song

The Cruise Inn, at the city's edge,
Extends a breezy prospect of the sea
From tables fixed like islands near a hedge
Of foam-white flowers, and to deaden thought,
Marimba medleys from a local band,
To whose gay pace my love now drummed a hand.
I watched an old Greek freighter quitting port.

You hardly smell the salt breeze in this country
Except you come down to the harbor's edge.
Not like the smaller islands to the south.
There the green wave spreads on the printless beach.
I think of wet hair and a grape-red mouth.
The hand which wears her husband's ring, lies
On the table idly, a brown leaf on the sand.
The other brushes off two coupling flies.
"Sometimes I wonder if you've lost your speech."
Above our heads, the rusty cries
Of gulls revolving in the wind.
Wave after wave of memory silts the mind.

The gulls seem happy in their element.
We are lapped gently in the sentiment
Of a small table by the harbor's edge.
Hearts learn to die well that have died before.
My sun-puffed carcass, its eyes full of sand,
Rolls, spun by breakers on a southern shore.
"This way is best, before we both get hurt."

Look how I turn there, featureless, inert.
That weary phrase moves me to stroke her hand
While winds play with the corners of her skirt.

Better to lie, to swear some decent pledge,
To resurrect the buried heart again;
To twirl a glass and smile, as in pain,
At a small table by the water's edge.
"Yes, this is best, things might have grown much worse . . ."

And that is all the truth, it could be worse;
All is exhilaration on the eve,
Especially, when the self-seeking heart
So desperate for some mirror to believe
Finds in strange eyes the old original curse.
So cha cha cha, begin the long goodbyes,
Leave the half-tasted sorrows of each pledge,
As the salt wind brings brightness to her eyes,
At a small table by the water's edge.

I walk with her into the brightening street;
Stores rattling shut, as brief dusk fills the city.
Only the gulls, hunting the water's edge
Wheel like our lives, seeking something worth pity.

An old lady writes me in a spidery style,
Each character trembling, and I see a veined hand
Pellucid as paper, travelling on a skein
Of such frail thoughts its thread is often broken;
Or else the filament from which a phrase is hung
Dims to my sense, but caught, it shines like steel,
As touch a line, and the whole web will feel.
She describes my father, yet I forget her face
More easily than my father's yearly dying;
Of her I remember small, buttoned boots and the place
She kept in our wooden church on those Sundays
Whenever her strength allowed;
Gray haired, thin voiced, perpetually bowed.

"I am Mable Rawlins," she writes, "and know both your parents";
He is dead, Miss Rawlins, but God bless your tense:
"Your father was a dutiful, honest,
Faithful and useful person."
For such plain praise what fame is recompense?
"A horn-painter, he painted delicately on horn,
He used to sit around the table and paint pictures."
The peace of God needs nothing to adorn
It, no glory nor ambition.
"He is twenty-eight years buried," she writes, "he was called home,
And is, I am sure, doing greater work."

The strength of one frail hand in a dim room
Somewhere in Brooklyn, patient and assured,
Restores my sacred duty to the Word.
"Home, home," she can write, with such short time to live,
Alone as she spins the blessings of her years;
Not withered of beauty if she can bring such tears,

Nor withdrawn from the world that breaks its lovers so;
Heaven is to her the place where painters go,
All who bring beauty on frail shell or horn,
There was all made, thence their lux-mundi drawn,
Drawn, drawn, till the thread is resilient steel,
Lost though it seems in darkening periods,
And there they return to do work that is God's.

So this old lady writes, and again I believe,
I believe it all, and for no man's death I grieve.

K with quick laughter, honey skin and hair
and always money. In what beach shade, what year
has she so scented with her gentleness
I cannot watch bright water but think of her
and that fine morning when she sang o' rare
Ben's lyric of "the bag o' the bee"
and "the nard in the fire"
                              "nard in the fire"
against the salty music of the sea
the fresh breeze tangling each honey tress
                              and what year was the fire?
Girls' faces dim with time, Andreuille all gold . . .
Sunday. The grass peeps through the breaking pier.
Tables in the trees, like entering Renoir.
Maintenant je n'ai plus ni fortune, ni pouvoir . . .
But when the light was setting through thin hair,
holding whose hand by what trees, what old wall.

Two honest women, Christ, where are they gone?
Out of that wonder, what do I most recall?
The darkness closing round a fisherman's oar.
The sound of water gnawing at bright stone.

The shoulders of a shining nereid
Glide in warm shallows, nearing the white sand;
Thighs tangled in the golden weed,
Did fin flash there, or woman's hand?
Weed dissolves to burnished hair,
Foam now, where was milk-white breast,
Did thigh or dolphin cleave the air?
Half-woman and half-fish, or best
Both fish and woman, let them keep
Their elusive mystery.
Hurt, the wound shuts itself in sleep,
As water closes round the oar,
And as no oar can wound the sea.
Confused, the senses waken
To a renewed delight,
She to herself has taken
Sea-music and sea-light.

A SEA-CHANTEY

Là, tout n'est qu'ordre et beauté,
Luxe, calme, et volupté.

Anguilla, Adina,
Antigua, Cannelles,
Andreuille, all the l's,
Voyelles, of the liquid Antilles,
The names tremble like needles
Of anchored frigates,
Yachts tranquil as lilies,
In ports of calm coral,
The lithe, ebony hulls
Of strait-stitching schooners,
The needles of their masts
That thread archipelagoes
Refracted embroidery
In feverish waters
Of the sea-farer's islands,
Their shorn, leaning palms,
Shaft of Odysseus,
Cyclopic volcanoes,
Creak their own histories,
In the peace of green anchorage;
Flight, and Phyllis,
Returned from the Grenadines,
Names entered this Sabbath,
In the port-clerk's register;
Their baptismal names,
The sea's liquid letters,
Repos donnez a cils . . .
And their blazing cargoes
Of charcoal and oranges;

Quiet, the fury of their ropes.
Daybreak is breaking
On the green chrome water,
The white herons of yachts
Are at Sabbath communion,
The histories of schooners
Are murmured in coral,
Their cargoes of sponges
On sandspits of islets
Barques white as white salt
Of acrid Saint Maarten,
Hulls crusted with barnacles,
Holds foul with great turtles,
Whose ship-boys have seen
The blue heave of Leviathan,
A sea-faring, Christian,
And intrepid people.

Now an apprentice washes his cheeks
With salt water and sunlight.

In the middle of the harbor
A fish breaks the Sabbath
With a silvery leap.
The scales fall from him
In a tinkle of church-bells;
The town streets are orange
With the week-ripened sunlight,
Balanced on the bowsprit
A young sailor is playing
His grandfather's chantey
On a trembling mouth-organ.
The music curls, dwindling
Like smoke from blue galleys,
To dissolve near the mountains.

The music uncurls with
The soft vowels of inlets,
The christening of vessels,
The titles of portages,
The colors of sea-grapes,
The tartness of sea-almonds,
The alphabet of church-bells,
The peace of white horses,
The pastures of ports,
The litany of islands,
The rosary of archipelagoes,
Anguilla, Antigua,
Virgin of Guadeloupe,
And stone-white Grenada
Of sunlight and pigeons,
The amen of calm waters,
The amen of calm waters,
The amen of calm waters.

The orange tree, in various light,
Proclaims perfected fables now
That her last season's summer height
Bends from each overburdened bough.

She has her winters and her spring,
Her molt of leaves, which in their fall
Reveal, as with each living thing,
Zones truer than the tropical.

For if by night each golden sun
Burns in a comfortable creed,
By noon harsh fires have begun
To quail those splendors which they feed.

Or mixtures of the dew and dust
That early shone her orbs of brass,
Mottle her splendors with the rust
She sought all summer to surpass.

By such strange, cyclic chemistry
That dooms and glories all at once
As green yet aging orange tree,
The mind enspheres all circumstance.

No Florida loud with citron leaves
With crystal falls to heal this age
Shall calm the darkening fear that grieves
The loss of visionary rage.

Or if Time's fires seem to blight
The nature ripening into art,

Not the fierce noon or lampless night
Can quail the comprehending heart.

The orange tree, in various light
Proclaims that fable perfect now
That her last season's summer height
Bends from each overburdened bough.

ISLANDS

for Margaret

Merely to name them is the prose
Of diarists, to make you a name
For readers who like travellers praise
Their beds and beaches as the same;
But islands can only exist
If we have loved in them. I seek
As climate seeks its style, to write
Verse crisp as sand, clear as sunlight,
Cold as the curled wave, ordinary
As a tumbler of island water;
Yet, like a diarist, thereafter
I savor their salt-haunted rooms,
(Your body stirring the creased sea
Of crumpled sheets), whose mirrors lose
Our huddled, sleeping images,
Like words which love had hoped to use
Erased with the surf's pages.

So, like a diarist in sand,
I mark the peace with which you graced
Particular islands, descending
A narrow stair to light the lamps
Against the night surf's noises, shielding
A leaping mantle with one hand,
Or simply scaling fish for supper,
Onions, jack-fish, bread, red snapper;
And on each kiss the harsh sea-taste,
And how by moonlight you were made
To study most the surf's unyielding
Patience though it seems a waste.

FROM

The Castaway

(1965)

The starved eye devours the seascape for the morsel
Of a sail.

The horizon threads it infinitely.

Action breeds frenzy. I lie,
Sailing the ribbed shadow of a palm,
Afraid lest my own footprints multiply.

Blowing sand, thin as smoke,
Bored, shifts its dunes.
The surf tires of its castles like a child.

The salt-green vine with yellow trumpet-flower,
A net, inches across nothing.
Nothing: the rage with which the sandfly's head is filled.

Pleasures of an old man:
Morning: contemplative evacuation, considering
The dried leaf, nature's plan.

In the sun, the dog's feces
Crusts, whitens like coral.
We end in earth, from earth began.
In our own entrails, genesis.

If I listen I can hear the polyp build,
The silence thwanged by two waves of the sea.
Cracking a sea-louse, I make thunder split.

Godlike, annihilating Godhead, art
And self, I abandon
Dead metaphors: the almond's leaflike heart,

The ripe brain rotting like a yellow nut
Hatching
Its babel of sea-lice, sandfly and maggot,

That green wine bottle's gospel choked with sand,
Labeled, a wrecked ship,
Clenched seawood nailed and white as a man's hand.

Gnawing the highway's edges, its black mouth
Hums quietly: "Home, come home . . ."

Behind its viscous breath the very word "growth"
Grows fungi, rot;
White mottling its root.

More dreaded
Than canebrake, quarry, or sun-shocked gully-bed
Its horrors held Hemingway's hero rooted
To sure, clear shallows.

It begins nothing. Limbo of cracker convicts, Negroes.
Its black mood
Each sunset takes a smear of your life's blood.

Fearful, original sinuosities! Each mangrove sapling
Serpentlike, its roots obscene
As a six-fingered hand,

Conceals within its clutch the mossbacked toad,
Toadstools, the potent ginger-lily,
Petals of blood,

The speckled vulva of the tiger-orchid;
Outlandish phalloi
Haunting the travellers of its one road.

Deep, deeper than sleep
Like death,
Too rich in its decrescence, too close of breath,

In the fast-filling night, note
How the last bird drinks darkness with its throat,
How the wild saplings slip

Backward to darkness, go black
With widening amnesia, take the edge
Of nothing to them slowly, merge

Limb, tongue and sinew into a knot
Like chaos, like the road
Ahead.

A VILLAGE LIFE

for John Robertson

I

Through the wide, gray loft window,
I watched that winter morning, my first snow
crusting the sill, puzzle the black,
nuzzling tom. Behind my back
a rime of crud glazed my cracked coffee-cup,
a snowfall of torn poems piling up
heaped by a rhyming spade.
Starved, on the prowl,
I was a frightened cat in that gray city.
I floated, a cat's shadow, through the black wool
sweaters, leotards, and parkas of the fire-haired,
snow-shouldered Greenwich Village mädchen,
homesick, my desire
crawled across snow
like smoke, for its lost fire.

All that winter I haunted
your house on Hudson Street, a tiring friend,
demanding to be taken in, drunk, and fed.
I thought winter would never end.

I cannot imagine you dead.

But that stare, frozen,
a frosted pane in sunlight,
gives nothing back by letting nothing in,
your kindness or my pity.

No self-reflection lies
within those silent, ice-blue irises,
whose image is some snow-locked mountain lake
in numb Montana.

And since that winter I have learnt to gaze
on life indifferently as through a pane of glass.

II

Your image rattled on the subway glass
is my own death-mask in an overcoat;
under New York, the subterranean freight
of human souls, locked in an iron cell,
station to station cowed with swaying calm,
thunders to its end, each in its private hell,
each plumped, prime bulk still swinging by its arm
upon a hook. You're two years dead. And yet
I watch that silence spreading through our souls:
that horn-rimmed midget who consoles
his own deformity with Sartre on Genet.
Terror still eats the nerves, the Word
is gibberish, the plot Absurd.
The turnstile slots, like addicts, still consume
obols and aspirin, Charon in his grilled cell
grows vague about our crime, our destination.
Not all are silent, or endure
the enormity of silence; at one station,
somewhere off 33rd and Lexington,
a fur-wrapped matron screamed above the roar
of rattling iron. Nobody took her on,
we looked away. Such scenes
rattle our trust in nerves tuned like machines.
All drives as you remember it, the pace

of walking, running the rat race,
locked in a system, ridden by its rail,
within a life where no one dares to fail.
I watch your smile breaking across my skull,
the hollows of your face below my face
sliding across it like a pane of glass.
Nothing endures. Even in his cities
man's life is grass.
Times Square. We sigh and let off steam,
who should screech with the braking wheels, scream
like our subway-Cassandra, heaven-sent
to howl for Troy, emerge
blind from the blast of daylight, whirled
apart like papers from a vent.

III

Going away, through Queens we pass
a cemetery of miniature skyscrapers. The verge
blazes its rust, its taxi-yellow leaves. It's fall.
I stare through glass,
my own reflection there, at
empty avenues, lawns, spires, quiet
stones, where the curb's rim
wheels westward, westward, where thy bones . . .

Montana, Minnesota, your real
America, lost in tall grass, serene idyll.

IBIS

Flare of the ibis, rare vermilion,
A hieroglyphic of beak-headed Egypt
That haunts, they claim, the green swamp-traveller
Who catches it to watch its plumage fade,
Loses its colors in captivity,
Blanches into a pinkish, stilted heron
Among the garrulous fishwife gulls, bitterns and spoonbills
And ashen herons of the heronry.
She never pines, complains at being kept,
Yet, imperceptibly, fades from her fire,
Pointing no moral but the fact
Of flesh that has lost pleasure in the act,
Of domesticity, drained of desire.

OCTOPUS

Post coitum, omne animal . . . from love
The eight limbs loosen, like tentacles in water,
Like the slow tendrils of
The octopus.
        Fathoms down
They drift, numbed by the shock
Of an electric charge, drown
Vague as lidless fishes, separate
Like the anemone from rock
The sleek eel from its sea-cleft, drawn
By the darkening talons of the tide.
Pulse of the sea in the locked, heaving side.

LIZARD

Fear:
> the heraldic lizard, magnified,
Devouring its midge.
> > Last night I plucked
"as a brand from the burning," a murderous, pincered beetle
Floundering in urine like a shipwreck shallop
Rudderless, its legs frantic as oars.
Did I, by this act, set things right side up?
It was not death I dreaded but the fight
With nothing. The aged, flailing their claws
On flowery coverlets, may dread such salvation,
The impotence of rescue or compassion.
Rightening a beetle damns creation.
It may have felt more terror on its back
When my delivering fingers, huge as hell,
Shadowed the stiffening victim with their jaws
Than the brown lizard, Galapagos-large,
Waggling its horny tail at morning's morsel
Held for the midge.
> > Mercy has strange laws.
Withdraw and leave the scheme of things in charge.

MAN-O'-WAR BIRD

The idling pivot of the frigate bird
Sways the world's scales, tilts cobalt sea and sky,
Rightens, by its round eye, my drift
Through heaven when I shift
My study of the sun.
> > The easy wings
Depend upon the stress I give such things
As my importance to its piercing height, the peace

Of its slow, ravening circuit of a speck
Upon a beach prey to its beak
Like any predatory tern it seizes.
In that blue wildfire somewhere is an Eye
That weighs this world exactly as it pleases.

SEA CRAB

The sea crab's cunning, halting, awkward grace
is the syntactical envy of my hand;
obliquity burrowing to surface
from hot, plain sand.
Those who require vision, complexity,
tire of its distressing
limits: sea, sand, scorching sky.
Cling to this ground, though constellations race,
the horizon burn, the wave coil, hissing,
salt sting the eye.

THE WHALE, HIS BULWARK

To praise the blue whale's crystal jet,
To write, "O fountain!" honoring a spout
Provokes this curse:
                 "The high are humbled yet"
From those who humble Godhead, beasthood, verse.

Once, the Lord raised this bulwark to our eyes,
Once, in our seas, whales threshed,
The harpooner was common. Once, I heard
Of a baleine beached up the Grenadines, fleshed
By derisive, ant-like villagers: a prize
Reduced from majesty to pygmy-size.

Salt-crusted, mythological,
And dead.

The boy who told me couldn't believe his eyes,
And I believed him. When I was small
God and a foundered whale were possible.
Whales are rarer, God as invisible.
Yet, through His gift, I praise the unfathomable,
Though the boy may be dead, the praise unfashionable,
The tale apocryphal.

TARPON

At Cedros, thudding the dead sand
in spasms, the tarpon
gaped with a gold eye, drowned
thickly, thrashing with brute pain
this sea I breathe.
Stilled, its bulk,
screwed to the eye's lens, slowly
sought design. It dried like silk,
leisurely, altered to lead.
The belly, leprous, silver, bulged
like a cold chancre for the blade.
Suddenly it shuddered in immense
doubt, but the old jaw, gibbering, divulged
nothing but some new filaments
of blood. For every bloody stroke
with which a frenzied fisherman struck
its head my young son shook his head.
Could I have called out not to look
simply at the one world we shared?
Dead, and examined in detail,
a tarpon's bulk grows beautiful.

Bronze, with a brass-green mold, the scales
age like a corselet of coins,
a net of tarnished silver joins
the back's deep-sea blue to the tail's
wedged, tapering Y.
Set in a stone, triangular skull,
ringing with gold, the open eye
is simply, tiringly there.
A shape so simple, like a cross,
a child could draw it in the air.
A tarpon's scale, its skin's flake
washed at the sea's edge and held
against the light looks just like what
the grinning fisherman said it would:
dense as frost glass but delicate,
etched by a diamond, it showed
a child's drawing of a ship,
the sails' twin triangles, a mast.

Can such complexity of shape,
such bulk, terror and fury fit
in a design so innocent,
that through opaque, phantasmal mist,
moving, but motionlessly, it
sails where imagination sent?

GOATS AND MONKEYS

. . . even now, an old black ram
is tupping your white ewe.

Othello

The owl's torches gutter. Chaos clouds the globe.
Shriek, augury! His earthen bulk
buries her bosom in its slow eclipse.
His smoky hand has charred
that marble throat. Bent to her lips,
he is Africa, a vast, sidling shadow
that halves your world with doubt.
"Put out the light," and God's light is put out.

That flame extinct, she contemplates her dream
of him as huge as night, as bodiless,
as starred with medals, like the moon
a fable of blind stone.
Dazzled by that bull's bulk against the sun
of Cyprus, couldn't she have known
like Pasiphaë, poor girl, she'd breed horned monsters?
That like Eurydice, her flesh a flare
travelling the hellish labyrinth of his mind
his soul would swallow hers?

Her white flesh rhymes with night. She climbs, secure.

Virgin and ape, maid and malevolent Moor,
their immoral coupling still halves our world.
He is your sacrificial beast, bellowing, goaded,
a black bull snarled in ribbons of its blood.
And yet, whatever fury girded
on that saffron-sunset turban, moon-shaped sword

was not his racial, panther-black revenge
pulsing her chamber with raw musk, its sweat,
but horror of the moon's change,
of the corruption of an absolute,
like a white fruit
pulped ripe by fondling but doubly sweet.

And so he barbarously arraigns the moon
for all she had beheld since time began
for his own night-long lechery, amibition,
while barren innocence whimpers for pardon.

And it is still the moon, she silvers love,
limns lechery and stares at our disgrace.
Only annihilation can resolve
the pure corruption in her dreaming face.

A bestial, comic agony. We harden
with mockery at this blackamoor
who turns his back on her, who kills
what, like the clear moon, cannot abhor
her element, night; his grief
farcically knotted in a handkerchief
a sibyl's
prophetically stitched remembrancer
webbed and embroidered with the zodiac,
this mythical, horned beast who's no more
monstrous for being black.

VERANDA

for Ronald Bryden

Gray apparitions at veranda ends
like smoke, divisible, but one
your age is ashes, its coherence gone,

Planters whose tears were marketable gum, whose voices
scratch the twilight like dried fronds
edged with reflection,

Colonels, hard as the commonwealth's greenheart,
middlemen, usurers whose art
kept an empire in the red,

Upholders of Victoria's china seas
lapping embossed around a drinking mug,
bully-boy roarers of the Empire club,

To the tarantara of the bugler, the sunset furled
round the last post,
the "flamingo colors" of a fading world,

A ghost steps from you, my grandfather's ghost!
Uprooted from some rainy English shire,
you sought your Roman

End in suicide by fire.
Your mixed son gathered your charred, blackened bones,
in a child's coffin.

And buried them himself on a strange coast.
Sire,
why do I raise you up? Because

Your house has voices, your burnt house,
shrills with unguessed, lovely inheritors,
your genealogical roof tree, fallen, survives,
like seasoned timber through green, little lives.

I ripen towards your twilight, sir, that dream
where I am singed in that sea-crossing, steam
towards that vaporous world, whose souls,

like pressured trees brought diamonds out of coals.
The sparks pitched from your burning house are stars.
I am the man my father loved and was.

Whatever love you suffered makes amends
within them, father.
I climb the stair

And stretch a darkening hand to greet those friends
who share with you the last inheritance
of earth, our shrine and pardoner,

gray, ghostly loungers at veranda ends.

Night, our black summer, simplifies her smells
into a village; she assumes the impenetrable

musk of the Negro, grows secret as sweat,
her alleys odorous with shucked oyster shells,

coals of gold oranges, braziers of melon.
Commerce and tambourines increase her heat.

Hellfire or the whorehouse: crossing Park Street,
a surf of sailors' faces crests, is gone

with the sea's phosphorescence; the boîtes de nuit
twinkle like fireflies in her thick hair.

Blinded by headlamps, deaf to taxi klaxons,
she lifts her face from the cheap, pitch-oil flare

towards white stars, like cities, flashing neon,
burning to be the bitch she will become.

As daylight breaks the Indian turns his tumbril
of hacked, beheaded coconuts towards home.

Splitting from Jack Delaney's, Sheridan Square,
that winter night, stewed, seasoned in bourbon,
my body kindled by the whistling air
snowing the Village that Christ was reborn,
I lurched like any lush by his own glow
across towards Sixth, and froze before the tracks
of footprints bleeding on the virgin snow.
I tracked them where they led across the street
to the bright side, entering the wax-
sealed smell of neon, human heat,
some all-night diner with its wise-guy cook
his stub thumb in my bowl of stew and one
man's pulped and beaten face, its look
acknowledging all that, white-dark outside,
was possible: some beast prowling the block,
something fur-clotted, running wild
beyond the boundary of will. Outside,
more snow had fallen. My heart charred.
I longed for darkness, evil that was warm.
Walking, I'd stop and turn. What had I heard,
wheezing behind my heel with whitening breath?
Nothing. Sixth Avenue yawned wet and wide.
The night was white. There was nowhere to hide.

I looked now upon the world as a thing remote, which I had nothing to do with, no
expectation from, and, indeed, no desires about. In a word, I had nothing indeed to
do with it, nor was ever like to have; so I thought it looked as we may perhaps look
upon it hereafter, viz., as a place I had lived in but was come out of it; and well might
I say, as Father Abraham to Dives, "Between me and thee is a great gulf fixed."

Robinson Crusoe

Once we have driven past Mundo Nuevo trace
     safely to this beach house
perched between ocean and green, churning forest
     the intellect appraises
objects surely, even the bare necessities
     of style are turned to use,
like those plain iron tools he salvages
     from shipwreck, hewing a prose
as odorous as raw wood to the adze,
     out of such timbers
came our first book, our profane Genesis
     whose Adam speaks that prose
which, blessing some sea-rock, startles itself
     with poetry's surprise,
in a green world, one without metaphors;
     like Christofer he bears
in speech mnemonic as a missionary's
     the Word to savages,
its shape an earthen, water-bearing vessel's
     whose sprinkling alters us
into good Fridays who recite His praise,
     parroting our master's
style and voice, we make his language ours,
     converted cannibals
we learn with him to eat the flesh of Christ.

All shapes, all objects multiplied from his,
          our ocean's Proteus;
in childhood, his derelict's old age
          was like a god's. (Now pass
in memory, in serene parenthesis,
          the cliff-deep leeward coast
of my own island filing past the noise
          of stuttering canvas,
some noon-struck village, Choiseul, Canaries,
          with crocodile canoes,
a savage settlement from Henty's novels,
          Marryat or R.L.S.,
with one boy signaling at the sea's edge,
          though what he cried is lost;)
So time that makes us objects, multiplies
          our natural loneliness.

For the hermetic skill, that from earth's clays
          shapes something without use,
and separate from itself, lives somewhere else,
          sharing with every beach
a longing for those gulls that cloud the cays
          with raw, mimetic cries,
never surrenders wholly for it knows
          it needs another's praise
like hoar, half-cracked Ben Gunn, until it cries
          at last, "O happy desert!"
and learns again the self-creating peace
          of islands. So from this house
that faces nothing but the sea, his journals
          assume a household use,
We learn to shape from them, where nothing was
          the language of a race,
and since the intellect demands its mask
          that sun-cracked, bearded face

provides us with the wish to dramatize
      ourselves at nature's cost,
to attempt a beard, to squint through the sea-haze,
      posing as naturalists,
drunks, castaways, beachcombers, all of us
      yearn for those fantasies
of innocence, for our faith's arrested phase
      when the clear voice
startled itself saying "water, heaven, Christ,"
      hoarding such heresies as
God's loneliness moves in His smallest creatures.

I

The chapel's cowbell
Like God's anvil
Hammers ocean to a blinding shield;
Fired, the sea-grapes slowly yield
Bronze plates to the metallic heat.

Red, corrugated iron
Roofs roar in the sun.
The wiry, ribbed air
Above earth's open kiln
Writhes like a child's vision
Of hell, but nearer, nearer.

Below, the picnic plaid
Of Scarborough is spread
To a blue, perfect sky,
Dome of our hedonist philosophy.
Bethel and Canaan's heart
Lie open like a psalm.
I labor at my art.
My father, God, is dead.

Past thirty now I know
To love the self is dread
Of being swallowed by the blue
Of heaven overhead
Or rougher blue below.
Some lesion of the brain
From art or alcohol
Flashes this fear by day:

As startling as his shadow
Grows to the castaway.

Upon this rock the bearded hermit built
His Eden:
Goats, corn-crop, fort, parasol, garden,
Bible for Sabbath, all the joys
But one
Which sent him howling for a human voice.
Exiled by a flaming sun
The rotting nut, bowled in the surf
Became his own brain rotting from the guilt
Of heaven without his kind,
Crazed by such paradisal calm
The spinal shadow of a palm
Built keel and gunwale in his mind.

The second Adam since the fall
His germinal
Corruption held the seed
Of that congenital heresy that men fail
According to their creed.
Craftsman and castaway
All heaven in his head,
He watched his shadow pray
Not for God's love but human love instead.

II

We came here for the cure
Of quiet in the whelk's center,
From the fierce, sudden quarrel,
From kitchens where the mind
Like bread, disintegrates in water,

To let a salt sun scour
The brain as harsh as coral
To bathe like stones in wind,
To be, like beast or natural object, pure.

That fabled, occupational
Compassion, supposedly inherited with the gift
Of poetry had fed
With a rat's thrift on faith, shifted
Its trust to corners, hoarded
Its mania like bread,
Its brain a white, nocturnal bloom
That in a drunken, moonlit room
Saw my son's head
Swaddled in sheets
Like a lopped nut, lolling in foam.

O love, we die alone!
I am borne by the bell
Backward to boyhood
To the gray wood
Spire, harvest and marigold,
To those whom a cruel
Just God could gather
To His blue breast, His beard
A folding cloud,
As He gathered my father.
Irresolute and proud,
I can never go back.

I have lost sight of hell,
Of heaven, of human will,
My skill
Is not enough,

I am struck by this bell
To the root.
Crazed by a racking sun,
I stand at my life's noon,
On parched, delirious sand
My shadow lengthens.

III

Art is profane and pagan,
The most it has revealed
Is what a crippled Vulcan
Beat on Achilles' shield.
By these blue, changing graves
Fanned by the furnace blast
Of heaven, may the mind
Catch fire till it cleaves
Its mold of clay at last.

Now Friday's progeny,
The brood of Crusoe's slave,
Black little girls in pink
Organdy, crinolines,
Walk in their air of glory
Beside a breaking wave;
Below their feet the surf
Hisses like tambourines.

At dusk when they return
For vespers, every dress
Touched by the sun will burn
A seraph's, an angel's,

And nothing I can learn
From art or loneliness
Can bless them as the bell's
Transfiguring tongue can bless.

CODICIL

Schizophrenic, wrenched by two styles,
one a hack's hired prose, I earn
my exile. I trudge this sickle, moonlit beach for miles,

tan, burn
to slough off
this love of ocean that's self-love.

To change your language you must change your life.

I cannot right old wrongs.
Waves tire of horizon and return.
Gulls screech with rusty tongues

Above the beached, rotting pirogues,
they were a venomous beaked cloud at Charlotteville.

Once I thought love of country was enough,
now, even I chose, there's no room at the trough.

I watch the best minds root like dogs
for scraps of favor.
I am nearing middle-

age, burnt skin
peels from my hand like paper, onion-thin,
like Peer Gynt's riddle.

At heart there's nothing, not the dread
of death. I know too many dead.
They're all familiar, all in character,

even how they died. On fire,
the flesh no longer fears that furnace mouth
of earth,

that kiln or ashpit of the sun,
nor this clouding, unclouding sickle moon
whitening this beach again like a blank page.

All its indifference is a different rage.

FROM

The Gulf

(1969)

THE CORN GODDESS

Silence asphalts the highway, our tires hiss
like serpents, of God's touching weariness,
his toil unfinished, while in endless rows
the cabbage fields, like lilies, spin in air;
his flags rot, and the monkey god's nerves rattle
lances in rage. Human rags tend cattle
more venal every year, and chrome-tooled cars
lathered like estate horses nose the shallows.
At dusk the Presbyterian cattle-bell
collects lean, charcoal-brittle elders,
stalled in their vision of a second hell,
as every crossroad crucifies its sect
of bell-voiced, bell-robed sisters, gold-gelders
baying for self-respect. But, over braziers
of roasting corn while their shucked souls
evenly char, the sybil glows. Her seal's skin
shines like drizzled asphalt, in that grin
all knowledges burnt out. Jeer, but their souls
catch an elation fiercer than your desolate
envy; from their fanned, twisting coals
their shrieks crackle and fly. The sparks
are sorrowing upward though they die.

MOON

Resisting poetry I am becoming a poem.
O lolling Orphic head silently howling,
my own head rises from its surf of cloud.

Slowly my body grows a single sound,
slowly I become
a bell,
an oval, disembodied vowel,
I grow, an owl,
an aureole, white fire.

I watch the moonstruck image of the moon burn,
a candle mesmerized by its own aura,
and turn
my hot, congealing face, towards that forked mountain
which wedges the drowned singer.

That frozen glare,
that morsured, classic petrifaction.
Haven't you sworn off such poems for this year,
and no more on the moon?

Why are you gripped by demons of inaction?
Whose silence shrieks so soon?

The sun's brass clamp electrifies a skull
kept shone since he won Individual
of the Year, their first year on the road,
as Vercingetorix And His Barbarous Horde;
lurching from lounge to air-conditioned lounge
with the crazed soldier ant's logistic skill
of pause as capture, he stirs again to plunge,
his brain's antennae on fire through the black ants
milling and mulling through each city fissure;
banlon-cool limers, shopgirls, Civil Servants.
"Caesar," the hecklers siegheil, "Julius Seizure!"
He fakes an epileptic, clenched salute,
taking their tone, is no use getting vex,
some day those brains will squelch below his boot
as sheaves of swords hoist Vercingetorix!

So that day bursts to bugling cocks, the sun's gong
clangs the coup, a church, a bank explodes
and, bullet-headed with his cow-horned gang
of marabunta hordes, he hits the road.
Dust powders the white dead in Woodford Square;
his black, khaki canaille, panting for orders,
surge round the kiosk, then divide to hear
him clomp up silence louder than the roars
of rapine. Silence. Dust. A microphone
crackles the tinfoil quiet. On its paws
the beast mills, basilisk-eyed, for its one
voice. He clears his gorge and feels the bile
of rhetoric rising. Enraged that every clause

"por la patria, la muerte" resounds
the same, he fakes a frothing fit and shows his wounds,
while, as the cold sheaves heighten, his eyes fix
on one black, bush-haired convict's widening smile.

Through a great lion's head clouded by mange
a black clerk growls.
Next, a gold-wired peacock withholds a man,
a fan, flaunting its oval, jeweled eyes,
What metaphors!
What coruscating, mincing fantasies!

Hector Mannix, waterworks clerk San Juan, has entered a lion,
Boysie, two golden mangoes bobbing for breastplates, barges
like Cleopatra down her river, making style.
"Join us" they shout, "O God, child, you can't dance?"
but somewhere in that whirlwind's radiance
a child, rigged like a bat, collapses, sobbing.

But I am dancing, look, from an old gibbet
my bull-whipped body swings, a metronome!
Like a fruit-bat dropped in the silk cotton's shade
my mania, my mania is a terrible calm.

Upon your penitential morning,
some skull must rub its memory with ashes,
some mind must squat down howling in your dust,
some hand must crawl and recollect your rubbish,
someone must write your poems.

There'll be no miracle tonight; by the third drink
you can tell. The nerves deaden from steel
or a hollow sax. I look through the window:
a bus goes by like an empty hospital,
and turn. The stripper's spinning, pink
tits, falsies in a false light, her crotch's
mechanical lurch is her own rut, and think
of the night I almost burned my balls
off with some abrasive, powdery chemical
and in the next ward of the teaching hospital
would listen all night to the clenched, stuck
howl of a child dying of lockjaw. Clench, hold
on to what you have. After a while, this whole
slow grinding circus doesn't give a fuck.
There is nowhere to go. You'd better go.

Wind-haired, mufflered
against dawn, you watched the herd
of migrants ring the deck
from steerage. Only the funnel
bellowing, the gulls who peck
waste from the plowed channel
knew that you had not come
to England; you were home.

Even her wretched weather
was poetry. Your scarred leather
suitcase held that first
indenture, to her Word,
but, among cattle docking, that rehearsed
calm meant to mark you from the herd
shook, calflike, in her cold.

Never to go home again,
for this was home! The windows
leafed through history to the beat
of a school ballad, but the train
soon changed its poetry to the prose
of narrowing, pinched eyes you could not enter,
to the gas-ring, the ringing Students' Center,
to the soiled, icy sheet.

One night, near rheum-eyed windows
your memory kept pace with winter's
pages, piled in drifts,

till Spring, which slowly lifts
the heart, broke into prose
and suns you had forgotten
blazoned from barrows.

And earth began to look
as you remembered her,
herons, like seagulls, flock-
ed to the salted furrow,
the bellowing, smoky bullock
churned its cane sea,
a world began to pass
through your pen's eye,
between bent grasses and one word
for the bent rice.

And now, some phrase
caught in the parenthesis
of highway quietly states
its title, and an ochre trace
of flags and carat huts opens
at Chapter One,
the bullock's strenuous ease is mirrored
in a clear page of prose,
a forest is compressed in a blue coal,
or burns in graphite fire,
invisibly your ink nourishes
leaf after leaf the furrowed villages
where the smoke flutes
and the brittle pages
of the Ramayana stoke the mulch fires,

the arrowing, metal
highways head nowhere,
the tabla and the sitar amplified,

the Path unrolling like a dirty bandage,
the cinema-hoardings leer
in language half the country cannot read.

Yet, when dry winds rattle
the flags whose bamboo lances bend
to Hanuman, when, like chattel
folded in a cloth knot, the debased
brasses are tremblingly placed
on flaking temple lintels,
when the god stamps his bells
and smoke writhes its blue arms
for your lost India,

the old men, threshing rice,
rheum-eyed, pause,
their brown gaze flecked with chaff,
their loss chafed by the raw
whine of the cinema-van calling the countryside
to its own dark devotions,
summoning the drowned from oceans
of deep cane. The hymn
to Mother India whores its lie.
Your memory walks by its soft-spoken
path, as flickering, broken,
Saturday jerks past like a cheap film.

On one hand, harrowed England,
iron, an airfield's mire,
on the other, fire-
gutted trees, a hand
raking the carriage windows.

Where was my randy white grandsire from?
He left here a century ago
to found his "farm,"
and, like a thousand others,
drunkenly seed their archipelago.
Through dirty glass
his landscape fills through my face.

Black with despair
he set his flesh on fire,
blackening, a tree of flame.
That's hell enough for here.
His blood burns through me as this engine races,
my skin sears like a hairshirt with his name.

On the bleak Sunday platform
the guiltless, staring faces
divide like tracks before me as I come.
Like you, grandfather, I cannot change places,
I am half-home.

Formal, informal, by a country's cast
topography delineates its verse,
erects the classic bulk, for rigid contrast
of sonnet, rectory or this manor house
dourly timbered against these sinuous
Downs, defines the formal and informal prose
of Edward Thomas's poems which make this garden
return its subtle scent of Edward Thomas
in everything here hedged or loosely grown.
Lines which you once dismissed as tenuous
because they would not howl or overwhelm,
as crookedly grave-bent, or cuckoo-dreaming,
seemingly dissoluble as this Sussex down
harden in their indifference, like this elm.

for Jack and Barbara Harrison

I

The airport coffee tastes less of America.
Sour, unshaven, dreading the exertion
of tightening, racked nerves fueled with liquor,

some smoky, resinous bourbon,
the body, buckling at its casket hole,
a roar like last night's blast racing its engines,

watches the fumes of the exhausted soul
as the trans-Texas jet, screeching, begins
its flight and friends diminish. So, to be aware

of the divine union the soul detaches
itself from created things. "We're in the air,"
the Texan near me grins. All things: these matches

from LBJ's campaign hotel, this rose
given me at dawn in Austin by a child,
this book of fables by Borges, its prose

a stalking, moonlit tiger. What was willed
on innocent, sun-streaked Dallas, the beast's claw
curled round that hairspring rifle is revealed

on every page as lunacy or feral law;
circling that wound we leave Love Field.
Fondled, these objects conjure hotels,

quarrels, new friendships, brown limbs
nakedly molded as these autumn hills
memory penetrates as the jet climbs

the new clouds over Texas; their home means
an island suburb, forest, mountain water;
they are the simple properties for scenes

whose joy exhausts like grief, scenes where we learn,
exchanging the least gifts, this rose, this napkin,
that those we love are objects we return,

that this lens on the desert's wrinkled skin
has priced our flesh, all that we love in pawn
to that brass ball, that the gifts, multiplying

clutter and choke the heart, and that I shall
watch love reclaim its things as I lie dying.
My very flesh and blood! Each seems a petal

shriveling from its core. I watch them burn,
by the nerves' flare I catch their skeletal
candor! Best never to be born

the great dead cry. Their works shine on our shelves,
by twilight we tour their gilded, gravestone spines,
and read until the lamplit page revolves

to a white stasis whose detachment shines
like a propeller's rainbowed radiance.
Circling like us; no comfort for their loves!

The cold glass darkens. Elizabeth wrote once
that we make glass the image of our pain;
I watch clouds boil past the cold, sweating pane

above the Gulf. All styles yearn to be plain
as life. The face of the loved object under glass
is plainer still. Yet somehow, at this height,

above this cauldron boiling with its wars,
our old earth, breaking to familiar light,
that cloud-bound mummy with self-healing scars

peeled of her cerements again looks new;
some cratered valley heals itself with sage,
through that gray, fading massacre a blue

lighthearted creek flutes of some siege
to the amnesia of drumming water.
Their cause is crystalline: the divine union

of these detached, divided States, whose slaughter
darkens each summer now, as one by one,
the smoke of bursting ghettos clouds the glass

down every coast where filling-station signs
proclaim the Gulf, an air, heavy with gas,
sickens the state, from Newark to New Orleans.

Yet the South felt like home. Wrought balconies,
the sluggish river with its tidal drawl,
the tropic air charged with the extremities

of patience, a heat heavy with oil,
canebrakes, that legendary jazz. But fear
thickened my voice, that strange, familiar soil

prickled and barbed the texture of my hair,
my status as a secondary soul.
The Gulf, your gulf, is daily widening,

each blood-red rose warns of that coming night
when there's no rock cleft to go hidin' in
and all the rocks catch fire, when that black might,

their stalking, moonless panthers turn from Him
whose voice they can no more believe, when the black X's
mark their passover with slain seraphim.

IV

The Gulf shines, dull as lead. The coast of Texas
glints like a metal rim. I have no home
as long as summer bubbling to its head

boils for that day when in the Lord God's name
the coals of fire are heaped upon the head
of all whose gospel is the whip and flame,

age after age, the uninstructing dead.

Our hammock swung between Americas
we miss you, Liberty. Che's
bullet-riddled body falls,
and those who cried the Republic must first die
to be reborn are dead,
the freeborn citizen's ballot in the head.
Still, everybody wants to go to bed
with Miss America. And, if there's no bread,
let them eat cherry pie.

But the old choice of running, howling, wounded
wolf-deep in her woods,
while the white papers snow on
genocide is gone;
no face can hide
its public, private pain,
wincing, already statued.

Some splintered arrowhead lodged in her brain
sets the black singer howling in his bear trap
shines young eyes with the brightness of the mad,
tires the old with her residual sadness;
and yearly lilacs in her dooryards bloom,
and the cherry orchard's surf
blinds Washington and whispers
to the assassin in his furnished room
of an ideal America, whose flickering screens
show, in slow herds, the ghosts of the Cheyennes
scuffling across the staked and wired plains
with whispering, rag-bound feet,

while the farm couple framed in their Gothic door
like Calvin's saints, waspish, pragmatic, poor,
gripping the devil's pitchfork
stare rigidly towards the immortal wheat.

June 6, 1968

Those five or six young guys
hunched on the stoop
that oven-hot summer night
whistled me over. Nice
and friendly. So, I stop.
MacDougal or Christopher
Street in chains of light.

A summer festival. Or some
saint's. I wasn't too far from
home, but not too bright
for a nigger, and not too dark,
I figured we were all
one, wop, nigger, jew,
besides, this wasn't Central Park.
I'm coming on too strong? You figure
right! They beat this yellow nigger
black and blue.

Yeah. During all this, scared
in case one used a knife,
I hung my olive-green, just-bought
sports coat on a fire-plug.
I did nothing. They fought
each other, really. Life
gives them a few kicks,
that's all. The spades, the spicks.

My face smashed in, my bloody mug
pouring, my olive-branch jacket saved
from cuts and tears,
I crawled four flights upstairs.

Sprawled in the gutter, I
remember a few watchers waved
loudly, and one kid's mother shouting
like "Jackie" or "Terry,"
"Now that's enough!"
It's nothing really.
They don't get enough love.

You know they wouldn't kill
you. Just playing rough,
like young America will.
Still, it taught me something
about love. If it's so tough,
forget it.

The unheard, omnivorous
jaws of this rain forest
not merely devour all,
but allow nothing vain;
they never rest,
grinding their disavowal
of human pain.

Long, long before us,
those hot jaws like an oven
steaming, were open
to genocide; they devoured
two minor yellow races and
half of a black;
in the word made flesh of God
all entered that gross, un-
discriminating stomach;

the forest is unconverted,
because that shell-like noise
which roars like silence, or
ocean's surpliced choirs
entering its nave, to a censer
of swung mist, is not
the rustling of prayer
but nothing; milling air,
a faith, infested, cannibal,

which eats gods, which devoured
the god-refusing Carib, petal
by golden petal, then forgot,
and the Arawak
who leaves not the lightest fern-trace
of his fossil to be cultured
by black rock,

but only the rusting cries
of a rainbird, like a hoarse
warrior summoning his race
from vaporous air
between this mountain ridge
and the vague sea
where the lost exodus
of corials sunk without trace—

There is too much nothing here.

CHE

In this dark-grained news-photograph, whose glare
is rigidly composed as Caravaggio's,
the corpse glows candle-white on its cold altar—

its stone Bolivian Indian butcher's slab—
stare till its waxen flesh begins to harden
to marble, to veined, Andean iron;
from your own fear, *cabron*, its pallor grows;

it stumbled from your doubt, and for your pardon
burnt in brown trash, far from the embalming snows.

A newsclip; the invasion of Biafra:
black corpses wrapped in sunlight
sprawled on the white glare entering what's its name—
the central city?

        Someone who's white
illuminates the news behind the news,
his eyes flash with, perhaps, pity:
"The Ibos, you see, are like the Jews,
very much the situation in Hitler's Germany,
I mean the Hausas' resentment." I try to see.

I never knew you Christopher Okigbo,
I saw you when an actor screamed "The tribes!
the tribes!" I catch
the guttering, flare-lit
faces of Ibos,
stuttering, bug-eyed
prisoners of some drumhead tribunal.

The soldiers' helmeted shadows
could have been white, and yours
one of those sun-wrapped bodies on the white road
entering . . . the tribes, the tribes, their shame—
that central city, Christ, what is its name?

HOMECOMING: ANSE LA RAYE

for Garth St. Omer

Whatever else we learned
at school, like solemn Afro-Greeks eager for grades,
of Helen and the shades
of borrowed ancestors,
there are no rites
for those who have returned,
only, when her looms fade,
drilled in our skulls, the doom-
surge-haunted nights,
only this well-known passage
under the coconuts' salt-rusted
swords, these rotted
leathery sea-grape leaves,
the seacrabs' brittle helmets, and
this barbecue of branches, like the ribs
of sacrificial oxen on scorched sand;
only this fish-gut reeking beach
whose spindly, sugar-headed children race
whose starved, pot-bellied children race
pelting up from the shallows
because your clothes,
your posture
seem a tourist's.
They swarm like flies
round your heart's sore.

Suffer them to come,
entering your needle's eye,
knowing whether they live or die,
what others make of life will pass them by
like that far silvery freighter

threading the horizon like a toy;
for once, like them,
you wanted no career
but this sheer light, this clear,
infinite, boring, paradisal sea,
but hoped it would mean something to declare
today, I am your poet, yours,
all this you knew,
but never guessed you'd come
to know there are homecomings without home.

You give them nothing.
Their curses melt in air.
The black cliffs scowl,
the ocean sucks its teeth,
like that dugout canoe
a drifting petal fallen in a cup,
with nothing but its image,
you sway, reflecting nothing.
The freighter's silvery ghost
is gone, the children gone.
Dazed by the sun
you trudge back to the village
past the white, salty esplanade
under whose palms, dead
fishermen move their draughts in shade,
crossing, eating their islands,
and one, with a politician's
ignorant, sweet smile, nods,
as if all fate
swayed in his lifted hand.

Woman, wasp-waisted, then wasp-tongued,
hissing to enemies how much I wronged
you, how just you were! We would secrete
in every cell, each separate room
the stink and stigma of my name,
and nothing, not the bedside flame
charring in coils by the child's net
could calm your virulent regret
or my last effort, lust. You cried
against the poison charged inside
his flesh and yours, I prayed we'd clasp
each other fierce as coupling wasps,
as bittersweet it seemed to flesh
to die in self-stung martyrdom,
for mind and body bitten black
with shame to take its poison back,
to build, even in hate, a home,
in that hexagonal lace mesh
shuddering, exchanging venom.

STAR

If, in the light of things, you fade
real, yet wanly withdrawn
to our determined and appropriate
distance, like the moon left on
all night among the leaves, may
you invisibly delight this house,
O star, doubly compassionate, who came
too soon for twilight, too late
for dawn, may your faint flame
strive with the worst in us
through chaos
with the passion of
plain day.

The sun goes slowly blind.
It is this mountain, shrouding
the valley of the shadow,

widening like amnesia
evening dims the mind.
I shake my head in darkness,

it is a tree branched with cries,
a trash-can full of print.
Now, through the reddening squint

of leaves leaden as eyes,
a skein of drifting hair
like a twig, fallen on snow,

branches the blank pages.
I bring it close, and stare
in slow vertiginous darkness,

and now I drift elsewhere,
through hostile images,
of white and black, and look,

like a thaw-sniffing stallion, the head
of Pasternak emerges with its forelock,
his sinewy wrist a fetlock

pawing the frozen spring,
till his own hand has frozen
on the white page, heavy.

I ride through a white childhood
whose pines glittered with bracelets,
when I heard wolves, feared the black wood,

every wrist-aching brook
and the ice maiden
in Hawthorne's fairy book.

The hair melts into dark,
a question mark that led
where the untethered mind

strayed from its first track,
Now Hardy's somber head
over which hailstorms broke

looms, like a weeping rock,
like wind, the tresses drift
and its familiar trace

tingles across the face
with its light lashes.
I feared the depth of whiteness,

I feared the numbing kiss
of those women of winter,
Bathsheba, Lara, Tess

whose tragedy made less
of life, whose love was more
than love or literature.

THE WALK

After hard rain the eaves repeat their beads,
those trees exhale your doubt like mantled tapers,
drop after drop, like a child's abacus
beads of cold sweat file from high tension wires,

pray for us, pray for this house, borrow your neighbor's
faith, pray for this brain that tires,
and loses faith in the great books it reads;
after a day spent prone, hemorrhaging poems,

each phrase peeled from the flesh in bandages,
arise, stroll on under a sky
sodden as kitchen laundry,

while the cats yawn behind their window frames,
lions in cages of their choice,
no further though, than your last neighbor's gates
figured with pearl. How terrible is your own

fidelity, O heart, O rose of iron!
When was your work more like a housemaid's novel,
some drenched soap-opera which gets
closer than yours to life? Only the pain,

the pain is real. Here's your life's end,
a clump of bamboos whose clenched
fist loosens its flowers, a track
that hisses through the rain-drenched

grove: abandon all, the work,
the pain of a short life. Startled, you move;
your house, a lion rising, paws you back.

I

They'll keep on asking, why did you remain?
Not for the applauding rain
of hoarse and hungry thousands at whose center
the politician opens like a poisonous flower,
not for the homecoming lecturer
gripping his lectern like a witness, ready to explain
the root's fixation with earth,
nor for that new race of dung beetles, frock-coated, iridescent
crawling over the people.
Before the people became popular
he loved them.

Nor to spite some winter-bitten novelist
praised for his accuracy of phlegm,
but for something rooted, unwritten
that gave us its benediction,
its particular pain,
that may move its clouds from that mountain,
that is packing its bags on that fiction
of our greatness, which, like the homecoming rain,
veers to a newer sea.

II

I loved them all, the names
of shingled, rusting towns, whose dawn
touches like metal,
I should have written poems on the Thames,

shivered through cities furred and cracked with ice,
spat, for their taste, in some barge-burdened river.

III

Convinced of the power of provincialism,
I yielded quietly my knowledge of the world
to a gray tub steaming with clouds of seraphim,
the angels and flags of the world,
and answer those who hiss, like steam, of exile,
this coarse soap-smelling truth:

I sought more power than you, more fame than yours,
I was more hermetic, I knew the commonweal,
I pretended subtly to lose myself in crowds
knowing my passage would alter their reflection,
I was that muscle shouldering the grass
through ordinary earth,
commoner than water I sank to lose my name,
this was my second birth.

FROM

Another Life

(1973)

An old story goes that Cimabue was struck with admiration when he saw the shepherd boy, Giotto, sketching sheep. But, according to the true biographies, it is never the sheep that inspire a Giotto with the love of painting: but rather, his first sight of the paintings of such a man as Cimabue. What makes the artist is the circumstance that in his youth he was more deeply moved by the sight of works of art than by that of the things which they portray.

MALRAUX, *Psychology of Art*

I

Verandas, where the pages of the sea
are a book left open by an absent master
in the middle of another life—
I begin here again,
begin until this ocean's
a shut book, and, like a bulb
the white moon's filaments wane.

Begin with twilight, when a glare
which held a cry of bugles lowered
the coconut lances of the inlet,
as a sun, tired of empire, declined.
It mesmerized like fire without wind,
and as its amber climbed
the beer-stein ovals of the British fort
above the promontory, the sky
grew drunk with light.
                                    There
was your heaven! The clear
glaze of another life,
a landscape locked in amber, the rare
gleam. The dream
of reason had produced its monster:
a prodigy of the wrong age and color.

All afternoon the student
with the dry fever of some draftsman's clerk
had magnified the harbor, now twilight
eager to complete itself,
drew a girl's figure to the open door

of a stone boathouse with a single stroke, then fell
to a reflecting silence. This silence waited
for the verification of detail:
the gables of the Saint Antoine Hotel
aspiring from jungle, the flag
at Government House melting its pole,
and for the tidal amber glare to glaze
the last shacks of the Morne till they became
transfigured sheerly by the student's will,
a cinquecento fragment in gilt frame.

The vision died,
the black hills simplified
to hunks of coal,
but if the light was dying through the stone
of that converted boathouse on the pier,
a girl, blowing its embers in her kitchen,
could feel its epoch entering her hair.

Darkness, soft as amnesia, furred the slope.
He rose and climbed towards the studio.
The last hill burned,
the sea crinkled like foil,
a moon ballooned up from the Wireless Station. O
mirror, where a generation yearned
for whiteness, for candor, unreturned.

The moon maintained her station,
her fingers stroked a chiton-fluted sea,
her disc whitewashed the shells
of gutted offices barnacling the wharves
of the burnt town, her lamp
baring the ovals of toothless façades,
along the Roman arches, as he passed
her alternating ivories lay untuned,

her age was dead, her sheet
shrouded the antique furniture, the mantel
with its plaster of paris Venus, which
his yearning had made marble, half-cracked
unsilvering mirror of black servants,
like the painter's kerchiefed, ear-ringed portrait: Albertina.

Within the door, a bulb
haloed the tonsure of a reader crouched
in its pale tissue like an embryo,
the leisured gaze
turned towards him, the short arms
yawned briefly, welcome. Let us see.
Brown, balding, a lacertilian
jut to its underlip,
with spectacles thick as a glass paperweight
over eyes the hue of sea-smoothed bottle glass,
the man wafted the drawing to his face
as if dusk were myopic, not his gaze.
Then, with slow strokes the master changed the sketch.

II

In its dimension the drawing could not trace
the sociological contours of the promontory;
once, it had been an avenue of palms
strict as Hobbema's aisle of lowland poplars,
now, leveled, bulldozed, and metaled for an airstrip,
its terraces like tree-rings told its age.
There, patriarchal banyans,
bearded with vines from which black schoolboys gibboned,
brooded on a lagoon seasoned with dead leaves,
mangroves knee-deep in water
crouched like whelk-pickers on brown, spindly legs

scattering red soldier crabs
scrabbling for redcoats' meat.
The groves were sawn
symmetry and contour crumbled,
down the arched barrack balconies
where colonels in the whiskey-colored light
had watched the green flash, like a lizard's tongue,
catch the last sail, tonight
row after row of orange stamps repeated
the villas of promoted Civil Servants.

The moon came to the window and stayed there.
He was her subject, changing when she changed,
from childhood he'd considered palms
ignobler than imagined elms,
the breadfruit's splayed
leaf coarser than the oak's,
he had prayed
nightly for his flesh to change,
his dun flesh peeled white by her lightning strokes!
Above the cemetery where
the airstrip's tarmac ended
her slow disc magnified
the life beneath her like a reading-glass.

Below the bulb
a green book, laid
face downward. Moon,
and sea. He read
the spine. FIRST POEMS:
CAMPBELL. The painter
almost absently
reversed it, and began to read:

"Holy be
the white head of a Negro,
sacred be
the black flax of a black child . . ."

And from a new book,
bound in sea-green linen, whose lines
matched the exhilaration which their reader,
rowing the air around him now, conveyed,
another life it seemed would start again
while past the droning, tonsured head
the white face
of a dead child stared from its window-frame.

III

They sang, against the rasp and cough of shovels,
against the fists of mud pounding the coffin,
the diggers' wrists rounding off every phrase,
their iron hymn, "The Pilgrims of the Night."
In the sea-dusk, the live child waited
for the other to escape, a flute
of frail, seraphic mist,
but their black, Bible-paper voices fluttered shut, silence
reentered every mold, it wrapped the edges
of sea-eaten stone, mantled the blind
eternally gesturing angels, strengthened the flowers
with a different patience, and left
or lost its hoarse voice in the shells
that trumpeted from the graves. The world
stopped swaying and settled in its place.
A black lace glove swallowed his hand.
The engine of the sea began again.

A night-black hearse, tasseled and heavy, lugged
an evening of blue smoke across the field,
like an old wreath the mourners broke apart
and drooped like flowers over the streaked stones
deciphering dates. The gravekeeper with his lantern-jaw
(years later every lantern-swinging porter
guarding infinite rails repeated this) opened
the yellow doorway to his lodge. Wayfarer's station.
The child's journey was signed.
The ledger drank its entry.
Outside the cemetery gates life stretched from sleep.

Gone to her harvest of flax-headed angels,
of seraphs blowing pink-palated conchs,
gone, so they sang, into another light:
But was it her?
Or Thomas Alva Lawrence's dead child,
another Pinkie, in her rose gown floating?
Both held the same dark eyes,
slow, haunting coals, the same curved
ivory hand touching the breast,
as if, answering death, each whispered "Mc?"

IV

Well, everything whitens,
all that town's characters, its cast of thousands
arrested in one still!
As if a sudden flashbulb showed their deaths.
The trees, the road he walks home, a white film,
tonight in the park the children leap into statues,
their outcries round as moonlight,
their flesh like flaking stone,
poor negatives!

They have soaked too long in the basin of the mind,
they have drunk the moon-milk
that X-rays their bodies,
the bone tree shows
through the starved skins,
and one has left, too soon,
a reader out of breath,
and once that begins, how shall I tell them,
while the tired filaments of another moon,
one that was younger,
fades, with the elate extinction of a bulb?

CHAPTER 2

I

At every first communion, the moon
would lend her lace to a barefooted town
christened, married and buried in borrowed white,
in fretwork borders of carpenter's Gothic,
in mansard bonnets, pleated jalousies,
when, with her laces laid aside,
she was a servant, her sign
a dry park of disconsolate palms, like brooms,
planted by the Seventh Edward, Prince of Wales,
with drooping ostrich crests, ICH DIEN, I SERVE.

I sweep. I iron. The smell of drizzled asphalt
like a flat-iron burning,
odors of smoke, the funereal berried ferns
that made an undertaker's parlor of our gallery.
Across the pebbled backyard, woodsmoke thins,
epiphany of ascension. The soul, like fire,
abhors what it consumes. In the upstairs rooms
smell of blue soap that puckered the black nurse's palms,
those hands which held our faces like a vase;
the coffee-grinder, grumbling,
ground its teeth,
waking at six.
                    The cracked egg hisses.
The sheets of Monday
are fluttering from the yard.
The week sets sail.

Maman,
only on Sundays was the Singer silent,
then,
tobacco smelt stronger, was more masculine.
Sundays
the parlor smelt of uncles,
the lamppoles rang,
the drizzle shivered its maracas,
like mandolins the tightening wires of rain,
then
from striped picnic buses, *jour marron*,
gold bangles tinkled like good-morning in Guinea
and a whore's laughter opened like sliced fruit.

Maman,
you sat folded in silence,
as if your husband might walk up the street,
while in the forests the cicadas pedaled their machines,
and silence, a black maid in white,
barefooted, polished and repolished
the glass across his fading watercolors,
the dumb Victrola cabinet,
the panels and the gleam of blue-winged teal
beating the mirror's lake.
In silence,
the revered, silent objects ring like glass,
at my eyes' touch, everything tightened, tuned,
Sunday,
the dead Victrola;

Sunday, a child
breathing with lungs of bread;
Sunday, the sacred silence of machines.

Maman,
your son's ghost circles your lost house, looking in
incomprehensibly at its dumb tenants
like fishes busily inaudible behind glass,
while the carpenter's Gothic joke, A, W, A, W,
Warwick and Alix involved in its eaves
breaks with betrayal.
You stitched us clothes from the nearest elements,
made shirts of rain and freshly ironed clouds,
then, singing your iron hymn, you riveted
your feet on Monday to the old machine.

Then Monday plunged her arms up to the elbows
in a foam tub, under a blue-soap sky,
the wet fleets sailed the yard, and every bubble
with its bent, mullioned window, opened
its mote of envy in the child's green eye
of that sovereign-headed, pink-cheeked bastard Bubbles
in the frontispiece of Pears Cyclopedia.
Rising in crystal spheres, world after world.

They melt from you, your sons.
Your arms grow full of rain.

III

Old house, old woman, old room,
old planes, old buckling membranes of the womb,
translucent walls,
breathe through your timbers; gasp
arthritic, curling beams,
cough in old air
shining with motes, stair
polished and repolished by the hands of strangers,

die with defiance flecking your gray eyes,
motes of a sunlit air,
your timbers humming with constellations of carcinoma,
your bed frames glowing with radium,
cold iron dilating the fever of your body,
while the galvanized iron snaps in spasms of pain,
but a house gives no outcry,
it bears the depth of forest, of ocean and mother.
Each consuming the other
with memory and unuse.

Why should we weep for dumb things?

This radiance of sharing extends to the simplest objects,
to a favorite hammer, a paintbrush, a toothless,
gum-sunken old shoe,
to the brain of a childhood room, retarded,
lobotomized of its furniture,
stuttering its inventory of accidents:
why this chair cracked,
when did the tightened scream
of that bedspring finally snap,
when did that unsilvering mirror finally
surrender her vanity,
and, in turn, these objects assess us,
that yellow paper flower with the eyes of a cat,
that stain, familiar as warts or some birthmark,
as the badge of some loved defect,

while the thorns of the bougainvillea
molt like old fingernails,
and the flowers keep falling,
and the flowers keep opening,
the allamandas' fallen bugles, but nobody charges.

Skin wrinkles like paint,
the forearm of a balustrade freckles,
crows' feet radiate
from the shut eyes of windows,
and the door, mouth clamped, reveals nothing,
for there is no secret,
there is no other secret
but a pain so alive that
to touch every ledge of that house edges a scream
from the burning wires, the nerves
with their constellation of cancer,
the beams with their star-seed of lice,
pain shrinking every room,
pain shining in every womb,
while the blind, dumb
termites, with jaws of the crabcells consume,
in silent thunder,
to the last of all Sundays,
consume.

Finger each object, lift it
from its place, and it screams again
to be put down
in its ring of dust, like the marriage finger
frantic without its ring;
I can no more move you from your true alignment,
mother, than we can move objects in paintings.

Your house sang softly of balance,
of the rightness of placed things.

CHAPTER 3

I

Each dusk the leaf flared on its iron tree,
the lamplighter shouldered his ladder, a sickle
of pale light fell on the curb.

The child tented his cotton nightdress tight
across his knees. A kite
whose twigs showed through. Twilight
enshrined the lantern of his head.

Hands swing him heavenward.
The candle's yellow leaf next to his bed
re-letters *Tanglewood Tales* and Kingsley's *Heroes*,
gilding their backs,

the ceiling reels with magic lantern shows.
The black lamplighter with Demeter's torch
ignites the iron trees above the shacks.
Boy! Who was Ajax?

II

Ajax,
          lion-colored stallion from Sealey's stable,
          by day a cart-horse, a thoroughbred
          on race-days, once a year,
          plunges the thunder of his neck, and sniffs
          above the garbage smells, the scent
          of battle, and the shouting,
          he saith among the kitchen peels "Aha!"

debased, bored animal,
its dung cakes pluming, gathers
the thunder of its flanks, and drags
its chariot to the next block, where

Berthilia,
the frog-like, crippled crone,
a hump on her son's back, is carried
to her straw mat, her day-long perch,
Cassandra, with her drone unheeded.
Her son, Pierre, carries night-soil in buckets,
she spurs him like a rider,
horsey-back, horsey-back;
when he describes his cross he sounds content,
he is everywhere admired. A model son.

Choiseul,
surly chauffeur from Clauzel's garage,
bangs Troy's gate shut!
It hinges on a scream. His rusty
commonlaw wife's. Hands hard as a crank handle,
he is obsequious, in love with engines.
They can be reconstructed. Before
human complications, his horny hands are thumbs.
Now, seal your eyes, and think of Homer's grief.

Darnley,
skin freckled like a mango leaf,
feels the sun's fingers press his lids.
His half-brother Russell steers him by the hand.
Seeing him, I practice blindness.
Homer and Milton in their owl-blind towers,
I envy him his great affliction. Sunlight
whitens him like a negative.

Emanuel
        Auguste, out in the harbor, lone Odysseus,
        tattooed ex-merchant sailor, rows alone
        through the rosebloom of dawn to chuckling oars
        measured, dip, pentametrical, reciting
        through narrowed eyes as his blades scissor silk,

            "Ah moon / (bend, stroke)
            of my delight / (bend, stroke)
            that knows no wane.
            The moon of heaven / (bend, stroke)
            is rising once again,"

        defiling past Troy town, his rented oars
        remembering what seas, what smoking shores?

FARAH & RAWLINS, temple with
        plate-glass front, gutted, but girded by
        Ionic columns, before which mincing

Gaga
        the town's transvestite, housemaid's darling
        is window-shopping, swirling his plastic bag,
        before his houseboy's roundtrip to Barbados,
        most Greek of all, the love that hath no name, and

Helen?
        Janie, the town's one clear-complexioned whore,
        with two tow-headed children in her tow,
        she sleeps with sailors only, her black
        hair electrical
        as all that trouble over Troy,
        rolling broad-beamed she leaves
        a plump and pumping vacancy,

"O promise me," as in her satin sea-heave follow
cries of

Ityn! Tin! Tin!
  from Philomène, the bird-brained idiot girl,
  eyes skittering as the sea-swallow
  since her rape,
  laying on lust, in her unspeakable tongue,
  her silent curse.

Joumard,
  the fowl-thief with his cockerel's strut,
  heads home like Jason, in his fluttering coat
  a smoke-drugged guinea-hen,
  the golden fleece,

Kyrie! kyrie! twitter
  a choir of surpliced blackbirds in the pews
  of telephone wires, bringing day to

Ligier,
  reprieved murderer, tangled in his pipe smoke
  wrestling Laocoön,
  bringing more gold to

Midas,
  Monsieur Auguste Manoir,
  pillar of business and the Church
  rising to watch the sunlight work for him,
  gilding the wharf's warehouses with his name.

Nessus,
  nicknamed N'homme Maman Migrain
  (your louse's mother's man),

rises in sackcloth, prophesying
fire and brimstone on the gilt wooden towers of
offices, ordures, on
Peter & Co. to burn like Pompeii, on J.
Q. Charles's stores, on the teetering, scabrous City of
Refuge, my old grandmother's barracks, where, once

Submarine,
the seven-foot-high bum-boatman,
loose, lank and gangling as a frayed cheroot,
once asking to see a ship's captain, and refused,
with infinite courtesy bending, inquired
"So what the hell is your captain?
A fucking microbe?"

Troy town awakens,
in its shirt of fire, but on our street

Uncle Eric
sits in a shadowed corner,
mumbling, hum-eyed,
writing his letters to the world,
his tilted hand scrambling for foothold.

Vaughan,
battling his itch, waits for the rumshop's
New Jerusalem, while Mister

Weekes,
slippered black grocer in gold-rimmed spectacles,
paddles across a rug of yellow sunshine
laid at his feet by the shadows of tall houses,
towards his dark shop,
propelled in his tranced passage by one star:
Garvey's imperial emblem of Africa United,

felt slippers muttering in Barbadian brogue,
and, entering his shop,
is mantled like a cleric
in a soutane of onion smells, saltfish and garlic,
salt-flaked Newfoundland cod hacked by a cleaver
on a scarred counter where a bent half-penny
shows Edward VII, Defender of the Faith, Emperor of India,
next to a Lincoln penny, IN GOD WE TRUST
"and in God one, b'Christ," thinks Mr. Weekes,
opening his Bible near the paradise plums,
arm crooked all day over a window open
at the New Jerusalem, for Colored People Only.
At Exodus.

Xodus, bearing back the saxophonist,
        Yes, whose ramshorn is his dented saxophone,
        bearing back to the green grasses of Guinea,

Zandoli,
        nicknamed The Lizard,
        rodent-exterminator, mosquito-murderer,
        equipment slung over a phthisic shoulder,
        safariing from Mary Ann Street's café,
        wiping a gum-bright grin, out for the week's assault on
        roaches, midges, jiggers, rodents, bugs and larvae,
        singing, refumigating
        Jerusalem, for Colored People Only.

These dead, these derelicts,
        that alphabet of the emaciated,
        they were the stars of my mythology.

CHAPTER 4

—Jerusalem, the golden
With milk and honey blest

Thin water glazed
                the pebbled knuckles of the Baptist's feet
In Craven's book.
Their halos shone like the tin guards of lamps.
Verocchio. Leonardo painted the kneeling angel's hair.
Kneeling in our plain chapel,
I envied them their frescoes.
Italy flung round my shoulders like a robe,
I ran among dry rocks, howling, "Repent!"
Zinnias, or else some coarser marigold,
brazenly rigid in their metal bowls
or our porch's allamandas trumpeted
from the Vermeer white napery of the altar:
LET US COME INTO HIS PRESENCE WITH THANKSGIVING
AND INTO HIS COURTS WITH PRAISE.
                        Those bowls,
in whose bossed brass the stewards were repeated
and multiplied, as in an insect's eye,
some jeweled insect in a corner of Crivelli,
were often ours, as were the trumpet flowers
between the silvered chargers with the Host
and ruby blood.
                Collect, epistle, lesson,
the Jacobean English rang, new-minted
the speech of simple men,
evangelists, reformers, abolitionists,
their text was cold brook water,
they fell to foreign fevers,
I would be a preacher,
I would write great hymns.

Arnold, staid melancholy of those Sabbath dusks,
I know those rigorous teachers of your youth,
Victorian gravures of the Holy Land,
thorn-tortured Palestine,
bearded disciples wrapped tight in malaria,
the light of desert fevers,
and those thin sunsets
with the consistency of pumpkin soup.
Gray chapel where parched and fiery Reverend Pilgrims
were shrieking twigs,
frock-coated beetles gesturing hellfire.
Are you cast down, cast down, my coal-black kin?
Be not afraid, the Lord shall raise you up.

The cloven hoof, the hairy paw
despite the passionate, pragmatic
Methodism of my infancy,
crawled through the thicket of my hair,
till sometimes the skin prickled
even in sunshine at "negromancy";
traumatic, tribal,
an atavism stronger than their Mass,
stronger than chapel, whose
tubers gripped the rooted middle-class,
beginning where Africa began:
in the body's memory.

I knew them all,
the "swell-foot," the epileptic "*mal-cadi*,"
cured by stinking compounds,
tisane, bush-bath, the exhausting emetic,
and when these failed, the incurably sored and sick
brought in a litter to the obeah-man.
One step beyond the city was the bush.
One step behind the churchdoor stood the devil.

One daybreak, as the iron light,
which guards dawn like a shopfront, lifted,
a scavenger washing the gutters stood
dumbstruck at the cross
where Chaussee Road and Grass Street intersect
before a rusting bloodstain.
A bubbling font at which
a synod of parsonical flies presided,
washing their hands. The scavenger Zandoli
slowly crossed himself.
The slowly sinking stain mapped no direction
in which the thing, a dog, perhaps, had crawled.
Light flushed its crimson like an obscene rose.
A knot of black communicants,
mainly old women, chorused round the wound.
The asphalt, like an artery, flowed, unstanched.

Monsieur Auguste Manoir, pillar of the Church,
lay on his back and watched dawn ring
his bed's gold quoits, and gild the view
of hills and roofs the hue of crusted blood,
heard the gray, iron harbor
open on a seagull's rusty hinge,
and knew, as soundlessly as sunlight,
that today he would die.

The blood of garbage mongrels had a thin,
watery excretion; this, a rich red
bubbled before their eyes.

Monsieur Manoir
urged his ringed, hairy hand to climb his stomach
to nuzzle at his heart.

Its crabbed jaw clenched the crucifix;
he heaved there, wheezing,
in the pose of one swearing eternal fealty,
hearing his blood race
like wine from a barrel when its bung has burst.

The blood coagulated like dregged wine.
Zandoli hefted a bucket
washing it wide. It
spread like a dying crab, clenching the earth.
Laved in a sudden wash of sweat, Manoir
struggled to scream for help.
His wife, in black, bent at communion.
Released, he watched the light deliriously dancing
on the cold, iron roofs of his warehouses
whose corrugations rippled with his name.

His hands still smelled of fish, of his beginnings,
hands that he'd ringed with gold, to hide their smell,
sometimes he'd hold them out,
puckered with lotions, powdered, to his wife,
a peasant's hands, a butcher's,
their acrid odor of saltfish and lard.
Drawn by the sweat,
a fly prayed at his ear-well:

Bon Dieu, pardon,
Demou, merci,
l'odeur savon,
l'odeur parfum
pas sait guérir
l'odeur péché,
l'odeur d'enfer,
pardonnez–moi
Auguste Manoir!

If there was one thing Manoir's watchman hated
more than the merchant, it was the merchant's dog,
more wolf than dog. It would break loose
some nights, rooting at the warehouse,
paws scuffing dirt like hands for some lost bone.
Before he struck it, something dimmed its eyes.
Its head dilating like an obscene rose,
humming and gemmed with flies, the dog
tottered through the tiled hallway of the house
towards its bed.

Under a scabrous roof whose fences
held the colors of dried blood, Saylie,
the wrinkled washerwoman, howled
in gibberish, in the devil's Latin.
Stepping back from the stench
as powerful as a cloud of smoke
the young priest chanted:
per factotem mundi,
per eum qui habet potestatem
mittendi te in gehennam . . .
six men with difficulty pinning her down,
gasping like divers coming up for breath,
her wild eyes rocketing,
as Beherit and Eazaz wrestled in her smoke.

The stores opened for business.
A stench of rumor filtered through the streets.
He was the first black merchant baron.
They would say things, of course, they would think things,
those children of his fellow villagers
descending the serpentine roads from the Morne,
they'd say his name in whispers now, "Manoir."

The priest prayed swiftly, averting his head,
she had, he knew, contracted with the devil,
now, dying, his dog's teeth tugged at her soul
like cloth in a wringer when the cogs have caught,
their hands pulled at its stuff through her clenched teeth,
"Name him!" The priest intoned, "Name! *Déparlez!*"
The bloodstain in the street dried quick as sweat.
"Manoir," she screamed, "that dog, Auguste Manoir."

I

AUGUSTE MANOIR, MERCHANT: LICENSED TO SELL
INTOXICATING LIQUOR, RETAILER, DRY GOODS, etc.
his signs peppered the wharves.
From the canted barracks of the City of Refuge,
from his grandmother's tea-shop, he would watch
on black hills of imported anthracite
the frieze of coal-black carriers, *charbonniers*,
erect, repetitive as hieroglyphs
descending and ascending the steep ramps,
building the pyramids,
songs of Egyptian bondage,
                            when they sang,
the burden of the panniered anthracite,
one hundredweight to every woman
tautened, like cable, the hawsers in their necks.
There was disease inhaled in the coal-dust.
Silicosis. Herring-gulls
white as the uniforms of tally clerks,
screeching, numbered and tagged the loads.

"Boy! Name the great harbors of the world!"
"Sydney! Sir."
"San Fransceesco!"
"Naples, sah!"
"And what about Castries?"
"Sah, Castries ees a coaling station and
der twenty-seventh best harba in der worl'!
In eet the entire Breetesh Navy can be heeden!"
"What is the motto of Saint Lucia, boy?"

"*Statio haud malefida carinis.*"
"Sir!"
"Sir!"
"And what does that mean?"
"Sir, a safe anchorage for sheeps!"

High on the Morne,
flowers medaled the gravestones of the Inniskillings,
too late. Bamboos burst like funereal gunfire.
Noon smoke of cannon fodder,
as black bat cries recited Vergil's tag: "*Statio haud!*"
Safe in their anchorage, sloe-lidded sloops
admired their reflections: *Phyllis Mark,*
Albertha Compton, Lady Joy, The Jewel.

II

The teetering two-storyed house next door became a haven
for bat-like transients.
Tenants flashed in and out of its dark rooms.
Their cries shot from its eaves. A family of creoles.
The mother a yellow, formidable Martiniquaise,
handsome, obliquely masculine, with a mole, "*très égyptienne,*"
black sapodilla-seed eyes
under the ziggurat of her pompadour,
we called "The Captain's Wife."

Sometimes, when the wind's hand creaked her upstairs window open,
hiding in the dim angle of our bedroom
I'd try to catch her naked. Their son, Gentile,
had round, scared eyes, a mouth
that gibbered in perpetual terror,
even in sunshine he shivered like a foundling.
"Gentile, Gentile!" we called. His own name frightened him.

We all knew when the Captain had dry-docked.
There would be violent bursts of shrieking French,
and in my own bed, parallel, separated by a gulf
of air, I'd hear the Captain's Wife,
sobbing, denying.
Next day her golden face seemed shrunken,
then, when he ulysseed, she bloomed again,
the bat-swift transients returned,
so many, perhaps they quartered in the eaves.
Dressed in black lace, like an impatient widow,
I imagined that skin, pomegranate, under silks
the sheen of water, and that
sweet-sour stink vixens give off.

Serene, and unimaginably naked,
as her dark countrymen hung round her rooms,
we heard their laughter tinkling above the glasses.
They came when Foquarde travelled down the coast.
Her laugh rang like the jangling of bracelets.

III

Jewel, a single stack, diesel, forty-foot coastal vessel,
its cabin curtained with canvas meant to shield
passengers from the sun,
but through which rain and shining spray still drenched,
coughed like a relic out of Conrad. Twice a week
she loaded her cargo of pigs, charcoal, food, lumber,
squabbling or frightened peasants, the odd priest,
threading the island's jettied villages,
Anse-la-Raye, Canaries, Soufrière, Choiseul,
and back. She also carried mail.

In deep green village coves she rocked offshore,
threatening her breakdown,
while rust bled from her wash,
a litter of dugouts nuzzling at her flank,
off-loading goods and passengers.

Disembarkation was precarious,
the inshore swell had to be nicely timed,
against the lunge of struggling canoes
in which, feet planted squarely as a mast, one man
stood, swaying, heaving with the swell.

IV

Her course sheared perilously close to the ochre rocks
and bushy outcrops of the leeward coast,
sometimes so closely that it seemed to us
"that all the shoreline's leaves were magnified
deliberately, with frightening detail,"
yet the yellow coast uncoiling past her prow
like new rope from a bollard never lost interest,
especially when the coiled beach lay
between black coves blinding
half-moon of sand,
before some settlement which the passengers
however often they had made this journey
always gave different names,
"because it went on repeating itself exactly,"
palms, naked children fishing, wretched huts,
a stone church by a brown, clogged river,
the leper colony of Malgrétoute.

A church, hedged by an unconverted forest,
a beach without a footprint, clear or malformed,

no children, no one, on the hollow pier.
The Jewel hove to, ringing her leper's bell.
The passengers crossed themselves and turned,
inevitably, to the priest.
He'd rise as the canoe appeared.
Condemned. I searched his skin.
The surpliced water heaved.
The bell tinkled like Mass. The priest got off.

He sat still in the long canoe, the afternoon
swallowed the bell-rings slowly,
one hand steadying his hat,
the other gripping its stern.
After a while we lost him to the dark green
ocean of the leaves, a white speck, a sail,
out of our memory and our gratitude.

FROM BOOK II: **HOMAGE TO GREGORIAS**

*I saw them growing gaunt and pale in their unlighted studios. The Indian turning
green, the Negro's smile gone, the white man more perverted—more and more
forgetful of the sun they had left behind, trying desperately to imitate what came
naturally to those whose rightful place was in the net. Years later, having frittered
away their youth, they would return with vacant eyes, all initiative gone, without
heart to set themselves the only task appropriate to the milieu that was slowly
revealing to me the nature of its values: Adam's task of giving things their names.*

ALEJO CARPENTIER, *The Lost Steps*

I

A gaunt, gabled house,
gray, fretted, soars
above a verdigris canal which
sours with moss. A bridge,
lithe as a schoolboy's leap,
vaults the canal. Each
longitudinal window seems
a vertical sarcophagus, a niche
in which its family must sleep
erect, repetitive as saints
in their cathedral crypt,
like urgent angels in their fluted stone
sailing their stone dream.
And like their house,
all the Gregoriases
were pious, arrogant men,
of that first afternoon, when
Gregorias ushered me in there,
I recall an air of bugled orders,
cavalry charges of children
tumbling down the stair,
a bristling, courteous father,
but also something delicate,
a dessicating frailty which showed
in his worn mother, a taut tree
shorn to the dark house's use,
its hothouse, fragile atmosphere
laboring yearly to produce
the specimen, *Gregorias elongatus.*

In the spear-lowering light of the afternoon
I paced his hunter's stride,
there was a hierarchic arrogance in his bearing
which crested in the martial,
oracular mustaches of his father,
a Lewis gunner in the First World War,
now brown, prehensile fingers plucked his work,
lurid Madonnas, pietistic crucifixions
modeled on common Catholic lithographs,
but with the personal flourish of a witness.
Widowed, his father's interest in life declined,
his battle finished. The brown twigs broke apart.

Around that golden year which I described
Gregorias and that finished soldier quartered
in a brown, broken-down bungalow
whose yard was indistinguishable from bush,
between the broad-leaved jungle and the town.
Shaky, half-rotted treaders, sighing, climbed
towards a sun-warped veranda, one half of which
Gregorias had screened into a studio,
shading a varnished, three-legged table
crawling with exhausted paint-tubes, a lowering quart
of *Pirate* rum, and gray, dog-eared, turpentine-stained editions
of the Old Masters. One day the floor collapsed.
The old soldier sank suddenly to his waist
wearing the veranda like a belt.
Gregorias buckled with laughter telling this,
but shame broke the old warrior.
The dusk lowered his lances through the leaves.
In another year the soldier shrank and died.
Embittered, Gregorias wanted carved on his stone:
PRAISE YOUR GOD, DRINK YOUR RUM, MIND YOUR OWN BUSINESS.

We were both fatherless now, and often drunk.

Drunk,
          on a half-pint of joiner's turpentine,
drunk,
             while the black, black-sweatered, horn-soled fishermen drank
             their *l'absinthe* in sand backyards standing up,
             on the clear beer of sunrise,
             on cheap, tannic Canaries muscatel,
             on glue, on linseed oil, on kerosene,
             as Van Gogh's shadow rippling on a cornfield,
             on Cézanne's boots grinding the stones of Aix
             to shales of slate, ochre and Vigie blue,
             on Gauguin's hand shaking the gin-colored dew
             from the umbrella yams,
             garrulous, all day, sun-struck,
till dusk glazed vision with its darkening varnish.
Days welded by the sun's torch into days!
Gregorias plunging whole-suit in the shallows,
painting under water, roaring, and spewing spray,
Gregorias gesturing, under the coconuts
wickerwork shade—tin glare—wickerwork shade,
days woven into days, a stinging haze
of thorn trees bent like green flames by the Trades,
under a sky tacked to the horizon, drumskin tight,
as shaggy combers leisurely beard the rocks,
while the asphalt sweats its mirages and the beaks
of fledgling ginger lilies
gasped for rain.
Gregorias, the easel rifled on his shoulder, marching
towards an Atlantic flashing tinfoil,
singing "O Paradiso,"
till the western breakers labored to that music,
his canvas crucified against a tree.

But drunkenly, or secretly, we swore,
disciples of that astigmatic saint,
that we would never leave the island
until we had put down, in paint, in words,
as palmists learn the network of a hand,
all of its sunken, leaf-choked ravines,
every neglected, self-pitying inlet
muttering in brackish dialect, the ropes of mangroves
from which old soldier crabs slipped
surrendering to slush,
each ochre track seeking some hilltop and
losing itself in an unfinished phrase,
under sand shipyards where the burnt-out palms
inverted the design of unrigged schooners,
entering forests, boiling with life,
goyave, corrosol, bois-canot, sapotille.

Days!
The sun drumming, drumming,
past the defeated pennons of the palms,
roads limp from sunstroke,
past green flutes of grass
the ocean cannonading, come!
Wonder that opened like the fan
of the dividing fronds
on some noon-struck Sahara,
where my heart from its rib-cage yelped like a pup
after clouds of sanderlings rustily wheeling
the world on its ancient,
invisible axis,
the breakers slow-dolphining over more breakers,
to swivel our easels down, as firm
as conquerors who had discovered home.

For no one had yet written of this landscape
that it was possible, though there were sounds
given to its varieties of wood;

the *bois-canot* responded to its echo,
when the axe spoke, weeds ran up to the knee
like bastard children, hiding in their names,

whole generations died, unchristened,
growths hidden in green darkness, forests
of history thickening with amnesia,

so that a man's branched, naked trunk,
its roots crusted with dirt,
swayed where it stopped, remembering another name;

breaking a lime leaf,
cracking an acrid ginger-root,
a smell of tribal medicine stained the mind,

stronger than ocean's rags,
than the reek of the maingot forbidden pregnant women,
than the smell of the horizon's rusting rim,

here was a life older than geography,
as the leaves of edible roots opened their pages
at the child's last lesson, Africa, heart-shaped,

and the lost Arawak hieroglyphs and signs
were razed from slates by sponges of the rain,
their symbols mixed with lichen,

the archipelago like a broken root,
divided among tribes, while trees and men
labored assiduously, silently to become

whatever their given sounds resembled,
ironwood, logwood-heart, golden apples, cedars,
and were nearly

ironwood, logwood-heart, golden apples, cedars,
men . . .

All have actually parted from the house, but all truly have remained. And it's not the memory of them that remains, but they themselves. Nor is it that they remain in the house but that they continue because of the house. The functions and the acts go from the house by train or by plane or on horseback, walking or crawling. What continues in the house is the organ, the gerundial or circular agent. The steps, the kisses, the pardons, the crimes have gone. What continues in the house is the foot, the lips, the eyes, the heart. Negations and affirmations, good and evil have scattered. What continues in the house is the subject of the act.

CESAR VALLEJO, *Poemas Humanos*

I

When the oil-green water glows but doesn't catch,
only its burnish, something wakes me early,
draws me out breezily to the pebbly shelf
of shallows where the water chuckles
and the ribbed boats sleep like children,
buoyed on their creases. I have nothing to do,
the burnished kettle is already polished,
to see my own blush burn,
and the last thing the breeze needs is my exhilaration.

I lie to my body with useless chores.
The ducks, if they ever slept, waddle knowingly.
The pleats of the shallows are neatly creased
and decorous and processional,
they arrive at our own harbor from the old Hospital
across the harbor. When the first canoe,
silent, will not wave at me,
I understand, we are acknowledging
our separate silences, as the one silence,
I know that they know my peace as I know theirs.
I am amazed that the wind is tirelessly fresh.
The wind is older than the world.

It is always one thing at a time.
Now, it is always girlish.
I am happy enough to see it as a kind
of dimpled, impish smiling.
When the sleep-smelling house stirs
to that hoarse first cough, that child's first cry,

that rumbled, cavernous questioning of my mother,
I come out of the cave
like the wind emerging,
like a bride, to her first morning.

I shall make coffee.
The light, like a fiercer dawn,
will singe the downy edges of my hair,
and the heat will plate my forehead till it shines.
Its sweat will share the excitement of my cunning.
Mother, I am in love.
Harbor, I am waking.
I know the pain in your budding, nippled limes,
I know why your limbs shake, windless, pliant trees.
I shall grow gray as this light.
The first flush will pass.
But there will always be morning,
and I shall have this fever waken me,
whoever I lie to, lying close to, sleeping
like a ribbed boat in the last shallows of night.

But even if I love not him but the world,
and the wonder of the world in him, of him in the world,
and the wonder that he makes the world waken to me,
I shall never grow old in him,
I shall always be morning to him,
and I must walk and be gentle as morning.
Without knowing it, like the wind,
that cannot see her face,
the serene humility of her exultation,
that having straightened the silk sea smooth, having noticed
that the comical ducks ignore her, that
the childish pleats of the shallows are set straight,
that everyone, even the old, sleeps in innocence,
goes in nothing, naked, as I would be,

if I had her nakedness, her transparent body.
The bells garland my head. I could be happy,
just because today is Sunday. No, for more.

II

Then Sundays, smiling, carried in both hands
a toweled dish bubbling with the good life
whose fervor steaming, beaded her clear brow,
from which damp skeins were brushed,
and ladled out her fullness to the brim.
And all those faded prints that pressed their scent
on her soft, house-warm body,
glowed from her flesh with work,
her hands that held the burnish of dry hillsides
freckled with fire-light,
hours that ripened till the fullest hour
could burst with peace.

"Let's go for a little walk," she said, one afternoon,
"I'm in a walking mood." Near the lagoon,
dark water's lens had made the trees one wood
arranged to frame this pair whose pace
unknowingly measured loss,
each face was set towards its character.
Where they now stood, others before had stood,
the same lens held them, the repeated wood,
then there grew on each one
the self-delighting, self-transfiguring stone
stare of the demi-god.
Stunned by their images they strolled on, content
that the black film of water kept the print
of their locked images when they passed on.

And which of them in time would be betrayed
was never questioned by that poetry
which breathed within the evening naturally,
but by the noble treachery of art
that looks for fear when it is least afraid,
that coldly takes the pulse-beat of the heart
in happiness; that praised its need to die
to the bright candor of the evening sky,
that preferred love to immortality;
so every step increased that subtlety
which hoped that their two bodies could be made
one body of immortal metaphor.
The hand she held already had betrayed
them by its longing for describing her.

CHAPTER 15

I

Still dreamt of, still missed,
especially on raw, rainy mornings, your face shifts
into anonymous schoolgirl faces, a punishment,
since sometimes, you condescend to smile,
since at the corners of the smile there is forgiveness.

Besieged by sisters, you were a prize
of which they were too proud, circled
by the thorn thicket of their accusation,
what grave deep wrong, what wound have you brought Anna?

The rain season comes with its load.
The half-year has travelled far. Its back hurts.
It drizzles wearily.

It is twenty years since,
after another war, the shell-cases are where?
But in our brassy season, our imitation autumn,
your hair puts out its fire,
your gaze haunts innumerable photographs,

now clear, now indistinct,
all that perusing generality,
that vengeful conspiracy with nature,

all that sly informing of objects,
and behind every line, your laugh
frozen into a lifeless photograph.

In that hair I could walk through the wheatfields of Russia,

your arms were downed and ripening pears,
for you became, in fact, another country,

you are Anna of the wheatfield and the weir,
you are Anna of the solid winter rain,
Anna of the smoky platform and the cold train,
in that war of absence, Anna of the steaming stations,

gone from the marsh-edge,
from the drizzled shallows
puckering with gooseflesh,
Anna of the first green poems that startlingly hardened,

of the mellowing breasts now,
Anna of the lurching, long flamingos
of the harsh salt lingering in the thimble
of the bather's smile,

Anna of the darkened house, among the reeking shell-cases
lifting my hand and swearing us to her breast,
unbearably clear-eyed.

You are all Annas, enduring all goodbyes,
within the cynical station of your body,
Christie, Karenina, big-boned and passive,

that I found life within some novel's leaves
more real than you, already chosen
as his doomed heroine. You knew, you knew.

II

Who were you, then?
The golden partisan of my young Revolution,
my braided, practical, seasoned commissar,

your back, bent at its tasks, in the blue kitchen,
or hanging flags of laundry, feeding the farm's chickens,
against a fantasy of birches,

poplars or whatever.
As if a pen's eye could catch that virginal litheness,
as if shade and sunlight leoparding the blank page
could be so literal,

foreign as snow,
far away as first love,
my Akhmatova!

Twenty years later, in the odor of burnt shells,
you can remind me of "A Visit to the Pasternaks,"
so that you are suddenly the word "wheat,"

falling on the ear, against the frozen silence of a weir,
again you are bending
over a cabbage garden, tending
a snowdrift of rabbits,
or pulling down the clouds from the thrumming clotheslines.

If dreams are signs,
then something died this minute,
its breath blown from a different life,

from a dream of snow, from paper
to white paper flying, gulls and herons
following this plow. And now,

you are suddenly old, white-haired,
like the herons, the turned page. Anna, I wake
to the knowledge that things sunder
from themselves, like peeling bark,

to the emptiness
of a bright silence shining after thunder.

III

"Any island would drive you crazy,"
I knew you'd grow tired
of all that iconography of the sea

like the young wind, a bride
riffling daylong the ocean's catalogue
of shells and algae,

everything, this flock
of white, novitiate herons
I saw in the grass of a gray parish church,

like nurses, or young nuns after communion,
their sharp eyes sought me out
as yours once, only.

And you were heron-like,
a water-haunter,
you grew bored with your island,

till, finally, you took off,
without a cry,
a novice in your nurse's uniform,

years later I imagined you
walking through trees to some gray hospital,
serene communicant,
but never "lonely,"

like the wind, never to be married,
your faith like folded linen, a nun's, a nurse's,
why should you read this now?

No woman should read verses
twenty years late. You go about your calling, candle-like
carrying yourself down a dark aisle

of wounded, married to the sick,
knowing one husband, pain,
only with the heron-flock, the rain,

the stone church, I remembered . . .
Besides, the slender, virginal New Year's
just married, like a birch
to a few crystal tears,

and like a birch bent at the register
who cannot, for a light's flash, change her name,
she still writes '65 for '66;

so, watching the tacit
ministering herons, each at its
work among the dead, the stone church, the stones,

I made this in your honor, when
vows and affections failing
your soul leapt like a heron sailing
from the salt, island grass

into another heaven.

IV

Anna replies:

I am simple,
I was simpler then.
It was simplicity
which seemed so sensual.

What could I understand,
the world, the light? The light
in the mud-stained sea-wash,
the light in a gull's creak

letting the night in?
They were simple to me,
I was not within them as simply
as I was within you.

It was your selflessness
which loved me as the world,
I was a child, as much
as you, but you brought the tears

of too many contradictions,
I became a metaphor, but
believe me I was unsubtle as salt.

And I answer, Anna,
twenty years after,
a man lives half of life,
the second half is memory,

the first half, hesitation
for what should have happened
but could not, or

what happened with others
when it should not.

A gleam. Her burning grip. The brass shell-cases,
oxidized, the brass reeking of cordite,
forty-one years after the Great War. The gleam
of brass reburnished in the allamanda,
through the barbed wire of bougainvillea thorns
beyond the window, on the sun-chevroned porch
I watched the far cannon-smoke of cloud
above the Morne, wounded, struck-dumb,
as she drew my hand firmly to the firstness
of the crisp, fragile cloth across her breast,
in a locked silence, she the nurse,
I the maimed soldier. There have been
other silences, none as deep. There has since
been possession, none as sure.

FROM BOOK IV: THE ESTRANGING SEA

Who order'd that their longing's fire
Should be, as soon as kindled, cool'd?
Who renders vain their deep desire?—
A God, a God their severance ruled!
And bade betwixt their shores to be
The unplumb'd, salt, estranging sea.

ARNOLD, "To Marguerite"

CHAPTER 20

—*Down their carved names*
the raindrop ploughs

HARDY

I

Smug, behind glass, we watch the passengers,
like cattle breaking, disembark.
One life, one marriage later I watched Gregorias stride
across the tarmac at Piarco, that familiar lope
that melancholy hunter's stride
seemed broken, part of the herd.
                              Something inside
me broke subtly, like a vein. I saw him grope
desperately, vaguely for his friend,
for something which a life's bewilderment could claim
as stable. I shouted, "Apilo!"
Panic and wonder struggled for the grin.

"O the years, O . . ."
                              The highway canes unrolled in
silence past the car glass, like glass
the years divided. We fished for the right level, shrill,
hysterical, until, when it subsided,
a cautionary silence glazed each word.
Was he as broken down as I had heard,
driven deep in debt,
unable to hold down a job, painting so badly
that those who swore his genius vindicated
everything once, now saw it as a promise never kept?
Viciously, near tears, I wished him dead.

I wished him a spiteful martyrdom, in revenge
for their contempt, their tiring laughter.
After I told him, he laughed and said, "I tried it once."

"One morning I lay helplessly in bed,
everything drained, gone. The children crying.
I couldn't take any more. I had dreamed of dying.
I sent for Peggy, you remember her?
She's in the States now. Anyhow,
I sent her to the bathroom for a blade . . .
When she had brought it, I asked her to go.
I lay there with the razor-blade in my hand . . .
I tried to cut my wrist . . . I don't know why
I stopped. I wanted very, very much to die . . .
Only some nights before, I had had a dream . . .
I dreamt . . ."
                    And what use what he dreamt?
"We lived in a society which denied itself heroes"
(Naipaul), poor scarred carapace
shining from those abrasions it has weathered,
wearing his own humility like a climate,
a man exhausted, racked by his own strength,
Gregorias, I saw, had entered life.

They shine, they shine,
such men. After the vision
of their own self-exhaustion bores them,
till, slowly unsurprised at their own greatness,
needing neither martyrdom nor magnificence,
"I see, I see," is what Gregorias cried,
living within that moment where he died.

Rereading Pasternak's *Safe Conduct*
as always again when life
startles under the lamplight,

I saw him brutally as Mayakovsky,
nostalgia, contempt raged for his death,
and the old choir of frogs,
those spinsterish, crackling cicadas.
Yet, even in such books
the element has burnt out,
honor and revelation are
a votive flame, and what's left
is too much like a wreath,
a smoky, abrupt recollection.
I write of a man whom life,
not death or memory, grants fame,
in my own pantheon, so, while
this fiery particle
thrives fiercely in another,
even if fueled by liquor
to venerate the good,
honor the humbly great,
to render in "an irresponsible citizen"
the simple flame.

Too late, too late.

II

The rain falls like knives
on the kitchen floor.
The sky's heavy drawer
was pulled out too suddenly.
The raw season is on us.

For days it has huddled on the kitchen sill,
tense, a smoke-and-orange kitten
flexing its haunches,

coiling its yellow scream
and now, it springs.
Nimble fingers of lightning
have picked the watershed,
the wires fling their beads.
Tears, like slow crystal beetles, crawl the pane.

On such days, when the postman's bicycle
whirrs dryly like the locust
that brings rain, I dread my premonitions.
A gray spot, a waterdrop
blisters my hand.
A sodden letter thunders in my hand.
The insect gnaws steadily at its leaf,
an eaten letter crumbles in my hand,
as he once held my drawing to his face,
as though dusk were myopic, not his gaze.

"Harry has killed himself. He was found dead
in a house in the country. He was dead for two days."

III

The fishermen, like thieves, shake out their silver,
the lithe knives wriggle on the drying sand.
They go about their work,
their chronicler has gone about his work.

At Garand, at Piaille, at L'Anse la Verdure,
the sky is gray as pewter, without meaning.
It thunders and the kitten scuttles back
into the kitchen bin
of coal, its tines sheathing, unsheathing,
its yellow eyes the color of fool's gold.

He had left this note.
No meaning, and no meaning.

All day, on the tin roofs
the rain berates the poverty of life,
all day the sunset bleeds like a cut wrist.

IV

Well, there you have your seasons, prodigy!
For instance, the autumnal fall of bodies,
deaths, like a comic, brutal repetition,
and in the Book of Hours, that seemed so far,
the light and amber of another life,
there is a Reaper busy about his wheat,
one who stalks nearer, and will not look up
from the scythe's swish in the orange evening grass,
and the fly at the front of your ear
sings, Hurry, hurry!
Never to set eyes on this page,
ah Harry, never to read our names,
like a stone blurred with tears I could not read
among the pilgrims, and the mooning child
staring from the window of the high studio.

Brown, balding, with a lacertilian
jut to his underlip,
with spectacles thick as a glass paperweight
and squat, blunt fingers,
waspish, austere, swift with asperities,
with a dimpled pot for a belly from the red clay of Piaille.
Eyes like the glint of sea-smoothed bottle glass,
his knee-high khaki stockings,
brown shoes lacquered even in desolation.

People entered his understanding
like a wayside country church,
they had built him themselves.
It was they who had smoothed the wall
of his clay-colored forehead,
who made of his rotundity an earthy
useful object
holding the clear water of their simple troubles,
he who returned their tribal names
to the adze, mattock, midden, and cookingpot.
A tang of white rum on the tongue of the mandolin,
a young bay, parting its mouth,
a heron silently named or a night-moth,
or the names of villages plaited into one map,
in the evocation of scrubbed backyard smoke,
and he is a man no more
but the fervor and intelligence
of a whole country.

Leonce, Placide, Alcindor,
Dominic, from whose plane vowels were shorn
odorous as forest,
ask the charcoal-burner to look up
with his singed eyes,
ask the lip-cracked fisherman three miles at sea
with nothing between him and Dahomey's coast
to dip rain-water over his parched boards
for Monsieur Simmons, *pour* Msieu Harry Simmons,
let the husker on his pyramid of coconuts
rest on his tree.

Blow out the eyes in the unfinished portraits.

And the old woman who danced
with a spine like the "glory cedar,"

so lissome that her veins bulged evenly
upon the tightened drumskin of the earth,
her feet nimbler than the drummer's fingers,
let her sit in her corner and become evening
for a man the color of her earth,
for a cracked claypot full of idle brushes,
and the tubes curl and harden,
except the red,
except the virulent red!

His island forest, open and enclose him
like a rare butterfly between its leaves.

CHAPTER 21

I

Why?
You want to know why?
Go down to the shacks then,
like shattered staves
bound in old wire
at the hour when
the sun's wrist bleeds in
the basin of the sea,
and you will sense it,

or follow the path
of the caked piglet through
the sea-village's midden,
past the repeated
detonations of spray,
where the death-rattle
gargles in the shale,
and the crab,
like a letter, slides
into its crevice,
and you may understand this,

smell the late, ineradicable reek
of stale rags like rivers
at daybreak, or the dark corner
of the salt-caked shop where the cod-
barrel smells of old women,
and you can start then,

to know how the vise
of horizon tightens
the throat, when the first sulphur star
catches the hum
of insects round the gas lantern
like flies round a sore.
No more? Then hang round the lobby
of the one cinema too early

in the hour between two illusions
where you startle at the chuckle
of water under the shallop
of the old schooner basin,
or else it is still under all
the frighteningly formal
marches of banana groves,
the smell from the armpits of cocoa,

from the dead, open mouths
of husked nuts
on the long beach at twilight,
old mouths filled with water,
or else with no more to say.

11

So you have ceased to ask yourself,
nor do these things ask you,
for the bush too is an answer
without a question,
as the sea is a question, chafing,
impatient for answers,
and we are the same.
They do not ask us, master,

do you accept this?
A nature reduced to the service
of praising or humbling men,
there is a yes without a question,
there is assent founded on ignorance,
in the mangroves plunged to the wrist, repeating
the mangroves plunging to the wrist,
there are spaces
wider than conscience.

Yet, when I continue to see
the young deaths of others,
even of lean old men, perpetually young,
when the alphabet I learnt as a child
will not keep its order,
see the young wife, self-slain
like scentful clove in the earth,
a skin the color of cinnamon,
there is something which balances,
I see him bent under the weight of the morning,
against its shafts,
devout, angelical,
the easel rifling his shoulder,
the master of Gregorias and myself,
I see him standing over the bleached roofs
of the salt-streaked villages,
each steeply pricked
by its own wooden star.

I who dressed too early for the funeral of this life,
who saw them all, as pilgrims of the night.

And do I still love her, as I love you?
I have loved all women who have evolved from her,
fired by two marriages
to have her gold ring true.
And on that hill, that evening,
when the deep valley grew blue with forgetting,
why did I weep,
why did I kneel,
whom did I thank?
I knelt because I was my mother,
I was the well of the world,
I wore the stars on my skin,
I endured no reflections,
my sign was water,
tears and the sea,
my sign was Janus,
I saw with twin heads,
and everything I say is contradicted.

I was fluent as water,
I would escape
with the linear elation of an eel,
a vase of water in its vase of clay,
my clear tongue licked the freshness of the earth,
and when I leapt from that shelf
of rock, an abounding bolt of lace,
I leapt for the pride of that race
at Sauteurs! An urge more than mine,
so, see them as heroes or as the Gadarene swine,
let it be written, I shared, I shared,
I was struck like rock, and I opened
to His gift!
I laughed at my death-gasp in the rattle

of the sea-shoal.
You want to see my medals? Ask the stars.
You want to hear my history? Ask the sea.
And you, master and friend,
forgive me!
Forgive me, if this sketch should ever thrive,
or profit from your gentle, generous spirit.
When I began this work, you were alive,
and with one stroke, you have completed it!

O simultaneous stroke of chord and light,
O tightened nerves to which the soul vibrates,
some flash of lime-green water, edged with white—
"I have swallowed all my hates."

IV

For I have married one whose darkness is a tree,
bayed in whose arms I bring my stifled howl,
love and forgive me!
Who holds my fears at dusk like birds which take
the lost or moonlit color of her leaves,
in whom our children
and the children of friends settle
simply, like rhymes,
in whose side, in the grim times
when I cannot see light for the deep leaves,
sharing her depth, the whole lee ocean grieves.

CHAPTER 22

I

Miasma, acedia, the enervations of damp,
as the teeth of the mold gnaw, greening the carious stump
of the beaten, corrugated silver of the marsh light,
where the red heron hides, without a secret,
as the cordage of mangrove tightens
bland water to bland sky
heavy and sodden as canvas,
where the pirogue foundered with its caved-in stomach
(a hulk, trying hard to look like
a paleolithic, half-gnawed memory of pre-history)
as the too green acid grasses set the salt teeth on edge,
acids and russets and watercolored water,
let the historian go mad there
from thirst. Slowly the water rat takes up its reed pen
and scribbles. Leisurely, the egret
on the mud tablet stamps its hieroglyph.

The explorer stumbles out of the bush crying out for myth.
The tired slave vomits his past.
The Mediterranean accountant, with the nose of the water rat,
ideograph of the egret's foot,
calculates his tables,
his eyes reddening like evening in the glare of the brass lamp;
the Chinese grocer's smile is leaden with boredom:
so many lbs. of cod,
          so many bales of biscuits,
on spiked shop paper,
the mummified odor of onions,
spikenard, and old Pharaohs peeling like onionskin
to the archaeologist's finger—all that

is the muse of history. Potsherds,
and the crusted amphora of cutthroats.

Like old leather,
tannic, stinking, peeling in a self-contemptuous
curl away from itself,
the yellowing poems, the spiked brown paper,
the myth of the golden Carib,
like a worn-out film,
the lyrical arrow in the writhing Arawak maiden
broken under the leaf-light.
                              The astigmatic geologist
stoops, with the crouch of the heron,
deciphering—not a sign.
All of the epics are blown away with the leaves,
blown with the careful calculations on brown paper;
these were the only epics: the leaves.

No horsemen here, no cuirasses
crashing, no fork-bearded Castilians,
only the narrow, silvery creeks of sadness
like the snail's trail,
only the historian deciphering, in invisible ink,
its patient slime,
no cataracts abounding down gorges
like bolts of lace,
while the lizards are taking a million years to change,
and the lopped head of the coconut rolls to gasp on the sand,
its mouth open at the very moment
of forgetting its name.

That child who sets his half-shell afloat
in the brown creek that is Rampanalgas River—
my son first, then two daughters—
towards the roar of waters,

towards the Atlantic with a dead almond leaf for a sail,
with a twig for a mast,
was, like his father, this child,
a child without history, without knowledge of its pre-world,
only the knowledge of water runneling rocks,
and the desperate whelk that grips the rock's outcrop
like a man whom the waves can never wash overboard;
that child who puts the shell's howl to his ear,
hears nothing, hears everything
that the historian cannot hear, the howls
of all the races that crossed the water,
the howls of grandfathers drowned
in that intricately swiveled Babel,
hears the fellaheen, the Madrasi, the Mandingo, the Ashanti,
yes, and hears also the echoing green fissures of Canton,
and thousands without longing for this other shore
by the mud tablets of the Indian Provinces,
robed ghostly white and brown, the twigs of uplifted hands,
of manacles, mantras, of a thousand kaddishes,
whorled, drilling into the shell,
see, in the evening light by the saffron, sacred Benares,
how they are lifting like herons,
robed ghostly white and brown,
and the crossing of water has erased their memories.
And the sea, which is always the same,
accepts them.
And the shore, which is always the same,
accepts them.

In the shallop of the shell,
in the round prayer,
in the palate of the conch,
in the dead sail of the almond leaf
are all of the voyages.

And those who gild cruelty,
who read from the entrails of disemboweled Aztecs
the colors of Hispanic glory
greater than Greece,
greater than Rome,
than the purple of Christ's blood,
the golden excrement on barbarous altars
of their beaked and feathered king,
and the feasts of human flesh,
those who remain fascinated,
in attitudes of prayer,
by the festering roses made from their fathers' manacles,
or upraise their silver chalices flecked with vomit,
who see a golden, cruel, hawk-bright glory
in the conquistador's malarial eye,
crying, at least here
something happened—
they will absolve us, perhaps, if we begin again,
from what we have always known, nothing,
from that carnal slime of the garden,
from the incarnate subtlety of the snake,
from the Egyptian moment of the heron's foot
on the mud's entablature,
by this augury of ibises
flying at evening from the melting trees,
while the silver-hammered charger of the marsh light
brings towards us, again and again, in beaten scrolls,
nothing, then nothing,
and then nothing.

Here, rest. Rest, heaven. Rest, hell.
Patchwork, sunfloor, seafloor of pebbles at Resthaven, at Rampanalgas.
Sick of black angst.
Too many penitential histories passing
for poems. Avoid:
        1857 Lucknow and Cawnpore.
The process of history machined through fact,
for the poet's cheap alcohol,
lines like the sugarcane factory's mechanization of myth
ground into rubbish.
        1834 Slavery abolished.
A century later slavishly revived
for the nose of the water rat, for the literature of the factory,
in the masochistic veneration of
chains, and the broken rum jugs of cutthroats.
Exegesis, exegesis, writers
giving their own sons homework.

Ratoon, ratoon,
immigrant hordes downed soughing,
sickled by fever, *mal d'estomac*,
earth-eating slaves fitted with masks against despair,
not mental despondence but helminthiasis.

Pour la dernière fois, nommez! Nommez!

Abouberika Torre commonly called Joseph Samson.
Hammadi Torrouke commonly called Louis Modeste.
Mandingo sergeants offered Africa back,
the boring process of repatriation,
while to the indentured Indians
the plains of Caroni seemed like the Gangetic plain,
our fathers' bones. Which father?

Burned in the pyre of the sun.
On the ashpit of the sand.
Also you, Grandfather. Rest, heaven, rest, hell.
I sit in the roar of that sun
like a lotus yogi folded on his bed of coals,
my head is circled with a ring of fire.

IV

O sun, on that morning,
did I not mutter towards your
holy, repetitive resurrection, "Hare
hare Krishna," and then, politely,
"Thank you, life"? Not
to enter the knowledge of God
but to know that His name
had lain too familiar on my tongue,
as this one would say "bread,"
or "sun," or "wine," I staggered,
shaken at my remorse, as one
would say "bride," or "bread,"
or "sun," or "wine," to believe—
and that you would rise again,
when I am not here, to catch
the air afire, that you need not
look for me, or need this prayer.

v

So, I shall repeat myself,
prayer, same prayer, towards fire, same fire,
as the sun repeats itself and the thundering waters

for what else is there
but books, books and the sea,
verandas and the pages of the sea,
to write of the wind and the memory of wind-whipped hair
in the sun, the color of fire?

I was eighteen then, now I am forty-one,
I have had a serpent for companion,
I was a heart full of knives,
but, my son, my sun,

holy is Rampanalgas and its high-circling hawks,
holy are the rusted, tortured, rust-caked, blind almond trees,
your great-grandfather's, and your father's torturing limbs,
holy the small, almond-leaf-shadowed bridge
by the small red shop, where everything smells of salt,
and holiest the break of the blue sea below the trees,
and the rock that takes blows on its back
and is more rock,
and the tireless hoarse anger of the waters
by which I can walk calm, a renewed, exhausted man,
balanced at its edge by the weight of two dear daughters.

VI

Holy were you, Margaret,
and holy our calm.
What can I do now

but sit in the sun to burn
with an ageing mirror that blinds,
combing, uncombing my hair—

escape? No, I am inured
only to the real, which
burns. Like the flesh

of my children afire.
Inured. Inward. As rock,
I wish, as the real

rock I make real,
to have burnt out desire,
lust, except for the sun

with her corona of fire.
Anna, I wanted to grow white-haired
as the wave, with a wrinkled

brown rock's face, salted,
seamed, an old poet,
facing the wind

and nothing, which is,
the loud world in his mind.

CHAPTER 23

I

At the Malabar Hotel cottage
I would wake every morning surprised
by the framed yellow jungle of
the groyned mangroves meeting
the groyned mangroves repeating
their unbroken water line.
Years. The island had not moved
from anchor.
              Generations of waves,
generations of grass, like foam
petaled and perished in an instant.

I lolled in the shallows like an aging hammerhead
afraid of my own shadow, hungering there.
When my foot struck sand, the sky rang,
as I inhaled, a million leaves drew inward.
I bent towards what I remembered,
all was inevitably shrunken,
it was I who first extended my hand
to nameless arthritic twigs,
and a bush would turn in the wind
with a toothless giggle, and
certain roots refused English.
But I was the one in awe.

This was a new pain,
I mean the mimosa's averring
"You mightn't remember me,"
like the scars of that scrofulous sea-grape
where Gregorias had crucified a canvas,

and there, still dancing like the old woman
was the glory, the *gloricidia*.
I would not call up Anna.
I would not visit his grave.

II

They had not changed, they knew only
the autumnal hint of hotel rooms
the sea's engine of air-conditioners,
and the waitress in national costume
and the horsemen galloping past the single wave
across the line of Martinique, the horse or *la mer*
out of Gauguin by the Tourist Board.
Hotel, hotel, hotel, hotel, hotel and a club: The Bitter End.
This is not bitter, it is harder
to be a prodigal than a stranger.

III

I looked from old verandas at
verandas, sails, the eternal summer sea
like a book left open by an absent master.
And what if it's all gone,
the hill's cut away for more tarmac,
the groves all sawn,
and bungalows proliferate on the scarred, hacked hillside,
the magical lagoon drained
for the Higher Purchase plan,
and they've bulldozed and bowdlerized our Vigie,
our *ocelle insularum*, our Sirmio
for a pink and pastel New Town where the shacks and huts stood
teetering and tough in unabashed unhope,

as twilight like amnesia blues the slope,
when over the untroubled ocean, the moon
will always swing its lantern
and evening fold the pages of the sea,
and peer like my lost reader silently
between the turning leaves
for the lost names
of Caribs, slaves and fishermen?

Forgive me, you folk,
who exercise a patience
subtler, stronger than the muscles
in the wave's wrist,
and you, sea, with the mouth
of that old gravekeeper
white-headed, lantern-jawed,
forgive our desertions, you islands
whose names dissolve like sugar
in a child's mouth. And you, Gregorias.
And you, Anna. Rest.

IV

But ah, Gregorias,
I christened you with that Greek name because
it echoes the blest thunders of the surf,
because you painted our first, primitive frescoes,
because it sounds explosive,
a black Greek's! A sun that stands back
from the fire of itself, not shamed, prizing
its shadow, watching it blaze!
You sometimes dance with that destructive frenzy
that made our years one fire.
Gregorias listen, lit,

we were the light of the world!
We were blest with a virginal, unpainted world
with Adam's task of giving things their names,
with the smooth white walls of clouds and villages
where you devised your inexhaustible,
impossible Renaissance,
brown cherubs of Giotto and Masaccio,
with the salt wind coming through the window,
smelling of turpentine, with nothing so old
that it could not be invented,
and set above it your crude wooden star,
its light compounded in that mortal glow:
Gregorias, Apilo!

April 1965–April 1972

FROM

Sea Grapes

(1976)

That little sail in light
which tires of islands,
a schooner beating up the Caribbean

for home, could be Odysseus,
home-bound on the Aegean,
that father and husband's

longing, under gnarled sour grapes, is
like the adulterer hearing Nausicaa's name
in every gull's outcry;

This brings nobody peace. The ancient war
between obsession and responsibility
will never finish and has been the same

for the sea-wanderer or the one on shore
now wriggling on his sandals to walk home,
since Troy lost its old flame,

and the blind giant's boulder heaved the trough
from whose ground-swell the great hexameters come
to finish up as Caribbean surf.

The classics can console. But not enough.

The adulteress stoned to death,
is killed in our own time
by whispers, by the breath
that films her flesh with slime.

The first was Eve,
who horned God for the serpent,
for Adam's sake; which makes
everyone guilty or Eve innocent.

Nothing has changed
for men still sing the song that Adam sang
against the world he lost to vipers,

the song to Eve
against his own damnation;
he sang it in the evening of the world

with the lights coming on in the eyes
of panthers in the peaceable kingdom
and his death coming out of the trees,

he sings it, frightened
of the jealousy of God and at the price
of his own death,

the song ascends to God who wipes his eyes:

"Heart, you are in my heart as the bird rises,
heart, you are in my heart while the sun sleeps,
heart, you lie still in me as the dew is,
you weep within me, as the rain weeps."

PARTY NIGHT AT THE HILTON

In our upside-down hotel, in that air-conditioned
roomful of venal, vengeful party-hacks,
lunch-drunk, scotch-drunk, cigar and brandy-stoned,
arguing, insulting till coherence cracks,
poor voice on the rock of power, drained
of every sense but retching indignation
before these pimp Nkrumahs! Their minds
greased by infanticide, generation on generation
heaped in a famine of imagination,
while dacrons sleek their paunches and behinds
with air, hot air. Guilt, sweated
out in glut, while outside, a black wind,
circles the room with jasmine, like a whore's
perfume or second secretary's lotion. Fear those laws
which ex-slaves praise with passion. Pissed, dead
drunk, I soar to hellish light. In the lobby,
cigars with eyes like agents drilling me.

You should crawl into rocks away from
the stare of the fisherman,
you, yes, you!

Don't you remember the hustings by the beach
with their sulphurous lanterns,
and your lies in the throat of the sea?

You should get your arse baked till your back
is an old map of blisters,
and your lips crack

like the soil for the water you promised
on the dais, with the sound system
and the sisters calling you Jesus,

and come back with a sieve for your heart,
your brain like a rusted can,
and your bilge reeking,

turn your head, man, I'm speaking
now, I haven't spoken enough, I am speaking
so do what you want, man!

When the first roar came you were astounded,
it was sweeping your heart like a hurricane;
but what are your promises? A grounded

ribbed vessel that the naked
children play through. Listen, you

could still come with me again,
to watch the rain coming from far
like rain, not like votes,

like the ocean, like the wind,
not like an overwhelming majority,
you, who served the people a dung cake of maggots,

that rain cannot extinguish
the processional flambeaux of the poui,
the immortelles, feel it with me

again, you bastard papas,
how it seeps through the pores,
how it loads the sponge of the heart

with the grief of a people,
or smile at this rage, then,
buzzard in a conference coat,

bishop in a buzzard's surplice,
crows circling like shadows
over this page,

ministers administering
the last rights to a people,
cabinet, crowded with skeletons,

here's a swinging convocation of bishops
and ministers on the old beach.
Corbeaux. And nobody here with a flashbulb!

There's the wide desert, but no one marches
except in the pads of old caravans,
there is the ocean, but the keels incise
the precise, old parallels,
there's the blue sea above the mountains
but they scratch the same lines
in the jet trails,
so the politicians plod
without imagination, circling
the same somber gardens
with its fountain dry in the forecourt,
the gri-gri palms desiccating
dung pods like goats,
the same lines rule the White Papers,
the same steps ascend Whitehall,
and only the name of the fool changes
under the plumed white cork-hat
for the Independence Parades
revolving around, in calypso,
to the brazen joy of the tubas.

Why are the eyes of the beautiful
and unmarked children
in the uniforms of the country
bewildered and shy,
why do they widen in terror
of the pride drummed into their minds?
Were they truer, the old songs,
when the law lived far away,
when the veiled queen, her girth
as comfortable as cushions,
upheld the orb with its stern admonitions?

We wait for the changing of statues,
for the change of parades.

Here he comes now, here he comes!
Papa! Papa! With his crowd,
the sleek, waddling seals of his Cabinet,
trundling up to the dais,
as the wind puts its tail between
the cleft of the mountains, and a wave
coughs once, abruptly.
Who will name this silence
respect? Those forced, hoarse hosannas
awe? That tin-ringing tune
from the pumping, circling horns
the New World? Find a name
for that look on the faces
of the electorate. Tell me
how it all happened, and why
I said nothing.

Forged from the fire of Exodus
the iron of the tribe,

bright as the lion light, Isaiah,
the anger of the tribe

that the crack must come
and sunder the stone

and the sky-stone fall
on Babylon, Babylon,

the crack in the prison wall
in the chasm of tenements

when the high, high C, Joshua
cry, as I for my tribe:

but in the black markets
lizard-smart poets

selling copper tributes
changing skin with the tribe

and the tribe still buys it
the dreams and the lies

that there'll come to market
as the brethren divide

like the Red Sea to Moses
halt by Aaron's rod

the rod which is both serpent
and staff of brotherhood

more cripples like questions
on the snakes of black tires

Solomon in black glasses
hiding his eyes

shaking hands all round
statistics and jiving

to the clapping of the tribe;
Economics and Exodus,

embrace us within
bracket and parenthesis

their snake arms of brotherhood
(the brackets of the bribe)

Want to open your mouth, then?
Shake your dread locks, brethren?

and see one door yawn wide,
then the lion-den of prison,

sky mortar like stone;
Brothers in Babylon, Doc! Uncle! Papa!

Behind the dark glasses
the fire is dying

the coal of my people;
no vision, no flame,

no deepness, no danger,
more music, less anger

more sorrow, less shame
more talk of the River

that wash out my name
let things be the same

forever and ever
the faith of my tribe.

NAMES

for Edward Brathwaite

I

My race began as the sea began,
with no nouns, and with no horizon,
with pebbles under my tongue,
with a different fix on the stars.

But now my race is here,
in the sad oil of Levantine eyes,
in the flags of the Indian fields,

I began with no memory,
I began with no future,
but I looked for that moment
when the mind was halved by a horizon,

I have never found that moment
when the mind was halved by a horizon
for the goldsmith from Benares,
the stone-cutter from Canton,
as a fishline sinks, the horizon
sinks in the memory.

Have we melted into a mirror,
leaving our souls behind?
The goldsmith from Benares,
the stone-cutter from Canton,
the bronzesmith from Benin.

A sea-eagle screams from the rock,
and my race began like the osprey

with that cry,
that terrible vowel,
that I!

Behind us all the sky folded,
as history folds over a fishline,
and the foam foreclosed
with nothing in our hands

but this stick
to trace our names on the sand
which the sea erased again, to our indifference.

II

And when they named these bays
bays,
was it nostalgia or irony?

In the uncombed forest,
in uncultivated grass
where was there elegance
except in their mockery?
Where were the courts of Castille,
Versailles' colonnades
supplanted by cabbage palms
with Corinthian crests,
belittling diminutives,
then, little Versailles
meant plans for a pigsty,
names for the sour apples
and green grapes
of their exile.

Their memory turned acid
but the names held,
Valencia glows
with the lanterns of oranges,
Mayaro's
charred candelabra of cocoa.
Being men, they could not live
except they first presumed
the right of every thing to be a noun.
The African acquiesced,
repeated, and changed them.

Listen, my children, say:
moubain: the hogplum,
cerise: the wild cherry,
baie-la: the bay,
with the fresh green voices
they were once themselves
in the way the wind bends
our natural inflections.

These palms are greater than Versailles,
for no man made them,
their fallen columns greater than Castille,
no man unmade them
except the worm, who has no helmet,
but was always the emperor,

and children, look at these stars
over Valencia's forest!

Not Orion,
not Betelgeuse,
tell me, what do they look like?
Answer, you damned little Arabs!
Sir, fireflies caught in molasses.

SAINTE LUCIE

I THE VILLAGES

Laborie, Choiseul, Vieuxfort, Dennery,
from these sun-bleached villages
where the church-bell caves in the sides
of one gray-scurfed shack that is shuttered
with warped boards, with rust
with crabs crawling under the house-shadow
where the children played house;
a net rotting among cans, the sea-net
of sunlight trolling the shallows
catching nothing all afternoon,
from these I am growing no nearer
to what secret eluded the children
under the house-shade, in the far bell, the noon's
stunned amethystine sea,
something always being missed
between the floating shadow and the pelican
in the smoke from over the next bay
in that shack on the lip of the sandpit
whatever the seagulls cried out for
with the gray drifting ladders of rain
and the great gray tree of the waterspout,
for which the dolphins kept diving, that
should have rounded the day.

II

Pomme arac,
otaheite apple,
pomme cythere,

pomme granate,
moubain,
z'anananas
the pine apple's
Aztec helmet,
pomme,
I have forgotten
what pomme for
the Irish potato,
cerise,
the cherry,
z'aman
sea-almonds
by the crisp
sea-bursts,
au bord de la 'ouviere.
Come back to me
my language.
Come back,
cacao,
grigri,
solitaire,
ciseau
the scissor-bird
no nightingales
except, once
in the indigo mountains
of Jamaica, blue depth,
deep as coffee,
flicker of pimento,
the shaft light
on a yellow ackee
the bark alone bare

jardins
en montagnes
en haut betassion
the wet leather reek
of the hill donkey

evening opens at
a text of fireflies,
in the mountain huts
ti cailles betassion
candles,
candleflies
the black night bending
cups in its hard palms
cool thin water
this is important water,
important?
imported?
water is important
also very important
the red rust drum
of evening deep
as coffee
the morning powerful
important coffee
the villages shut
all day in the sun.

In the empty schoolyard
teacher dead today
the fruit rotting
yellow on the ground
dyes from Gauguin
the pomme arac dyes
the earth purple,

the ochre roads
still waiting in the sun
for my shadow,
O so you is Walcott?
you is Roddy brother?
Teacher Alix son?
and the small rivers
with important names.

And the important corporal
in the country station
en betassion
looking towards the thick
green slopes of cocoa
the sun that melts
the asphalt at noon,
and the woman in the shade
of the breadfruit bent over
the lip of the valley,
below her, blue-green
the lost, lost valleys
of sugar, the bus-rides,
the fields of bananas
the tanker still rusts
in the lagoon at Roseau,
and around what corner

was uttered a single
yellow leaf,
from the frangipani
a tough bark, reticent,
but when it flowers
delivers hard lilies,
pungent, recalling
Martina, or Eunice

or Lucilla,
who comes down the steps
with the cool, side flow
as spring water eases
over shelves of rock
in some green ferny hole
by the road in the mountains,
her smile like the whole country
her smell, earth,
red-brown earth, her armpits
a reaping, her arms
saplings, an old woman
that she is now,
with other generations
of daughters flowing
down the steps,
gens betassion,
belle ti fille betassion,
until their teeth go,
and all the rest,

O Martinas, Lucillas,
I'm a wild golden apple
that will burst with love,
of you and your men,
those I never told enough
with my young poet's eyes
crazy with the country,
generations going,
generations gone,
moi c'est gens St. Lucie.
C'est la moi sorti;
is there that I born.

(Saint Lucian *conte* or narrative song, heard on the back of an open truck travelling to Vieuxfort, some years ago)

Ma Kilman, Bon Dieu kai punir 'ous,
Pour qui raison parcequi'ous entrer trop religion.
Oui, l'autre cote, Bon Dieu kai benir 'ous,
Bon Dieu kai benir 'ous parcequi 'ous faire charite l'argent.
Corbeau aille Curacao, i' voyait l'argent ba 'ous,
Ous prend l'argent cela
Ous mettait lui en cabaret.
Ous pas ka lire, ecrire, 'ous pas ka parler Anglais,
Ous tait supposer ca; cabaret pas ni benefice.
L'heure Corbeau devirait,
L'tait ni, I' tait ni l'argent,
L'heure i'rivait ici,
Oui, maman! Corbeau kai fou!

Iona dit Corbeau, pendant 'ous tait Curacao,
Moi fait deux 'tits mamaille, venir garder si c'est ca 'ous.
Corbeau criait "Mama! Bon soir, messieurs, mesdames,
Lumer lampe-la ba mwen
Pour moi garder ces mamailles-la!"
Corbeau virait dire: "Moi save toutes les negres ka semble,
I peut si pas ca moin,
Moi kai soigner ces mamailles-la!"

Oui, Corbeau partit, Corbeau descend Roseau,
Allait chercher travail, pourqui 'peut soigner ces mamailles-la,
Iona dit Corbeau pas tait descendre Roseau,
Mais i' descend Roseau, jamettes Roseau tomber derriere-i'

Phillipe Mago achetait un sax bai Corbeau,
I' pas ni temps jouer sax-la,
Sax-man comme lui prendre la vie-lui.

Samedi bon matin, Corbeau partit descendre en ville,
Samedi apres-midi, nous 'tendre la mort Corbeau.
Ca fait moi la peine; oui, ca brulait coeur-moin,
Ca penetrait moin, l'heure moin 'tendre la mort Corbeau.

Iona dit comme-ca: ca qui fait lui la peine,
Ca qui brulait coeur-lui: saxophone Corbeau pas jouer.
Moin 'tendre un corne cornait
a sur bord roseaux-a,
Moi dit: "Doux-doux, moin kai chercher volants ba 'ous"
L'heure moin 'rivait la, moin fait raconte epi Corbeau,
I' dit: "Corne-la qui cornait-a,
c'est Ionia ka cornait moin."

Guitar-man la ka dire:
"Nous tous les deux c'est guitar-man,
Pas prendre ca pour un rien,
C'est meme beat-la nous ka chember."

Iona mariee, Dimanche a quatre heures.
Mardi, a huit heures, i' aille l'hopital.
I' fait un bombe, mari-lui cassait bras-lui.
L'heure moi joindre maman-ous,
Moin kai conter toute ca 'ous 'ja faire moin.
Iona!
(N'ai dit maman-ous!)
Iona!
(Ous pas ka 'couter moin!)
Trois jours, trois nuits
Iona bouillit, Iona pas chuitte.
(N'ai dit maman-i' ca)

Toute moune ka dit Iona tourner,
C'est pas tourner Iona tourner, mauvais i' mauvais,
Iona!

IV IONA: MABOUYA VALLEY

for Eric Branford

Ma Kilman God will punish you,
for the reason that you've got too much religion,
on the other hand, God will bless you,
God will bless you because of your charity.

Corbeau went to Curacao
He sent you money back
You took the same money
and put it in a rum-shop
You can't read, you can't write, you can't speak English,
You should know that rum-shops make no profit,
When Corbeau come back
He had, yes he had money
when he arrived back here,
Yes Mama, Corbeau'll go crazy.

Iona told Corbeau while you were in Curacao
I made two little children, come and see if they're yours.
Corbeau cried out, "Mama, Goodnight ladies and gentlemen
Light the lamp there for me
For me to look at these kids,"
Corbeau came back and said "I know niggers resemble,
They may or may not be mine,
I'll mind them all the same."

Ah yes, Corbeau then left, he went down to Roseau,
He went to look for work, to mind the two little ones,
Iona told Corbeau, don't go down to Roseau
But he went down to Roseau, and Roseau's whores fell on him.
Phillipe Mago, brought Corbeau a saxophone,
He had no time to play the sax
A saxman just like him took away his living.

Saturday morning early, Corbeau goes into town.
Saturday afternoon we hear Corbeau is dead.
That really made me sad, that really burnt my heart;
That really went through me when I heard Corbeau was dead.

Iona said like this: it made her sorry too,
It really burnt her heart, that the saxophone will never play.

I heard a horn blowing
by the river reeds down there
Sweetheart, I said, I'll go looking
for flying fish for you.
When I got there, I came across Corbeau
He said that horn you heard
was Iona horning me.

The guitar man's saying
We both are guitar men,
Don't take it for anything,
We both holding the same beat.

Iona got married, Sunday at four o'clock.
Tuesday, by eight o'clock, she's in the hospital.
She made a fare, her husband broke her arm,
when I meet your mother I'll tell what you did me.
Iona,
(I'll tell your maman)

Iona
(You don't listen to me)
Three days and three nights
(Iona boiled, she's still not cooked)
(I'll tell her mother that)
They say Iona's changed
It isn't Iona's changed
she's wicked, wicked, that's all
Iona.

V FOR THE ALTARPIECE OF THE ROSEAU VALLEY CHURCH,
   SAINT LUCIA

I

The chapel, as the pivot of this valley,
round which whatever is rooted loosely turns
men, women, ditches, the revolving fields
of bananas, the secondary roads,
draws all to it, to the altar
and the massive altarpiece;
like a dull mirror, life
repeated there,
the common life outside
and the other life it holds
a good man made it.

Two earth-brown laborers
dance the botay in it, the drum sounds under
the earth, the heavy foot.

                    This is a rich valley,
It is fat with things.
Its roads radiate like aisles from the altar towards

those acres of bananas, towards
leaf-crowded mountains
rain-bellied clouds
in haze, in iron heat;

                  This is a cursed valley,
ask the broken mules, the swollen children,
ask the dried women, their gap-toothed men,
ask the parish priest, who, in the altarpiece
carries a replica of the church,
ask the two who could be Eve and Adam dancing.

II

Five centuries ago
in the time of Giotto
this altar might have had
in one corner, when God was young
ST OMER ME FECIT AETAT whatever his own age now,
GLORIA DEI and to God's Mother also.

It is signed with music.
It turns the whole island.
You have to imagine it empty on a Sunday afternoon
between adorations

Nobody can see it and it is there,
nobody adores the two who could be Eve and Adam dancing.

A Sunday at three o'clock
when the real Adam and Eve have coupled
and lie in re-christening sweat

his sweat on her still breasts,
her sweat on his paneled torso

that hefts bananas
that has killed snakes
that has climbed out of rivers,

now, as on the furred tops of the hills
a breeze moving the hairs on his chest

on a Sunday at three o'clock
when the snake pours itself
into a chalice of leaves.

The sugar factory is empty.

Nobody picks bananas,
no trucks raising dust on their way to Vieuxfort,
no helicopter spraying

the mosquito's banjo, yes,
and the gnat's violin, okay,

okay, not absolute Adamic silence,
the valley of Roseau is not the Garden of Eden,
and those who inhabit it, are not in heaven,

so there are little wires of music
some marron up in the hills, by Aux Lyons,
some christening.

A boy banging a tin by the river,
with the river trying to sleep.
But nothing can break that silence,

which comes from the depth of the world,
from whatever one man believes he knows of God
and the suffering of his kind,

it comes from the wall of the altarpiece
ST OMER AD GLORIAM DEI FECIT
in whatever year of his suffering.

III

After so many bottles of white rum in a pile,
after the flight of so many little fishes
from the brush that is the finger of St. Francis,

after the deaths
of as many names as you want,
Iona, Julian, Ti-Nomme, Cacao,
like the death of the cane-crop in Roseau Valley, St. Lucia.

After five thousand novenas
and the idea of the Virgin
coming and going like a little lamp

after all that,
your faith like a canoe at evening coming in,
like a relative who is tired of America,
like a woman coming back to your house

that sang in the ropes of your wrist
when you lifted this up;
so that, from time to time, on Sundays

between adorations, one might see,
if one were there, and not there,
looking in at the windows

the real faces of angels.

OHIO, WINTER

for James Wright

It's your country, Jim, and what
I imagine there may not exist:
summer grass clutching derailed freight
trains till they rust
and blacken like buffalo.
This winter is white as wheat
and width is its terror, you're
right; behind the clenched, white
barns all afternoon the night
hides with a knife; the road
grovels under a blizzard,
frost glazes the eyelid
of the windscreen, and every barn or
farm-light goes lonelier, lonelier.

THE CHELSEA

I

Nothing, not the hotel's beige dankness, not
the neon-flickered drifts of dirty rain,
the marigolds' drying fire from their pot
above a dead fireplace, meant ruin
anymore to him. The mirror's reflexes
are nerveless and indifferent as he is
to fame and money. He will find success
in the lost art of failure, so he says
to the flawless girl framed in the mirror's tarnish.
She's more than the hotel's bronze plaque of greats
who hit the bottle or the street, grew rich
or famous. Their fame curls like layers of beige
paint, just as those mirrored flowers will die.
The clear-eyed girl letting cold tap-water
run on, watches herself watching him lie.

II

Between the darkening drapes of the hotel
we'd watch the lion-colored twilight come
stalking up the sandstone, tall
bluff of the West Side Gymnasium,
the wide sky yawning as the tame light curled
around Manhattan, then felt the room fill
with a vague pity, as its objects furred
to indistinction, chair, bed, desk, turn soft
as drowsing lions. Love gives a selfish strength
if lonely lives, down the stale corridors,
still, as they turn the key, nod down the length

of their whole life at slowly closing doors,
In other's hell we made our happiness.
Across the window furnished room and loft
lamplit their intimacies. Happier lives,
settled in ruts, and great for wanting less.

LOVE AFTER LOVE

The time will come
when, with elation,
you will greet yourself arriving
at your own door, in your own mirror,
and each will smile at the other's welcome,

and say sit here. Eat.
You will love again the stranger who was your self,
Give wine. Give bread. Give back your heart
to itself, to the stranger who has loved you

all your life, whom you ignored
for another, who knows you by heart.
Take down the love-letters from the bookshelf

the photographs, the desperate notes,
peel your own image from the mirror.
Sit. Feast on your life.

So much rain, so much life like the swollen sky
of this black August. My sister, the sun,
broods in her yellow room and won't come out.

Everything goes to hell; the mountains fume
like a kettle, rivers overrun, still,
she will not rise and turn off the rain.

She's in her room, fondling old things,
my poems, turning her album. Even if thunder falls
like a crash of plates from the sky,

she does not come out.
Don't you know I love you but am hopeless
at fixing the rain? But I am learning slowly

to love the dark days, the steaming hills,
the air with gossiping mosquitoes,
and to sip the medicine of bitterness,

so that when you emerge, my sister,
parting the beads of the rain,
with your forehead of flowers and eyes of forgiveness,

all will not be as it was, but it will be true,
(you see they will not let me love
as I want), because my sister, then

I would have learnt to love black days like bright ones,
the black rain, the white hills, when once
I loved only my happiness and you.

If they ask what my favorite flower was,
there's one thing that you'll have to understand:
I learnt to love it by the usual ways
of those who swore to serve truth with one hand,
and one behind their back for cash or praise,
that I surrendered dreaming how I'd stand
in the rewarding autumn of my life,
just ankle-deep in money, thick as leaves,
to bring my poetry, poor, faithful wife
past her accustomed style, well, all the same,
though there's no autumn, nature played the game
with me each fiscal year, when the gold pouis
would guiltily start scattering largesse
like Christian bankers or wind-shook-down thieves.
What I soon learnt was they had changed the script,
left out the golden fall and turned to winter,
to some gray monochrome, much like this meter,
with no gold in it. So, I saw my toil
as a seedy little yard of scrub and root
that gripped for good, and what took in that soil,
was the cheap flower that you see at my foot,
the coarsest, commonest, toughest, nondescript,
resilient violet with its white spot center.

MIDSUMMER, TOBAGO

Broad sun-stoned beaches.

White heat.
A green river.

A bridge,
scorched yellow palms

from the summer-sleeping house
drowsing through August.

Days I have held,
days I have lost,

days that outgrow, like daughters,
my harboring arms.

TO RETURN TO THE TREES

for John Figueroa

Senex, an oak.
Senex, this old sea-almond
unwincing in spray

in this geriatric grove
on the sea-road to Cumana.
To return to the trees,

to decline like this tree,
this burly oak
of Boanerges Ben Jonson!

Or, am I lying
like this felled almond
when I write I look forward to age

a gnarled poet
bearded with the whirlwind,
his meters like thunder?

It is not only the sea,
no, for on windy, green mornings
I read the changes on Morne Coco Mountain,

from flagrant sunrise
to its ashen end;
gray has grown strong to me,

it's no longer neutral,
no longer the dirty flag
of courage going under,

it is speckled with hues
like quartz, it's as
various as boredom,

gray is now a crystal
haze, a dull diamond,
stone-dusted and stoic,

gray is the heart at peace,
tougher than the warrior
as it bestrides factions,

it is the great pause
when the pillars of the temple
rest on Samson's palms

and are held, held,
that moment
when the heavy rock of the world

like a child sleeps
on the trembling shoulders of Atlas
and his own eyes close,

the toil that is balance.
Seneca, that fabled bore,
and his gnarled, laborious Latin

I can read only in fragments
of broken bark, his
heroes tempered by whirlwinds,

who see with the word
senex, with its two eyes,
through the boles of this tree,

beyond joy,
beyond lyrical utterance,
this obdurate almond

going under the sand
with this language, slowly,
by sand grains, by centuries.

FROM

The
Star-Apple
Kingdom

(1979)

THE SCHOONER *FLIGHT*

1 *ADIOS, CARENAGE*

In idle August, while the sea soft,
and leaves of brown islands stick to the rim
of this Caribbean, I blow out the light
by the dreamless face of Maria Concepcion
to ship as a seaman on the schooner *Flight.*
Out in the yard turning gray in the dawn,
I stood like a stone and nothing else move
but the cold sea rippling like galvanize
and the nail holes of stars in the sky roof,
till a wind start to interfere with the trees.
I pass me dry neighbor sweeping she yard
as I went downhill, and I nearly said:
"Sweep soft, you witch, 'cause she don't sleep hard,"
but the bitch look through me like I was dead.
A route taxi pull up, park-lights still on.
The driver size up my bags with a grin:
"This time, Shabine, like you really gone!"
I ain't answer the ass, I simply pile in
the back seat and watch the sky burn
above Laventille pink as the gown
in which the woman I left was sleeping,
and I look in the rearview and see a man
exactly like me, and the man was weeping
for the houses, the streets, that whole fucking island.

Christ have mercy on all sleeping things!
From that dog rotting down Wrightson Road
to when I was a dog on these streets;
if loving these islands must be my load,
out of corruption my soul takes wings.

But they had started to poison my soul
with their big house, big car, big-time bohbohl,
coolie, nigger, Syrian, and French Creole,
so I leave it for them and their carnival—
I taking a sea bath, I gone down the road.
I know these islands from Monos to Nassau,
a rusty head sailor with sea-green eyes
that they nickname Shabine, the patois for
any red nigger, and I, Shabine, saw
when these slums of empire was paradise.
I'm just a red nigger who love the sea,
I had a sound colonial education,
I have Dutch, nigger, and English in me,
and either I'm nobody, or I'm a nation.

But Maria Concepcion was all my thought
watching the sea heaving up and down
as the port side of dories, schooners, and yachts
was painted afresh by the strokes of the sun
signing her name with every reflection;
I knew when dark-haired evening put on
her bright silk at sunset, and, folding the sea,
sidled under the sheet with her starry laugh,
that there'd be no rest, there'd be no forgetting.

Is like telling mourners round the graveside
about resurrection, they want the dead back,
so I smile to myself as the bow rope untied
and the *Flight* swing seaward: "Is no use repeating
that the sea have more fish. I ain't want her
dressed in the sexless light of a seraph,
I want those round brown eyes like a marmoset, and
till the day when I can lean back and laugh,
those claws that tickled my back on sweating
Sunday afternoons, like a crab on wet sand."

As I worked, watching the rotting waves come
past the bow that scissor the sea like silk,
I swear to you all, by my mother's milk,
by the stars that shall fly from tonight's furnace,
that I loved them, my children, my wife, my home;
I loved them as poets love the poetry
that kills them, as drowned sailors the sea.

You ever look up from some lonely beach
and see a far schooner? Well, when I write
this poem, each phrase go be soaked in salt;
I go draw and knot every line as tight
as ropes in this rigging; in simple speech
my common language go be the wind,
my pages the sails of the schooner *Flight*.
But let me tell you how this business begin.

2 RAPTURES OF THE DEEP

Smuggled Scotch for O'Hara, big government man,
between Cedros and the Main, so the Coast Guard couldn't touch us,
and the Spanish pirogues always met us halfway,
but a voice kept saying: "Shabine, see this business
of playing pirate?" Well, so said, so done!
That whole racket crash. And I for a woman,
for her laces and silks, Maria Concepcion.
Ay, ay! Next thing I hear, some Commission of Inquiry
was being organized to conduct a big quiz,
with himself as chairman investigating himself.
Well, I knew damn well who the suckers would be,
not that shark in shark skin, but his pilot fish,
khaki-pants red niggers like you and me.
What worse, I fighting with Maria Concepcion,
plates flying and thing, so I swear: "Not again!"

It was mashing up my house and my family.
I was so broke all I needed was shades and a cup
or four shades and four cups in four-cup Port of Spain,
all the silver I had was the coins on the sea.

You saw them ministers in *The Express*,
guardians of the poor—one hand at their back,
and one set o' police only guarding their house,
and the Scotch pouring in through the back door.
As for that minister-monster who smuggled the booze,
that half-Syrian saurian, I got so vex to see
that face thick with powder, the warts, the stone lids
like a dinosaur caked with primordial ooze
by the lightning of flashbulbs sinking in wealth,
that I said: "Shabine, this is shit, understand!"
But he get somebody to kick my crutch out his office
like I was some artist! That bitch was so grand,
couldn't get off his high horse and kick me himself.
I have seen things that would make a slave sick
in this Trinidad, the Limers' Republic.

I couldn't shake the sea noise out of my head,
the shell of my ears sang Maria Concepcion,
so I start salvage diving with a crazy Mick,
name O'Shaugnessy, and a limey named Head;
but this Caribbean so choke with the dead
that when I would melt in emerald water,
whose ceiling rippled like a silk tent,
I saw them corals: brain, fire, sea fans,
dead-men's-fingers, and then, the dead men.
I saw that the powdery sand was their bones
ground white from Senegal to San Salvador,
so, I panic third dive, and surface for a month
in the Seamen's Hostel. Fish broth and sermons.
When I thought of the woe I had brought my wife,

when I saw my worries with that other woman,
I wept under water, salt seeking salt,
for her beauty had fallen on me like a sword
cleaving me from my children, flesh of my flesh!

There was this barge from St. Vincent, but she was too deep
to float her again. When we drank, the limey
got tired of my sobbing for Maria Concepcion.
He said he was getting the bends. Good for him!
The pain in my heart for Maria Concepcion,
the hurt I had done to my wife and children,
was worse than the bends. In the rapturous deep
there was no cleft rock where my soul could hide
like the boobies each sunset, no sandbar of light
where I could rest, like the pelicans know,
so I got raptures once, and I saw God
like a harpooned grouper bleeding, and a far
voice was rumbling, "Shabine, if you leave her,
if you leave her, I shall give you the morning star."
When I left the madhouse I tried other women
but, once they stripped naked, their spiky cunts
bristled like sea eggs and I couldn't dive.
The chaplain came round. I paid him no mind.
Where is my rest place, Jesus? Where is my harbor?
Where is the pillow I will not have to pay for,
and the window I can look from that frames my life?

3 SHABINE LEAVES THE REPUBLIC

I had no nation now but the imagination.
After the white man, the niggers didn't want me
when the power swing to their side.
The first chain my hands and apologize, "History";
the next said I wasn't black enough for their pride.

Tell me, what power, on these unknown rocks—
a spray-plane Air Force, the Fire Brigade,
the Red Cross, the Regiment, two, three police dogs
that pass before you finish bawling "Parade!"?
I met History once, but he ain't recognize me,
a parchment Creole, with warts
like an old sea bottle, crawling like a crab
through the holes of shadow cast by the net
of a grille balcony; cream linen, cream hat.
I confront him and shout, "Sir, is Shabine!
They say I'se your grandson. You remember Grandma,
your black cook, at all?" The bitch hawk and spat.
A spit like that worth any number of words.
But that's all them bastards have left us: words.

I no longer believed in the revolution.
I was losing faith in the love of my woman.
I had seen that moment Aleksandr Blok
crystallize in *The Twelve*. Was between
the Police Marine Branch and Hotel Venezuelana
one Sunday at noon. Young men without flags
using shirts, their chests waiting for holes.
They kept marching into the mountains, and
their noise ceased as foam sinks into sand.
They sank in the bright hills like rain, every one
with his own nimbus, leaving shirts in the street,
and the echo of power at the end of the street.
Propeller-blade fans turn over the Senate;
the judges, they say, still sweat in carmine,
on Frederick Street the idlers all marching
by standing still, the Budget turns a new leaf.
In the 12:30 movies the projectors best
not break down, or you go see revolution. Aleksandr Blok
enters and sits in the third row of pit eating choc-

olate cone, waiting for a spaghetti West-
ern with Clint Eastwood and featuring Lee Van Cleef.

4 THE FLIGHT, PASSING BLANCHISSEUSE

Dusk. The *Flight* passing Blanchisseuse.
Gulls wheel like from a gun again,
and foam gone amber that was white,
lighthouse and star start making friends,
down every beach the long day ends,
and there, on that last stretch of sand,
on a beach bare of all but light,
dark hands start pulling in the seine
of the dark sea, deep, deep inland.

5 SHABINE ENCOUNTERS THE MIDDLE PASSAGE

Man, I brisk in the galley first thing next dawn,
brewing li'l coffee; fog coil from the sea
like the kettle steaming when I put it down
slow, slow, 'cause I couldn't believe what I see:
where the horizon was one silver haze,
the fog swirl and swell into sails, so close
that I saw it was sails, my hair grip my skull,
it was horrors, but it was beautiful.
We float through a rustling forest of ships
with sails dry like paper, behind the glass
I saw men with rusty eyeholes like cannons,
and whenever their half-naked crews cross the sun,
right through their tissue, you traced their bones
like leaves against the sunlight; frigates, barkentines,
the backward-moving current swept them on,

and high on their decks I saw great admirals,
Rodney, Nelson, de Grasse, I heard the hoarse orders
they gave those Shabines, and that forest
of masts sail right through the *Flight*,
and all you could hear was the ghostly sound
of waves rustling like grass in a low wind
and the hissing weeds they trailed from the stern;
slowly they heaved past from east to west
like this round world was some cranked water wheel,
every ship pouring like a wooden bucket
dredged from the deep; my memory revolve
on all sailors before me, then the sun
heat the horizon's ring and they was mist.

Next we pass slave ships. Flags of all nations,
our fathers below deck too deep, I suppose,
to hear us shouting. So we stop shouting. Who knows
who his grandfather is, much less his name?
Tomorrow our landfall will be the Barbados.

6 *THE SAILOR SINGS BACK TO THE CASUARINAS*

You see them on the low hills of Barbados
bracing like windbreaks, needles for hurricanes,
trailing, like masts, the cirrus of torn sails;
when I was green like them, I used to think
those cypresses, leaning against the sea,
that take the sea noise up into their branches,
are not real cypresses but casuarinas.
Now captain just call them Canadian cedars.
But cedars, cypresses, or casuarinas,
whoever called them so had a good cause,
watching their bending bodies wail like women

after a storm, when some schooner came home
with news of one more sailor drowned again.
Once the sound "cypress" used to make more sense
than the green "casuarinas," though, to the wind
whatever grief bent them was all the same,
since they were trees with nothing else in mind
but heavenly leaping or to guard a grave;
but we live like our names and you would have
to be colonial to know the difference,
to know the pain of history words contain,
to love those trees with an inferior love,
and to believe: "Those casuarinas bend
like cypresses, their hair hangs down in rain
like sailors' wives. They're classic trees, and we,
if we live like the names our masters please,
by careful mimicry might become men."

7 THE FLIGHT ANCHORS IN CASTRIES HARBOR

When the stars self were young over Castries,
I loved you alone and I loved the whole world.
What does it matter that our lives are different?
Burdened with the loves of our different children?
When I think of your young face washed by the wind
and your voice that chuckles in the slap of the sea?
The lights are out on La Toc promontory,
except for the hospital. Across at Vigie
the marina arcs keep vigil. I have kept my own
promise, to leave you the one thing I own,
you whom I loved first: my poetry.
We here for one night. Tomorrow, the *Flight* will be gone.

It had one bitch on board, like he had me mark—
that was the cook, some Vincentian arse
with a skin like a gommier tree, red peeling bark,
and wash-out blue eyes; he wouldn't give me a ease,
like he feel he was white. Had an exercise book,
this same one here, that I was using to write
my poetry, so one day this man snatch it
from my hand, and start throwing it left and right
to the rest of the crew, bawling out, "Catch it,"
and start mincing me like I was some hen
because of the poems. Some case is for fist,
some case is for tholing pin, some is for knife—
this one was for knife. Well, I beg him first,
but he keep reading, "O my children, my wife,"
and playing he crying, to make the crew laugh;
it move like a flying fish, the silver knife
that catch him right in the plump of his calf,
and he faint so slowly, and he turn more white
than he thought he was. I suppose among men
you need that sort of thing. It ain't right
but that's how it is. There wasn't much pain,
just plenty blood, and Vincie and me best friend,
but none of them go fuck with my poetry again.

9 *MARIA CONCEPCION & THE BOOK OF DREAMS*

The jet that was screeching over the *Flight*
was opening a curtain into the past.
"Dominica ahead!"
                    "It still have Caribs there."
"One day go be planes only, no more boat."
"Vince, God ain't make nigger to fly through the air."

"Progress, Shabine, that's what it's all about.
Progress leaving all we small islands behind."
I was at the wheel, Vince sitting next to me
gaffing. Crisp, bracing day. A high-running sea.
"Progress is something to ask Caribs about.
They kill them by millions, some in war,
some by forced labor dying in the mines
looking for silver, after that niggers; more
progress. Until I see definite signs
that mankind change, Vince, I ain't want to hear.
Progress is history's dirty joke.
Ask that sad green island getting nearer."
Green islands, like mangoes pickled in brine.
In such fierce salt let my wound be healed,
me, in my freshness as a seafarer.

That night, with the sky sparks frosty with fire,
I ran like a Carib through Dominica,
my nose holes choked with memory of smoke;
I heard the screams of my burning children,
I ate the brains of mushrooms, the fungi
of devil's parasols under white, leprous rocks;
my breakfast was leaf mold in leaking forests,
with leaves big as maps, and when I heard noise
of the soldiers' progress through the thick leaves,
though my heart was bursting, I get up and ran
through the blades of balisier sharper than spears;
with the blood of my race, I ran, boy, I ran
with moss-footed speed like a painted bird;
then I fall, but I fall by an icy stream under
cool fountains of fern, and a screaming parrot
catch the dry branches and I drowned at last
in big breakers of smoke; then when that ocean
of black smoke pass, and the sky turn white,
there was nothing but Progress, if Progress is

an iguana as still as young leaf in sunlight.
I bawl for Maria, and her *Book of Dreams*.

It anchored her sleep, that insomniac's Bible,
a soiled orange booklet with a cyclop's eye
center, from the Dominican Republic.
Its coarse pages were black with the usual
symbols of prophecy, in excited Spanish;
an open palm upright, sectioned and numbered
like a butcher chart, delivered the future.
One night, in a fever, radiantly ill,
she say, "Bring me the book, the end has come."
She said: "I dreamt of whales and a storm,"
but for that dream, the book had no answer.

A next night I dreamed of three old women
featureless as silkworms, stitching my fate,
and I scream at them to come out my house,
and I try beating them away with a broom,
but as they go out, so they crawl back again,
until I start screaming and crying, my flesh
raining with sweat, and she ravage the book
for the dream meaning, and there was nothing;
my nerves melt like a jellyfish—that was when I broke—
they found me round the Savannah, screaming:

All you see me talking to the wind, so you think I mad.
Well, Shabine has bridled the horses of the sea;
you see me watching the sun till my eyeballs seared,
so all you mad people feel Shabine crazy,
but all you ain't know my strength, hear? The coconuts
standing by in their regiments in yellow khaki,
they waiting for Shabine to take over these islands,
and all you best dread the day I am healed
of being a human. All you fate in my hand,

ministers, businessmen, Shabine have you, friend,
I shall scatter your lives like a handful of sand,
I who have no weapon but poetry and
the lances of palms and the sea's shining shield!

10 *OUT OF THE DEPTHS*

Next day, dark sea. A arse-aching dawn.
"Damn wind shift sudden as a woman mind."
The slow swell start cresting like some mountain range
with snow on the top.
                            "Ay, Skipper, sky dark!"
"This ain't right for August."
                            "This light damn strange,
this season, sky should be clear as a field."

A stingray steeplechase across the sea,
tail whipping water, the high man-o'-wars
start reeling inland, quick, quick an archery
of flying fish miss us! Vince say: "You notice?"
and a black-mane squall pounce on the sail
like a dog on a pigeon, and it snap the neck
of the *Flight* and shake it from head to tail.
"Be Jesus, I never see sea get so rough
so fast! That wind come from God back pocket!"
"Where Cap'n headin? Like the man gone blind!"
"If we's to drong, we go drong, Vince, fock-it!"
"Shabine, say your prayers, if life leave you any!"

I have not loved those that I loved enough.
Worse than the mule kick of Kick-'Em-Jenny
Channel, rain start to pelt the *Flight* between
mountains of water. If I was frighten?
The tent poles of water spouts bracing the sky

start wobbling, clouds unstitch at the seams
and sky water drench us, and I hear myself cry,
"I'm the drowned sailor in her *Book of Dreams*."
I remembered them ghost ships, I saw me corkscrewing
to the sea bed of sea worms, fathom past fathom,
my jaw clench like a fist, and only one thing
hold me, trembling, how my family safe home.
Then a strength like it seize me and the strength said:
"I from backward people who still fear God."
Let Him, in His might, heave Leviathan upward
by the winch of His will, the beast pouring lace
from his sea-bottom bed; and that was the faith
that had fade from a child in the Methodist chapel
in Chisel Street, Castries, when the whale-bell
sang service and, in hard pews ribbed like the whale,
proud with despair, we sang how our race
survive the sea's maw, our history, our peril,
and now I was ready for whatever death will.
But if that storm had strength, was in Cap'n face,
beard beading with spray, tears salting his eyes,
crucify to his post, that nigger hold fast
to that wheel, man, like the cross held Jesus,
and the wounds of his eyes like they crying for us,
and I feeding him white rum, while every crest
with Leviathan-lash make the *Flight* quail
like two criminal. Whole night, with no rest,
till red-eyed like dawn, we watch our travail
subsiding, subside, and there was no more storm.
And the noon sea get calm as Thy Kingdom come.

II *AFTER THE STORM*

There's a fresh light that follows a storm
while the whole sea still havoc; in its bright wake

I saw the veiled face of Maria Concepcion
marrying the ocean, then drifting away
in the widening lace of her bridal train
with white gulls her bridesmaids, till she was gone.
I wanted nothing after that day.
Across my own face, like the face of the sun,
a light rain was falling, with the sea calm.

Fall gently, rain, on the sea's upturned face
like a girl showering; make these islands fresh
as Shabine once knew them! Let every trace,
every hot road, smell like clothes she just press
and sprinkle with drizzle. I finish dream;
whatever the rain wash and the sun iron:
the white clouds, the sea and sky with one seam,
is clothes enough for my nakedness.
Though my *Flight* never pass the incoming tide
of this inland sea beyond the loud reefs
of the final Bahamas, I am satisfied
if my hand gave voice to one people's grief.
Open the map. More islands there, man,
than peas on a tin plate, all different size,
one thousand in the Bahamas alone,
from mountains to low scrub with coral keys,
and from this bowsprit, I bless every town,
the blue smell of smoke in hills behind them,
and the one small road winding down them like twine
to the roofs below; I have only one theme:

The bowsprit, the arrow, the longing, the lunging heart—
the flight to a target whose aim we'll never know,
vain search for one island that heals with its harbor
and a guiltless horizon, where the almond's shadow
doesn't injure the sand. There are so many islands!
As many islands as the stars at night

on that branched tree from which meteors are shaken
like falling fruit around the schooner *Flight*.
But things must fall, and so it always was,
on one hand Venus, on the other Mars;
fall, and are one, just as this earth is one
island in archipelagoes of stars.
My first friend was the sea. Now, is my last.
I stop talking now. I work, then I read,
cotching under a lantern hooked to the mast.
I try to forget what happiness was,
and when that don't work, I study the stars.
Sometimes is just me, and the soft-scissored foam
as the deck turn white and the moon open
a cloud like a door, and the light over me
is a road in white moonlight taking me home.
Shabine sang to you from the depths of the sea.

Where are your monuments, your battles, martyrs?
Where is your tribal memory? Sirs,
in that gray vault. The sea. The sea
has locked them up. The sea is History.

First, there was the heaving oil,
heavy as chaos;
then, like a light at the end of a tunnel,

the lantern of a caravel,
and that was Genesis.
Then there were the packed cries,
the shit, the moaning:

Exodus.
Bone soldered by coral to bone,
mosaics
mantled by the benediction of the shark's shadow,

that was the Ark of the Covenant.
Then came from the plucked wires
of sunlight on the sea floor

the plangent harps of the Babylonian bondage,
as the white cowries clustered like manacles
on the drowned women,

and those were the ivory bracelets
of the Song of Solomon,
but the ocean kept turning blank pages

looking for History.
Then came the men with eyes heavy as anchors
who sank without tombs,

brigands who barbecued cattle,
leaving their charred ribs like palm leaves on the shore,
then the foaming, rabid maw

of the tidal wave swallowing Port Royal,
and that was Jonah,
but where is your Renaissance?

Sir, it is locked in them sea sands
out there past the reef's moiling shelf,
where the men-o'-war floated down;

strop on these goggles, I'll guide you there myself.
It's all subtle and submarine,
through colonnades of coral,

past the gothic windows of sea fans
to where the crusty grouper, onyx-eyed,
blinks, weighted by its jewels, like a bald queen;

and these groined caves with barnacles
pitted like stone
are our cathedrals,

and the furnace before the hurricanes:
Gomorrah. Bones ground by windmills
into marl and cornmeal,

and that was Lamentations—
that was just Lamentations,
it was not History;

then came, like scum on the river's drying lip,
the brown reeds of villages
mantling and congealing into towns,

and at evening, the midges' choirs,
and above them, the spires
lancing the side of God

as His son set, and that was the New Testament.

Then came the white sisters clapping
to the waves' progress,
and that was Emancipation—

jubilation, O jubilation—
vanishing swiftly
as the sea's lace dries in the sun,

but that was not History,
that was only faith,
and then each rock broke into its own nation;

then came the synod of flies,
then came the secretarial heron,
then came the bullfrog bellowing for a vote,

fireflies with bright ideas
and bats like jetting ambassadors
and the mantis, like khaki police,

and the furred caterpillars of judges
examining each case closely,
and then in the dark ears of ferns

and in the salt chuckle of rocks
with their sea pools, there was the sound
like a rumor without any echo

of History, really beginning.

for N.M.

There is a shattered palm
on this fierce shore,
its plumes the rusting helm-
et of a dead warrior.

Numb Antony, in the torpor
stretching her inert
sex near him like a sleeping cat,
knows his heart is the real desert.

Over the dunes
of her heaving,
to his heart's drumming
fades the mirage of the legions,

across love-tousled sheets,
the triremes fading.
At the carved door of her temple
a fly wrings its message.

He brushes a damp hair
away from an ear
as perfect as a sleeping child's.
He stares, inert, the fallen column.

He lies like a copper palm
tree at three in the afternoon
by a hot sea
and a river, in Egypt, Tobago.

Her salt marsh dries in the heat
where he foundered
without armor.
He exchanged an empire for her beads of sweat,

the uproar of arenas,
the changing surf
of senators, for
this silent ceiling over silent sand—

this grizzled bear, whose fur,
molting, is silvered—
for this quick fox with her
sweet stench. By sleep dismembered,

his head
is in Egypt, his feet
in Rome, his groin a desert
trench with its dead soldier.

He drifts a finger
through her stiff hair
crisp as a mare's fountaining tail.
Shadows creep up the palace tile.

He is too tired to move;
a groan would waken
trumpets, one more gesture,
war. His glare,

a shield
reflecting fires,
a brass brow that cannot frown
at carnage, sweats the sun's force.

It is not the turmoil
of autumnal lust,
its treacheries, that drove
him, fired and grimed with dust,

this far, not even love,
but a great rage without
clamor, that grew great
because its depth is quiet;

it hears the river
of her young brown blood,
it feels the whole sky quiver
with her blue eyelid.

She sleeps with the soft engine of a child,

that sleep which scythes
the stalks of lances, fells the
harvest of legions
with nothing for its knives,
that makes Caesars,

sputtering at flies,
slapping their foreheads
with the laurel's imprint,
drunkards, comedians.

All-humbling sleep, whose peace
is sweet as death,
whose silence has
all the sea's weight and volubility,

who swings this globe by a hair's trembling breath.

Shattered and wild and
palm-crowned Antony,
rusting in Egypt,
ready to lose the world,
to Actium and sand,

everything else
is vanity, but this tenderness
for a woman not his mistress
but his sleeping child.

The sky is cloudless. The afternoon is mild.

R.T.S.L.

(1917–1977)

As for that other thing
which comes when the eyelid is glazed
and the wax gleam
from the unwrinkled forehead
asks no more questions
of the dry mouth,

whether they open the heart like a shirt
to release a rage of swallows,
whether the brain
is a library for worms,
on the instant that knowledge
of the moment
when everything became so stiff,

so formal with ironical adieux,
organ and choir,
and I must borrow a black tie,
and at what moment in the oration
shall I break down and weep—

there was the startle of wings
breaking from the closing cage
of your body, your fist unclenching
these pigeons circling serenely
over the page,

and,
as the parentheses lock like a gate
1917 to 1977,
the semicircles close to form a face,

a world, a wholeness,
an unbreakable O,
and something that once had a fearful name
walks from the thing that used to wear its name,
transparent, exact representative,
so that we can see through it
churches, cars, sunlight,
and the Boston Common,
not needing any book.

FOREST OF EUROPE

for Joseph Brodsky

The last leaves fell like notes from a piano
and left their ovals echoing in the ear;
with gawky music stands, the winter forest
looks like an empty orchestra, its lines
ruled on these scattered manuscripts of snow.

The inlaid copper laurel of an oak
shines through the brown-bricked glass above your head
as bright as whiskey, while the wintry breath
of lines from Mandelstam, which you recite,
uncoils as visibly as cigarette smoke.

"The rustling of ruble notes by the lemon Neva."
Under your exile's tongue, crisp under heel,
the gutturals crackle like decaying leaves,
the phrase from Mandelstam circles with light
in a brown room, in barren Oklahoma.

There is a Gulag Archipelago
under this ice, where the salt, mineral spring
of the long Trail of Tears runnels these plains
as hard and open as a herdsman's face
sun-cracked and stubbled with unshaven snow.

Growing in whispers from the Writers' Congress,
the snow circles like cossacks round the corpse
of a tired Choctaw till it is a blizzard
of treaties and white papers as we lose
sight of the single human through the cause.

263

So every spring these branches load their shelves,
like libraries with newly published leaves,
till waste recycles them—paper to snow—
but, at zero of suffering, one mind
lasts like this oak with a few brazen leaves.

As the train passed the forest's tortured icons,
the floes clanging like freight yards, then the spires
of frozen years, the stations screeching steam,
he drew them in a single winter's breath
whose freezing consonants turned into stones.

He saw the poetry in forlorn stations
under clouds vast as Asia, through districts
that could gulp Oklahoma like a grape,
not these tree-shaded prairie halts but space
so desolate it mocked destinations.

Who is that dark child on the parapets
of Europe, watching the evening river mint
its sovereigns stamped with power, not with poets,
the Thames and the Neva rustling like banknotes,
then, black on gold, the Hudson's silhouettes?

From frozen Neva to the Hudson pours,
under the airport domes, the echoing stations,
the tributary of emigrants whom exile
has made as classless as the common cold,
citizens of a language that is now yours,

and every February, every "last autumn,"
you write far from the threshing harvesters
folding wheat like a girl plaiting her hair,
far from Russia's canals quivering with sunstroke,
a man living with English in one room.

The tourist archipelagoes of my South
are prisons too, corruptible, and though
there is no harder prison than writing verse,
what's poetry, if it is worth its salt,
but a phrase men can pass from hand to mouth?

From hand to mouth, across the centuries,
the bread that lasts when systems have decayed,
when, in his forest of barbed-wire branches,
a prisoner circles, chewing the one phrase
whose music will last longer than the leaves,

whose condensation is the marble sweat
of angels' foreheads, which will never dry
till Borealis shuts the peacock lights
of its slow fan from L.A. to Archangel,
and memory needs nothing to repeat.

Frightened and starved, with divine fever
Osip Mandelstam shook, and every
metaphor shuddered him with ague,
each vowel heavier than a boundary stone,
"to the rustling of ruble notes by the lemon Neva,"

but now that fever is a fire whose glow
warms our hands, Joseph, as we grunt like primates
exchanging gutturals in this winter cave
of a brown cottage, while in drifts outside
mastodons force their systems through the snow.

Koenig knew now there was no one on the river.
Entering its brown mouth choking with lilies
and curtained with midges, Koenig poled the shallop
past the abandoned ferry and the ferry piles
coated with coal dust. Staying aboard, he saw, up
in a thick meadow, a sand-colored mule,
untethered, with no harness, and no signs
of habitation round the ruined factory wheel
locked hard in rust, and through whose spokes the vines
of wild yam leaves leant from overweight;
the wild bananas in the yellowish sunlight
were dugged like aching cows with unmilked fruit.
This was the last of the productive mines.
Only the vegetation here looked right.
A crab of pain scuttled shooting up his foot
and fastened on his neck, at the brain's root.
He felt his reason curling back like parchment
in this fierce torpor. Well, he no longer taxed
and tired what was left of his memory;
he should thank heaven he had escaped the sea,
and anyway, he had demanded to be sent
here with the others—why get this river vexed
with his complaints? Koenig wanted to sing,
suddenly, if only to keep the river company—
this was a river, and Koenig, his name meant King.

They had all caught the missionary fever:
they were prepared to expiate the sins
of savages, to tame them as he would tame this river
subtly, as it flowed, accepting its bends;
he had seen how other missionaries met their ends—
swinging in the wind, like a dead clapper when

a bell is broken, if that sky was a bell—
for treating savages as if they were men,
and frightening them with talk of Heaven and Hell.
But I have forgotten our journey's origins,
mused Koenig, and our purpose. He knew it was noble,
based on some phrase, forgotten, from the Bible,
but he felt bodiless, like a man stumbling from
the pages of a novel, not a forest,
written a hundred years ago. He stroked his uniform,
clogged with the hooked burrs that had tried
to pull him, like the other drowning hands whom
his panic abandoned. The others had died,
like real men, by death. I, Koenig, am a ghost,
ghost-king of rivers. Well, even ghosts must rest.
If he knew he was lost he was not lost.
It was when you pretended that you were a fool.
He banked and leaned tiredly on the pole.
If I'm a character called Koenig, then I
shall dominate my future like a fiction
in which there is a real river and real sky,
so I'm not really tired, and should push on.

The lights between the leaves were beautiful,
and, as in that far life, now he was grateful
for any pool of light between the dull, usual
clouds of life: a sunspot haloed his tonsure;
silver and copper coins danced on the river;
his head felt warm—the light danced on his skull
like a benediction. Koenig closed his eyes,
and he felt blessed. It made direction sure.
He leant on the pole. He must push on some more.
He said his name. His voice sounded German,
then he said "river," but what was German
if he alone could hear it? *Ich spreche Deutsch*
sounded as genuine as his name in English,

Koenig in Deutsch, and, in English, King.
Did the river want to be called anything?
He asked the river. The river said nothing.

Around the bend the river poured its silver
like some remorseful mine, giving and giving
everything green and white: white sky, white
water, and the dull green like a drumbeat
of the slow-sliding forest, the green heat;
then, on some sandbar, a mirage ahead:
fabric of muslin sails, spiderweb rigging,
a schooner, foundered on black river mud,
was rising slowly up from the riverbed,
and a top-hatted native reading an inverted
newspaper.
          "Where's our Queen?" Koenig shouted.
"Where's our Kaiser?"
                    The nigger disappeared.
Koenig felt that he himself was being read
like the newspaper or a hundred-year-old novel.
"The Queen dead! Kaiser dead!" the voices shouted.
And it flashed through him those trunks were not wood
but that the ghosts of slaughtered Indians stood
there in the mangroves, their eyes like fireflies
in the green dark, and that like hummingbirds
they sailed rather than ran between the trees.
The river carried him past his shouted words.
The schooner had gone down without a trace.
"There was a time when we ruled everything,"
Koenig sang to his corrugated white reflection.
"The German Eagle and the British Lion,
we ruled worlds wider than this river flows,
worlds with dyed elephants, with tassled howdahs,
tigers that carried the striped shade when they rose
from their palm coverts; men shall not see these days

again; our flags sank with the sunset on the dhows
of Egypt; we ruled rivers as huge as the Nile,
the Ganges, and the Congo, we tamed, we ruled
you when our empires reached their blazing peak."
This was a small creek somewhere in the world,
never mind where—victory was in sight.
Koenig laughed and spat in the brown creek.
The mosquitoes now were singing to the night
that rose up from the river, the fog uncurled
under the mangroves. Koenig clenched each fist
around his barge-pole scepter, as a mist
rises from the river and the page goes white.

There were still shards of an ancient pastoral
in those shires of the island where the cattle drank
their pools of shadow from an older sky,
surviving from when the landscape copied such subjects as
"Herefords at Sunset in the Valley of the Wye."
The mountain water that fell white from the mill wheel
sprinkling like petals from the star-apple trees,
and all of the windmills and sugar mills moved by mules
on the treadmill of Monday to Monday, would repeat
in tongues of water and wind and fire, in tongues
of Mission School pickaninnies, like rivers remembering
their source, Parish Trelawny, Parish St. David, Parish
St. Andrew, the names afflicting the pastures,
the lime groves and fences of marl stone and the cattle
with a docile longing, an epochal content.
And there were, like old wedding lace in an attic,
among the boas and parasols and the tea-colored
daguerreotypes, hints of an epochal happiness
as ordered and infinite to the child
as the great house road to the Great House
down a perspective of casuarinas plunging green manes
in time to the horses, an orderly life
reduced by lorgnettes day and night, one disc the sun,
the other the moon, reduced into a pier glass:
nannies diminished to dolls, mahogany stairways
no larger than those of an album in which
the flash of cutlery yellows, as gamboge as
the piled cakes of teatime on that latticed
bougainvillea veranda that looked down toward
a prospect of Cuyp-like Herefords under a sky
lurid as a porcelain souvenir with these words:
"Herefords at Sunset in the Valley of the Wye."

Strange, that the rancor of hatred hid in that dream
of slow rivers and lilylike parasols, in snaps
of fine old colonial families, curled at the edge
not from age or from fire or the chemicals, no, not at all,
but because, off at its edges, innocently excluded
stood the groom, the cattle boy, the housemaid, the gardeners,
the tenants, the good Negroes down in the village,
their mouths in the locked jaw of silent scream.
A scream which would open the doors to swing wildly
all night, that was bringing in heavier clouds,
more black smoke than cloud, frightening the cattle
in whose bulging eyes the Great House diminished:
a scorching wind of a scream
that began to extinguish the fireflies,
that dried the water mill creaking to a stop
as it was about to pronounce Parish Trelawny
all over, in the ancient pastoral voice,
a wind that blew all without bending anything,
neither the leaves of the album nor the lime groves;
blew Nanny floating back in white from a feather
to a chimerical, chemical pin speck that shrank
the drinking Herefords to brown porcelain cows
on a mantelpiece, Trelawny trembling with dusk,
the scorched pastures of the old benign Custos; blew
far the decent servants and the lifelong cook,
and shriveled to a shard that ancient pastoral
of dusk in a gilt-edged frame now catching the evening sun
in Jamaica, making both epochs one.

He looked out from the Great House windows on
clouds that still held the fragrance of fire,
he saw the Botanical Gardens officially drown
in a formal dusk, where governors had strolled
and black gardeners had smiled over glinting shears
at the lilies of parasols on the floating lawns,

the flame trees obeyed his will and lowered their wicks,
the flowers tightened their fists in the name of thrift,
the porcelain lamps of ripe cocoa, the magnolia's jet
dimmed on the one circuit with the ginger lilies
and left a lonely bulb on the veranda,
and, had his mandate extended to that ceiling
of star-apple candelabra, he would have ordered
the sky to sleep, saying, I'm tired,
save the starlight for victories, we can't afford it,
leave the moon on for one more hour, and that's it.
But though his power, the given mandate, extended
from tangerine daybreaks to star-apple dusks,
his hand could not dam that ceaseless torrent of dust
that carried the shacks of the poor, to their root-rock music,
down the gullies of Yallahs and August Town,
to lodge them on thorns of maca, with their rags
crucified by cactus, tins, old tires, cartons;
from the black Warieka Hills the sky glowed fierce as
the dials of a million radios,
a throbbing sunset that glowed like a grid
where the dread beat rose from the jukebox of Kingston.
He saw the fountains dried of quadrilles, the water-music
of the country dancers, the fiddlers like fifes
put aside. He had to heal
this malarial island in its bath of bay leaves,
its forests tossing with fever, the dry cattle
groaning like winches, the grass that kept shaking
its head to remember its name. No vowels left
in the mill wheel, the river. Rock stone. Rock stone.

The mountains rolled like whales through phosphorous stars,
as he swayed like a stone down fathoms into sleep,
drawn by that magnet which pulls down half the world
between a star and a star, by that black power
that has the assassin dreaming of snow,

that poleaxes the tyrant to a sleeping child.
The house is rocking at anchor, but as he falls
his mind is a mill wheel in the moonlight,
and he hears, in the sleep of his moonlight, the drowned
bell of Port Royal's cathedral, sees the copper pennies
of bubbles rising from the empty eye-pockets
of green buccaneers, the parrot fish floating
from the frayed shoulders of pirates, sea horses
drawing gowned ladies in their liquid promenade
across the moss-green meadows of the sea;
he heard the drowned choirs under Palisadoes,
a hymn ascending to earth from a heaven inverted
by water, a crab climbing the steeple,
and he climbed from that submarine kingdom
as the evening lights came on in the institute,
the scholars lamplit in their own aquarium,
he saw them mouthing like parrot fish, as he passed
upward from that baptism, their history lessons,
the bubbles like ideas which he could not break:
Jamaica was captured by Penn and Venables,
Port Royal perished in a cataclysmic earthquake.

Before the coruscating façades of cathedrals
from Santiago to Caracas, where penitential archbishops
washed the feet of paupers (a parenthetical moment
that made the Caribbean a baptismal font,
turned butterflies to stone, and whitened like doves
the buzzards circling municipal garbage),
the Caribbean was borne like an elliptical basin
in the hands of acolytes, and a people were absolved
of a history which they did not commit;
the slave pardoned his whip, and the dispossessed
said the rosary of islands for three hundred years,
a hymn that resounded like the hum of the sea
inside a sea cave, as their knees turned to stone,

while the bodies of patriots were melting down walls
still crusted with mute outcries of La Revolución!
"San Salvador, pray for us, St. Thomas, San Domingo,
ora pro nobis, intercede for us, Sancta Lucia
of no eyes," and when the circular chaplet
reached the last black bead of Sancta Trinidad
they began again, their knees drilled into stone,
where Colón had begun, with San Salvador's bead,
beads of black colonies round the necks of Indians.
And while they prayed for an economic miracle,
ulcers formed on the municipal portraits,
the hotels went up, and the casinos and brothels,
and the empires of tobacco, sugar, and bananas,
until a black woman, shawled like a buzzard,
climbed up the stairs and knocked at the door
of his dream, whispering in the ear of the keyhole:
"Let me in, I'm finished with praying, I'm the Revolution.
I am the darker, the older America."

She was as beautiful as a stone in the sunrise,
her voice had the gutturals of machine guns
across khaki deserts where the cactus flower
detonates like grenades, her sex was the slit throat
of an Indian, her hair had the blue-black sheen of the crow.
She was a black umbrella blown inside out
by the wind of revolution, La Madre Dolorosa,
a black rose of sorrow, a black mine of silence,
raped wife, empty mother, Aztec virgin
transfixed by arrows from a thousand guitars,
a stone full of silence, which, if it gave tongue
to the tortures done in the name of the Father,
would curdle the blood of the marauding wolf,
the fountain of generals, poets, and cripples
who danced without moving over their graves
with each revolution; her Caesarean was stitched

by the teeth of machine guns, and every sunset
she carried the Caribbean's elliptical basin
as she had once carried the penitential napkins
to be the footbath of dictators, Trujillo, Machado,
and those whose faces had yellowed like posters
on municipal walls. Now she stroked his hair
until it turned white, but she would not understand
that he wanted no other power but peace,
that he wanted a revolution without any bloodshed,
he wanted a history without any memory,
streets without statues,
and a geography without myth. He wanted no armies
but those regiments of bananas, thick lances of cane,
and he sobbed, "I am powerless, except for love."
She faded from him, because he could not kill;
she shrank to a bat that hung day and night
in the back of his brain. He rose in his dream.

The soul, which was his body made as thin
as its reflection and invulnerable
without its clock, was losing track of time;
it walked the mountain tracks of the Maroons,
it swung with Gordon from the creaking gibbet,
it bought a pack of peppermints and cashews
from one of the bandanna'd mammies outside the ward,
it heard his breath pitched to the decibels
of the peanut vendors' carts, it entered a municipal wall
stirring the slogans that shrieked his name: SAVIOR!
and others: LACKEY! he melted like a spoon
through the alphabet soup of CIA, PNP, OPEC,
that resettled once he passed through with this thought:
I should have foreseen those seraphs with barbed-wire hair,
beards like burst mattresses, and wild eyes of garnet,
who nestled the Coptic Bible to their ribs, would
call me Joshua, expecting him to bring down Babylon

by Wednesday, after the fall of Jericho; yes, yes,
I should have seen the cunning bitterness of the rich
who left me no money but these mandates:

His aerial mandate, which
contained the crows whose circuit
was this wedding band that married him to his island.
His marine mandate, which
was the fishing limits
which the shark scissored like silk with its teeth
between Key West and Havana;
his terrestrial:
the bled hills rusted with bauxite;
paradisal:
the chimneys like angels sheathed in aluminum.

In shape like a cloud
he saw the face of his father,
the hair like white cirrus blown back
in a photographic wind,
the mouth of mahogany winced shut,
the eyes lidded, resigned
to the first compromise,
the last ultimatum,
the first and last referendum.

One morning the Caribbean was cut up
by seven prime ministers who bought the sea in bolts—
one thousand miles of aquamarine with lace trimmings,
one million yards of lime-colored silk,
one mile of violet, leagues of cerulean satin—
who sold it at a markup to the conglomerates,
the same conglomerates who had rented the water spouts
for ninety-nine years in exchange for fifty ships,
who retailed it in turn to the ministers

with only one bank account, who then resold it
in ads for the Caribbean Economic Community,
till everyone owned a little piece of the sea,
from which some made saris, some made bandannas;
the rest was offered on trays to white cruise ships
taller than the post office; then the dogfights
began in the cabinets as to who had first sold
the archipelago for this chain store of islands.

Now a tree of grenades was his star-apple kingdom,
over fallow pastures his crows patrolled,
he felt his fist involuntarily tighten
into a talon that was strangling five doves,
the mountains loomed leaden under martial law,
the suburban gardens flowered with white paranoia
next to the bougainvilleas of astonishing April;
the rumors were a rain that would not fall:
that enemy intelligence had alerted the roaches'
quivering antennae, that bats flew like couriers,
transmitting secrets between the embassies;
over dials in the war rooms, the agents waited
for a rifle crack from Havana; down shuttered avenues
roared a phalanx of Yamahas. They left
a hole in the sky that closed on silence.

He didn't hear the roar of the motorcycles
diminish in circles like those of the water mill
in a far childhood; he was drowned in sleep;
he slept, without dreaming, the sleep after love
in the mineral oblivion of night
whose flesh smells of cocoa, whose teeth are white
as coconut meat, whose breath smells of ginger,
whose braids are scented like sweet-potato vines
in furrows still pungent with the sun.
He slept the sleep that wipes out history,

he slept like the islands on the breast of the sea,
like a child again in her star-apple kingdom.

Tomorrow the sea would gleam like nails
under a zinc sky where the barren frangipani
was hammered, a horizon without liners;
tomorrow the heavy caravels of clouds would wreck
and dissolve in their own foam on the reefs
of the mountains, tomorrow a donkey's yawn
would saw the sky in half, and at dawn
would come the noise of a government groaning uphill.
But now she held him, as she holds us all,
her history-orphaned islands, she to whom
we came late as our muse, our mother,
who suckled the islands, who, when she grows old
with her breasts wrinkled like eggplants
is the head-tie mother, the bleached-sheets-on-the-river-rocks
    mother,
the gospel mother, the t'ank-you-parson mother
who turns into mahogany, the lignum-vitae mother,
her sons like thorns,
her daughters dry gullies that give birth to stones,
who was, in our childhood, the housemaid and the cook,
the young grand' who polished the plaster figure
of Clio, muse of history, in her seashell grotto
in the Great House parlor, Anadyomene washed
in the deep Atlantic heave of her housemaid's hymn.

In the indigo dawn the palms unclenched their fists,
his eyes opened the flowers, and he lay as still
as the waterless mill wheel. The sun's fuse caught,
it hissed on the edge of the skyline, and day exploded
its remorseless avalanche of dray carts and curses,
the roaring oven of Kingston, its sky as fierce
as the tin box of a patties cart. Down the docks

between the Levantine smells of the warehouses
nosed the sea wind with its odor of a dog's damp fur.
He lathered in anger and refreshed his love.
He was lathered like a horse, but the instant
the shower crowned him and he closed his eyes,
he was a bride under lace, remarrying his country,
a child drawn by the roars of the mill wheel's electorate,
those vows reaffirmed; he dressed, went down to breakfast,
and sitting again at the mahogany surface
of the breakfast table, its dark hide as polished
as the sheen of mares, saw his father's face
and his own face blent there, and looked out
to the drying garden and its seeping pond.

What was the Caribbean? A green pond mantling
behind the Great House columns of Whitehall,
behind the Greek façades of Washington,
with bloated frogs squatting on lily pads
like islands, islands that coupled as sadly as turtles
engendering islets, as the turtle of Cuba
mounting Jamaica engendered the Caymans, as, behind
the hammerhead turtle of Haiti-San Domingo
trailed the little turtles from Tortuga to Tobago;
he followed the bobbing trek of the turtles
leaving America for the open Atlantic,
felt his own flesh loaded like the pregnant beaches
with their moon-guarded eggs—they yearned for Africa,
they were lemmings drawn by magnetic memory
to an older death, to broader beaches
where the coughing of lions was dumbed by breakers.
Yes, he could understand their natural direction
but they would drown, sea eagles circling them,
and the languor of frigates that do not beat wings,
and he closed his eyes, and felt his jaw drop
again with the weight of that silent scream.

He cried out at the turtles as one screams at children
with the anger of love, it was the same scream
which, in his childhood, had reversed an epoch
that had bent back the leaves of his star-apple kingdom,
made streams race uphill, pulled the water wheel backwards
like the wheels in a film, and at that outcry,
from the raw ropes and tendons of his throat,
the sea buzzards receded and receded into specks,
and the osprey vanished.
                      On the knee-hollowed steps
of the crusted cathedral, there was a woman in black,
the black of moonless nights, within whose eyes
shone seas in starlight like the glint of knives
(the one who had whispered to the keyhole of his ear),
washing the steps, and she heard it first.
She was one of a flowing black river of women
who bore elliptical basins to the feet of paupers
on the Day of Thorns, who bore milk pails to cows
in a pastoral sunrise, who bore baskets on their heads
down the hemophilic red hills of Haiti,
now with the squeezed rag dripping from her hard hands
the way that vinegar once dropped from a sponge,
but she heard as a dog hears, as all the underdogs
of the world hear, the pitched shriek of silence.
Star-apples rained to the ground in that silence,
the silence was the green of cities undersea,
and the silence lasted for half an hour
in that single second, a seashell silence, resounding
with silence, and the men with barbed-wire beards saw
in that creak of light that was made between
the noises of the world that was equally divided
between rich and poor, between North and South,
between white and black, between two Americas,
the fields of silent Zion in Parish Trelawny,
in Parish St. David, in Parish St. Andrew,

leaves dancing like children without any sound,
in the valley of Tryall, and the white, silent roar
of the old water wheel in the star-apple kingdom;
and the woman's face, had a smile been decipherable
in that map of parchment so rivered with wrinkles,
would have worn the same smile with which he now
cracked the day open and began his egg.

FROM

The Fortunate Traveller

(1982)

Black clippers, tarred with whales' blood, fold their sails
entering New Bedford, New London, New Haven.
A white church spire whistles into space
like a swordfish, a rocket pierces heaven
as the thawed springs in icy chevrons race
down hillsides and Old Glories flail
the crosses of green farm boys back from 'Nam.
Seasons are measured still by the same
span of the veined leaf and the veined body
whenever the spring wind startles an uproar
of marching oaks with memories of a war
that peeled whole counties from the calendar.

The hillside is still wounded by the spire
of the white meetinghouse, the Indian trail
trickles down it like the brown blood of the whale
in rowanberries bubbling like the spoor
on logs burnt black as Bibles by hellfire.
The war whoop is coiled tight in the white owl,
stone-feathered icon of the Indian soul,
and railway lines are arrowing to the far
mountainwide absence of the Iroquois.
Spring lances wood and wound, and a spring runs
down tilted birch floors with their splintered suns
of beads and mirrors—broken promises
that helped make this Republic what it is.

The crest of our conviction grows as loud
as the spring oaks, rooted and reassured
that God is meek but keeps a whistling sword;
His harpoon is the white lance of the church,

His wandering mind a trail folded in birch,
His rage the vats that boiled the melted beast
when the black clippers brought (knotting each shroud
round the crosstrees) our sons home from the East.

Now, at the rising of Venus—the steady star
that survives translation, if one can call this lamp
the planet that pierces us over indigo islands—
despite the critical sand flies, I accept my function
as a colonial upstart at the end of an empire,
a single, circling, homeless satellite.
I can listen to its guttural death rattle in the shoal
of the legions' withdrawing roar, from the raj,
from the Reich, and see the full moon again
like a white flag rising over Fort Charlotte,
and sunset slowly collapsing like the flag.

It's good that everything's gone, except their language,
which is everything. And it may be a childish revenge
at the presumption of empires to hear the worm
gnawing their solemn columns into coral,
to snorkel over Atlantis, to see, through a mask,
Sidon up to its windows in sand, Tyre, Alexandria,
with their wavering seaweed spires through a glass-bottom boat,
and to buy porous fragments of the Parthenon
from a fisherman in Tobago, but the fear exists,
Delenda est Carthago on the rose horizon,

and the side streets of Manhattan are sown with salt,
as those in the North all wait for that white glare
of the white rose of inferno, all the world's capitals.
Here, in Manhattan, I lead a tight life
and a cold one, my soles stiffen with ice
even through woollen socks; in the fenced backyard,
trees with clenched teeth endure the wind of February,
and I have some friends under its iron ground.
Even when spring comes with its rain of nails,

with its soiled ice oozing into black puddles,
the world will be one season older but no wiser.

Fragments of paper swirl round the bronze general
of Sheridan Square, syllables of Nordic tongues
(as an Obeah priestess sprinkles flour on the doorstep
to ward off evil, so Carthage was sown with salt);
the flakes are falling like a common language
on my nose and lips, and rime forms on the mouth
of a shivering exile from his African province;
a blizzard of moths whirls around the extinguished lamp
of the Union general, sugary insects crunched underfoot.

You move along dark afternoons where death
entered a taxi and sat next to a friend,
or passed another a razor, or whispered "Pardon"
in a check-clothed restaurant behind her cough—
I am thinking of an exile farther than any country.
And, in this heart of darkness, I cannot believe
they are now talking over palings by the doddering
banana fences, or that seas can be warm.

How far I am from those cacophonous seaports
built round the single exclamation of one statue
of Victoria Regina! There vultures shift on the roof
of the red iron market, whose patois
is brittle as slate, a gray stone flecked with quartz.
I prefer the salt freshness of that ignorance,
as language crusts and blackens on the pots
of this cooked culture, coming from a raw one;
and these days in bookstores I stand paralyzed

by the rows of shelves along whose wooden branches
the free-verse nightingales are trilling "Read me! Read me!"
in various meters of asthmatic pain;

or I shiver before the bellowing behemoths
with the snow still falling in white words on Eighth Street,
those burly minds that barreled through contradictions
like a boar through bracken, or an old tarpon
bristling with broken hooks, or an old stag
spanieled by critics to a crag at twilight,

the exclamation of its antlers like a hat rack
on which they hang their theses. I am tired of words,
and literature is an old couch stuffed with fleas,
of culture stuffed in the taxidermist's hides.
I think of Europe as a gutter of autumn leaves
choked like the thoughts in an old woman's throat.
But she was home to some consul in snow-white ducks
doing out his service in the African provinces,
who wrote letters like this one home and feared malaria
as I mistrust the dark snow, who saw the lances of rain

marching like a Roman legion over the fens.
So, once again, when life has turned into exile,
and nothing consoles, not books, work, music, or a woman,
and I am tired of trampling the brown grass,
whose name I don't know, down an alley of stone,
and I must turn back to the road, its winter traffic,
and others sure in the dark of their direction,
I lie under a blanket on a cold couch,
feeling the flu in my bones like a lantern.

Under the blue sky of winter in Virginia
the brick chimneys flute white smoke through skeletal lindens,
as a spaniel churns up a pyre of blood-rusted leaves;
there is no memorial here to their Treblinka—
as a van delivers from the ovens loaves
as warm as flesh, its brakes jaggedly screech
like the square wheel of a swastika. The mania

of history veils even the clearest air,
the sickly-sweet taste of ash, of something burning.

And when one encounters the slow coil of an accent,
reflexes step aside as if for a snake,
with the paranoid anxiety of the victim.
The ghosts of white-robed horsemen float through the trees,
the galloping hysterical abhorrence of my race—
like any child of the Diaspora, I remember this
even as the flakes whiten Sheridan's shoulders,
and I remember once looking at my aunt's face,
the wintry blue eyes, the rusty hair, and thinking

maybe we are part Jewish, and felt a vein
run through this earth and clench itself like a fist
around an ancient root, and wanted the privilege
to be yet another of the races they fear and hate
instead of one of the haters and the afraid.
Above the spiny woods, dun grass, skeletal trees,
the chimney serenely fluting something from Schubert—
like the wraith of smoke that comes from someone burning—
veins the air with an outcry that I cannot help.

The winter branches are mined with buds,
the fields of March will detonate the crocus,
the olive battalions of the summer woods
will shout orders back to the wind. To the soldier's mind
the season's passage round the pole is martial,
the massacres of autumn sheeted in snow, as
winter turns white as a veterans hospital.
Something quivers in the blood beyond control—
something deeper than our transient fevers.

But in Virginia's woods there is also an old man
dressed like a tramp in an old Union greatcoat,

walking to the music of rustling leaves, and when
I collect my change from a small-town pharmacy,
the cashier's fingertips still wince from my hand
as if it would singe hers—well, yes, *je suis un singe,*
I am one of that tribe of frenetic or melancholy
primates who made your music for many more moons
than all the silver quarters in the till.

MAP OF THE NEW WORLD

I ARCHIPELAGOES

At the end of this sentence, rain will begin.
At the rain's edge, a sail.

Slowly the sail will lose sight of islands;
into a mist will go the belief in harbors
of an entire race.

The ten-years war is finished.
Helen's hair, a gray cloud.
Troy, a white ashpit
by the drizzling sea.

The drizzle tightens like the strings of a harp.
A man with clouded eyes picks up the rain
and plucks the first line of the *Odyssey*.

II THE COVE

Resound it, surge: the legend of Yseult
in languorous detonations of your surf.
I've smuggled in this bleached prow, rustling shoreward
to white sand guarded by fierce manchineel,
a secret
read by the shadow of a frigate hawk.

This inlet's a furnace.
The leaves flash silver signals to the waves.
Far from the curse of government by race,
I turn these leaves—this book's seditious fault—

to feel her skeins of sea mist cross my face,
and catch, on the wind's mouth, a taste of salt.

III SEA CRANES

"Only in a world where there are cranes and horses,"
wrote Robert Graves, "can poetry survive."
Or adept goats on crags. Epic
follows the plow, meter the ring of the anvil;
prophecy divines the figurations of storks, and awe
the arc of the stallion's neck.

The flame has left the charred wick of the cypress;
the light will catch these islands in their turn.

Magnificent frigates inaugurate the dusk
that flashes through the whisking tails of horses,
the stony fields they graze.
From the hammered anvil of the promontory
the spray settles in stars.

Generous ocean, turn the wanderer
from his salt sheets, the prodigal
drawn to the deep troughs of the swine-black porpoise.

Wrench his heart's wheel and set his forehead here.

for Pat Strachan

The thought-resembling moonlight at a cloud's edge
spreads like the poetry of some Roman outpost
to every corner of the Silver Age.
The moon, capitol of that white empire, is lost
in the black mass. Now, the hot core is Washington,
where once it was Whitehall. Her light burns
all night in office like Cato's ghost,
a concentration ringed with turbulence.
The wet dawn smells of seaweed. On this seawall
where there was a pier once, the concrete cracks
have multiplied like frontiers on a map
of Roman Europe. The same tides rise and fall,
froth, the moon's lantern hung in the same place.
On the sea road skirting the old Navy base,
the archaeologist, with his backpack, crouching
to collect cowries, startles the carbon skeleton
impressed on earth like the gigantic fern
of Caterpillar tracks. By Roman roads
along the sea grapes, their leaves the size
of armor-plates, the stripped hangars rust
where once the bombers left for target practice;
breakers bring rumors of the nuclear fleet
to shells the washed-out blue of pirates' eyes.

Beyond the choric gestures of the olive,
gnarled as sea almonds, over boulders dry
as the calcareous molars of a Cyclops,
past the maniacal frothing of a cave,
I climbed, carrying a body round my shoulders.
I held, for a blade, with armor-dented chops
a saw-toothed agave. Below me, on the sand,
the rooted phalanxes of coconuts,
Trojan and Spartan, stood with rustling helms;
hooking myself up by one bloody hand,
and groaning on each hoist, I made the height
where the sea crows circle, and heaved down the weight
on the stone acre of the promontory.
Up here, at last, was the original story,
nothing was here at all, just stones and light.

I walked to the cliff's edge for a wide look,
relishing this emptiness of sea and air,
the wind filling my mouth said the same word
for "wind," but here it sounded different,
shredding the sea to paper as it rent
sea, wind, and word from their corrupted root;
my memory rode its buffets like a bird.
The body that I had thrown down at my foot
was not really a body but a great book
still fluttering like chitons on a frieze,
till wind worked through the binding of its pages
scattering Hector's and Achilles' rages
to white, diminishing scraps, like gulls that ease
past the gray sphinxes of the crouching islands.

I held air without language in my hands.
My head was scoured of other people's monsters.
I reached this after half a hundred years.
I, too, signed on to follow that gold thread
which linked the spines down a dark library shelf,
around a narrowing catacomb where the dead,
in columns hemmed with gold around the plinth
of their calf-binding, wait, and came upon
my features melting in the Minotaur
at the dead end of the classic labyrinth,
and, with this blade of agave, hacked down
the old Greek bull. Now, crouched before blank stone,
I wrote the sound for "sea," the sign for "sun."

THE MAN WHO LOVED ISLANDS

A TWO-PAGE OUTLINE

A man is leaning on a cold iron rail
watching an islet from an island and so on,
say, Charlotte Amalie facing St. John,
which begins the concept of infinity
uninterrupted by any mortal sail,
only the thin ghost of a tanker drawing the horizon
behind it with the silvery slick of a snail,
and that's the first shot of this forthcoming film
starring James Coburn and his tanned, leathery, frail
resilience and his now whitening hair,
and his white, vicious grin. Now we were where?
On this island, one of the Virgins, the prota-
gonist established. Now comes the second shot,
and chaos of artifice still called the plot,
which has to get the hero off somewhere
else, 'cause there's no kick in contemplation
of silvery light upon wind-worried water
between here and the islet of Saint John,
and how they are linked like any silver chain
glinting against the hero's leather chest,
sold in the free gift ports, like noon-bright water.
The hero's momentary rest on the high rail
can be a good beginning. To start with rest
is good—the tanker can come later.
But we can't call it "The Man Who Loved Islands"
any more than some Zen-Karate film
would draw them with "The Hero Who Loves Water."
No soap. There must be something with diamonds,
emeralds, emeralds the color of the shallows there,
or sapphires, like blue, unambiguous air,

sapphires for Sophia, but we'll come to that.
Coburn looks great with or without a hat,
and there must be some minimum of slaughter
that brings in rubies, but you cannot hover
over that first shot like a painting. Action
is all of art, the thoughtless pace
of lying with style, so that when it's over,
that first great shot of Coburn's leathery face,
crinkled like the water which he contemplates,
could be superfluous, in the first place,
since that tired artifice called history,
which in its motion is as false as fiction,
requires an outline, a summary. I can think of none,
quite honestly. I'm no photographer; this
could be a movie. I mean things are moving,
the water for example, the light on the man's hair
that has gone white, even those crescent sands
are just as moving as his love of islands;
the tanker that seems still is moving, even
the clouds like galleons anchored in heaven,
and what is moving most of all of course
is the violent man lulled into this inaction
by the wide sea. Let's hold it on the sea
as we establish their ancient interaction,
a hint of the Homeric, a little poetry
before the whole mess hits the bloody fan.
All these islands that you love, I guaran-
tee we'll work them in as background, with
generous establishing shots from Jim's car and
even a few harbors and villages, *if*
we blow the tanker up and get the flames
blazing with oil, and Sophia, if she's free,
daintily smudged, with her slip daintily torn,
is climbing down this rope ladder, and we shoot up
from Coburn's P.O.V.—he's got the gems—

that's where we throw in Charlotte Amalie
and the waterfront bars, and this Danish alley
with the heavies chasing, and we can keep all the
business of Jim on the rail; that lyric stuff
goes with the credits if you insist on keeping it tend-
er; I can see it, but things must get rough
pretty damn fast, or else you lose them, pally,
or, tell you what, let's save it for THE END.

In their faint photographs
mottled with chemicals,
like the left hand of some spinster aunt,
they have drifted to the edge
of verandas in Whistlerian
white, their jungle turned tea-brown—
even its spiked palms—
their features pale,
to be penciled in:
bone-collared gentlemen
with spiked mustaches
and their wives embayed in the wickerwork
armchairs, all looking colored
from the distance of a century
beginning to groan sideways from the axe stroke!

Their bay horses blacken
like spaniels, the front lawn a beige
carpet, brown moonlight and a moon
so sallow, so pharmaceutical
that her face is a feverish child's,
some malarial angel
whose grave still cowers
under a fury of bush,
a mania of wild yams
wrangling to hide her from ancestral churchyards.

And the sigh of that child
is white as an orchid
on a crusted log
in the bush of Dominica,
a V of Chinese white

meant for the beat of a seagull
over a sepia souvenir of Cornwall,
as the white hush between two sentences.

Sundays! Their furnace
of boredom after church.
A maiden aunt canoes through lilies of clouds
in a Carib hammock, to a hymn's metronome,
and the child on the varnished, lion-footed couch
sees the hills dip and straighten with each lurch.
The green-leaved uproar of the century
turns dim as the Atlantic, a rumorous haze
behind the lime trees, breakers
advancing in decorous, pleated lace;
the cement grindstone of the afternoon
turns slowly, sharpening her senses,
the bay below is green as calalu, stewing Sargasso.

In that fierce hush
between Dominican mountains
the child expects a sound
from a butterfly clipping itself to a bush
like a gold earring to a black maid's ear—
one who goes down to the village, visiting,
whose pink dress wilts like a flower between the limes.

There are logs
wrinkled like the hand of an old woman
who wrote with a fine courtesy to that world
when grace was common as malaria,
when the gas lanterns' hiss on the veranda
drew the aunts out like moths
doomed to be pressed in a book, to fall
into the brown oblivion of an album,
embroiderers of silence

for whom the arches of the Thames,
Parliament's needles,
and the petit-point reflections of London Bridge
fade on the hammock cushions from the sun,
where one night
a child stares at the windless candle flame
from the corner of a lion-footed couch
at the erect white light,
her right hand married to *Jane Eyre*,
foreseeing that her own white wedding dress
will be white paper.

THE SPOILER'S RETURN

for Earl Lovelace

I sit high on this bridge in Laventille,
watching that city where I left no will
but my own conscience and rum-eaten wit,
and limers passing see me where I sit,
ghost in brown gabardine, bones in a sack,
and bawl: "Ay, Spoiler, boy! When you come back?"
And those who bold don't feel they out of place
to peel my limeskin back, and see a face
with eyes as cold as a dead macajuel,
and if they still can talk, I answer: "Hell."
I have a room there where I keep a crown,
and Satan send me to check out this town.
Down there, that Hot Boy have a stereo
where, whole day, he does blast my caiso;
I beg him two weeks' leave and he send me
back up, not as no bedbug or no flea,
but in this limeskin hat and floccy suit,
to sing what I did always sing: the truth.
Tell Desperadoes when you reach the hill,
I decompose, but I composing still:

I going to bite them young ladies, partner,
like a hogdog or a hamburger
and if you thin, don't be in a fright
is only big fat women I going to bite.

The shark, racing the shadow of the shark
across clear coral rocks, does make them dark—
that is my premonition of the scene
of what passing over this Caribbean.
Is crab climbing crab-back, in a crab-quarrel,

and going round and round in the same barrel,
is sharks with shirt-jacks, sharks with well-pressed fins,
ripping we small fry off with razor grins;
nothing ain't change but color and attire,
so back me up, Old Brigade of Satire,
back me up, Martial, Juvenal, and Pope
(to hang theirself I giving plenty rope),
join Spoiler' chorus, sing the song with me,
Lord Rochester, who praised the nimble flea:

Were I, who to my cost already am
One of those strange, prodigious creatures, Man,
A spirit free, to choose for my own share,
What case of flesh and blood I pleased to wear,
I hope when I die, after burial,
To come back as an insect or animal.

I see these islands and I feel to bawl,
"area of darkness" with V. S. Nightfall.

Lock off your tears, you casting pearls of grief
on a duck's back, a waxen dasheen leaf,
the slime crab's carapace is waterproof
and those with hearing aids turn off the truth,
and their dark glasses let you criticize
your own presumptuous image in their eyes.
Behind dark glasses is just hollow skull,
and black still poor, though black is beautiful.
So, crown and miter me Bedbug the First—
the gift of mockery with which I'm cursed
is just a insect biting Fame behind,
a vermin swimming in a glass of wine,
that, dipped out with a finger, bound to bite
its saving host, ungrateful parasite,
whose sting, between the cleft arse and its seat,

reminds Authority man is just meat,
a moralist as mordant as the louse
that the good husband brings from the whorehouse,
the flea whose itch to make all Power wince,
will crash a fête, even at his life's expense,
and these pile up in lime pits by the heap,
daily, that our deliverers may sleep.
All those who promise free and just debate,
then blow up radicals to save the state,
who allow, in democracy's defense,
a parliament of spiked heads on a fence,
all you go bawl out, "Spoils, things ain't so bad."
This ain't the Dark Age, is just Trinidad,
is human nature, Spoiler, after all,
it ain't big genocide, is just bohbohl;
safe and conservative, 'fraid to take side,
they say that Rodney commit suicide,
is the same voices that, in the slave ship,
smile at their brothers, "Boy, is just the whip,"
I free and easy, you see me have chain?
A little censorship can't cause no pain,
a little graft can't rot the human mind,
what sweet in goat-mouth sour in his behind.
So I sing with Attila, I sing with Commander,
what right in Guyana, right in Uganda.
The time could come, it can't be very long,
when they will jail calypso for picong,
for first comes television, then the press,
all in the name of Civic Righteousness;
it has been done before, all Power has
made the sky shit and maggots of the stars,
over these Romans lying on their backs,
the hookers swaying their enormous sacks,
until all language stinks, and the truth lies,
a mass for maggots and a fête for flies;

and, for a spineless thing, rumor can twist
into a style the local journalist—
as bland as a green coconut, his manner
routinely tart, his sources the Savannah
and all pretensions to a native art
reduced to giggles at the coconut cart,
where heads with reputations, in one slice,
are brought to earth, when they ain't eating nice;
and as for local Art, so it does go,
the audience have more talent than the show.

Is Carnival, straight Carnival that's all,
the beat is base, the melody bohbohl,
all Port of Spain is a twelve-thirty show,
some playing Kojak, some Fidel Castro,
some Rastamen, but, with or without locks,
to Spoiler is the same old khaki socks,
all Frederick Street stinking like a closed drain,
Hell is a city much like Port of Spain,
what the rain rots, the sun ripens some more,
all in due process and within the law,
as, like a sailor on a spending spree,
we blow our oil-bloated economy
on projects from here to eternity,
and Lord, the sunlit streets break Spoiler's heart,
to have natural gas and not give a fart,
to see them line up, pitch-oil tin in hand:
each independent, oil-forsaken island,
like jeering at some scrunter with the blues,
while you lend him some need-a-half-sole shoes,
some begging bold as brass, some coming meeker,
but from Jamaica to poor Dominica
we make them know they begging, every loan
we send them is like blood squeezed out of stone,
and giving gives us back the right to laugh

that we couldn't see we own black people starve,
and, more we give, more we congratulate
we-self on our own self-sufficient state.
In all them project, all them Five-Year Plan,
what happen to the Brotherhood of Man?
Around the time I dead it wasn't so,
we sang the Commonwealth of caiso,
we was in chains, but chains made us unite,
now who have, good for them, and who blight, blight;
my bread is bitterness, my wine is gall,
my chorus is the same: "I want to fall."
O, wheel of industry, check out your cogs!
Between the knee-high trash and khaki dogs
Arnold's Phoenician trader reach this far,
selling you half-dead batteries for your car;
the children of Tagore, in funeral shroud,
curry favor and chicken from the crowd;
as for the Creoles, check their house, and look,
you bust your brain before you find a book,
when Spoiler see all this, ain't he must bawl,
"area of darkness," with V. S. Nightfall?
Corbeaux like cardinals line the La Basse
in ecumenical patience while you pass
the Beetham Highway—Guard corruption's stench,
you bald, black justices of the High Bench—
and beyond them the firelit mangrove swamps,
ibises practicing for postage stamps,
Lord, let me take a taxi South again
and hear, drumming across Caroni Plain,
the tabla in the Indian half hour
when twilight fills the mud huts of the poor,
to hear the tattered flags of drying corn
rattle a sky from which all the gods gone,
their bleached flags of distress waving to me
from shacks, adrift like rafts on a green sea,

"Things ain't go change, they ain't go change at all,"
to my old chorus: "Lord, I want to bawl."
The poor still poor, whatever arse they catch.
Look south from Laventille, and you can watch
the torn brown patches of the Central Plain
slowly restitched by needles of the rain,
and the frayed earth, crisscrossed like old bagasse,
spring to a cushiony quilt of emerald grass,
and who does sew and sow and patch the land?
The Indian. And whose villages turn sand?
The fishermen doomed to stitching the huge net
of the torn foam from Point to La Fillette.

One thing with Hell, at least it organize
in soaring circles, when any man dies
he must pass through them first, that is the style,
Jesus was down here for a little while,
cadaverous Dante, big-guts Rabelais,
all of them wave to Spoiler on their way.
Catch us in Satan tent, next carnival:
Lord Rochester, Quevedo, Juvenal,
Maestro, Martial, Pope, Dryden, Swift, Lord Byron,
the lords of irony, the Duke of Iron,
hotly contending for the monarchy
in couplets or the old re-minor key,
all those who gave earth's pompous carnival
fatigue, and groaned "O God, I feel to fall!"
all those whose anger for the poor on earth
made them weep with a laughter beyond mirth,
names wide as oceans when compared with mine
salted my songs, and gave me their high sign.
All you excuse me, Spoiler was in town;
you pass him straight, so now he gone back down.

THE HOTEL NORMANDIE POOL

I

Around the cold pool in the metal light
of New Year's morning, I choose one of nine
cast-iron umbrellas set in iron tables
for work and coffee. The first cigarette
triggers the usual fusillade of coughs.
After a breeze the pool settles the weight
of its reflections on one line. Sunshine
lattices a blank wall with the shade of gables,
stirs the splayed shadows of the hills like moths.

Last night, framed in the binding of that window,
like the great chapter in some Russian novel
in which, during the war, the prince comes home
to watch the soundless waltzers dart and swivel,
like fishes in their lamplit aquarium,
I stood in my own gauze of swirling snow
and, through the parted hair of ribboned drapes,
felt, between gusts of music, the pool widen
between myself and those light-scissored shapes.

The dancers stiffened and, like fish, were frozen
in panes of ice blocked by the window frames;
one woman fanned, still fluttering on a pin,
as a dark fusillade of kettledrums
and a piercing cornet played "Auld Lang Syne"
while a battalion of drunk married men
reswore their vows. For this my fiftieth year,
I muttered to the ribbon-medaled water,
"Change me, my sign, to someone I can bear."

Now my pen's shadow, angled at the wrist
with the chrome stanchions at the pool's edge,
dims on its lines like birches in a mist
as a cloud fills my hand. A drop punctuates
the startled paper. The pool's iron umbrellas
ring with the drizzle. Sun hits the water.
The pool is blinding zinc. I shut my eyes,
and as I raise their lids I see each daughter
ride on the rayed shells of both irises.

The prayer is brief: That the transparent wrist
would not cloud surfaces with my own shadow,
and that this page's surface would unmist
after my breath as pools and mirrors do.
But all reflection gets no easier,
although the brown, dry needles of that palm
quiver to stasis and things resume their rhyme
in water, like the rubber ring that is a
red rubber ring inverted at the line's center.

Into that ring my younger daughter dived
yesterday, slithering like a young dolphin,
her rippling shadow hungering under her,
with nothing there to show how well she moved
but in my mind the veer of limb and fin.
Transparent absences! Love makes me look
through a clear ceiling into rooms of sand;
I ask the element that is my sign,
"Oh, let her lithe head through that surface break!"

Aquarian, I was married to water;
under that certain roof, I would lie still
next to my sister spirit, horizontal
below what stars derailed our parallel
from our far vow's undeviating course;

the next line rises as they enter it,
Peter, Anna, Elizabeth—Margaret
still sleeping with one arm around each daughter,
in the true shape of love, beyond divorce.

Time cuts down on the length man can endure
his own reflection. Entering a glass
I surface quickly now, prefer to breathe
the fetid and familiar atmosphere
of work and cigarettes. Only tyrants believe
their mirrors, or Narcissi, brooding on boards,
before they plunge into their images;
at fifty I have learnt that beyond words
is the disfiguring exile of divorce.

II

Across blue seamless silk, iron umbrellas
and a brown palm burn. A sandaled man comes out
and, in a robe of foam-frayed terry cloth,
with Roman graveness buries his room key,
then, mummy-oiling both forearms and face
with sunglasses still on, stands, fixing me,
and nods. Some petty businessman who tans
his pallor a negotiable bronze,
and the bright nod would have been commonplace

as he uncurled his shades above the pool's
reflecting rim—white towel, toga-slung,
foam hair repeated by the robe's frayed hem—
but, in the lines of his sun-dazzled squint,
a phrase was forming in that distant tongue
of which the mind keeps just a mineral glint,
the lovely Latin lost to all our schools:

"Quis te misit, Magister?" And its whisper went
through my cold body, veining it in stone.

On marble, concrete, or obsidian,
your visit, Master, magnifies the lines
of our small pool to that Ovidian
thunder of surf between the Baltic pines.
The light that swept Rome's squares and palaces,
washing her tangled fountains of green bronze
when you were one drop in a surf of faces—
a fleck of spittle from the she-wolf's tooth—
now splashes a palm's shadow at your foot.

Turn to us, Ovid. Our emerald sands
are stained with sewage from each tin-shacked Rome;
corruption, censorship, and arrogance
make exile seem a happier thought than home.
"Ah, for the calm proconsul with a voice
as just and level as this Roman pool,"
our house slaves sigh; the field slaves scream revenge;
one moves between the flatterer and the fool
yearning for the old bondage from both ends.

And I, whose ancestors were slave and Roman,
have seen both sides of the imperial foam,
heard palm and pine tree alternate applause
as the white breakers rose in galleries
to settle, whispering at the tilted palm
of the boy-god, Augustus. My own face
held negro Neros, chalk Caligulas;
my own reflection slid along the glass
of faces foaming past triumphal cars.

Master, each idea has become suspicious
of its shadow. A lifelong friend whispers

in his own house as if it might arrest him;
markets no more applaud, as was their custom,
our camouflaged, booted militias
roaring past on camions, the sugar-apples
of grenades growing on their belts; ideas
with guns divide the islands; in dark squares
the poems gather like conspirators.

Then Ovid said, "When I was first exiled,
I missed my language as your tongue needs salt,
in every watery shape I saw my child,
no bench would tell my shadow 'Here's your place';
bridges, canals, willow-fanned waterways
turned from my parting gaze like an insult,
till, on a tablet smooth as the pool's skin,
I made reflections that, in many ways,
were even stronger than their origin.

"Tiled villas anchored in their foaming orchards,
parched terraces in a dust cloud of words,
among clod-fires, wolfskins, starving herds,
Tibullus' flute faded, sweetest of shepherds.
Through shaggy pines the beaks of needling birds
pricked me at Tomis to learn their tribal tongue,
so, since desire is stronger than its disease,
my pen's beak parted till we chirped one song
in the unequal shade of equal trees.

"Campaigns enlarged our frontiers like clouds,
but my own government was the bare boards
of a plank table swept by resinous pines
whose boughs kept skittering from Caesar's eye
with every yaw. There, hammering out lines
in that green forge to fit me for the horse,
I bent on a solitude so tyrannous

against the once seductive surf of crowds
that no wife softens it, or Caesar's envy.

"And where are those detractors now who said
that in and out of the imperial shade
I scuttled, showing to a frowning sun
the fickle dyes of the chameleon?
Romans"—he smiled—"will mock your slavish rhyme,
the slaves your love of Roman structures, when,
from Metamorphoses to Tristia,
art obeys its own order. Now it's time."
Tying his toga gently, he went in.

There, at the year's horizon, he had stood,
as if the pool's meridian were the line
that doubled the burden of his solitude
in either world; and, as one leaf fell,
his echo rippled: "Why here, of all places,
a small, suburban tropical hotel,
its pool pitched to a Mediterranean blue,
its palms rusting in their concrete oasis?
Because to make my image flatters you."

III

At dusk, the sky is loaded like watercolor paper
with an orange wash in which every edge frays—
a painting with no memory of the painter—
and what this pool recites is not a phrase
from an invisible, exiled laureate,
where there's no laurel, but the scant applause
of one dry, scraping palm tree as blue eve-
ning ignites its blossoms from one mango flower,
and something, not a leaf, falls like a leaf,

as swifts with needle-beaks dart, panicking over
the pool's cloud-closing light. For an envoi,
write what the wrinkled god repeats to the boy-
god: "May the last light of heaven pity us
for the hardening lie in the face that we did not tell."
Dusk. The trees blacken like the pool's umbrellas.
Dusk. Suspension of every image and its voice.
The mangoes pitch from their green dark like meteors.
The fruit bat swings on its branch, a tongueless bell.

Anna, my daughter,
you have a black dog
that noses your heel,
selfless as a shadow;
here is a fable
about a black dog:
On the last sunrise
the shadow dressed with Him,
it stretched itself also—
they were two big men
with one job to do.
But life had been lent to one
only for this life.
They strode in silence toward
uncontradicting night.
The rats at the Last Supper
shared crumbs with their shadows,
the shadow of the bread
was shared by the bread;
when the candles lowered,
the shadow felt larger,
so He ordered it to leave;
He said where He was going
it would not be needed,
for there there'd be either
radiance or nothing.
It stopped when He turned
and ordered it home,
then it resumed the scent;
it felt itself stretching
as the sun grew small
like the eyes of the soldiers

receding into holes
under the petrified
serpents on their helmets;
the narrowing pupils
glinted like nailheads,
so before He lay back
it crept between the wood
as if it were the pallet
they had always shared;
it crept between the wood
and the flesh nailed to the wood
and it rose like a black flag
as the crossbeam hoisted
itself and the eyes
closed very slowly
extinguishing the shadow—
everything was nothing.
Then the shadow slunk away,
crawling low on its belly,
and it left there knowing
that never again
would He ever need it;
it reentered the earth,
it didn't eat for three days,
it didn't go out,
then it peeped out carefully
like a mole from its hole,
like a wolf after winter,
like a surreptitious serpent,
looking for those forms
that could give back its shape;
then it ran out when the bells
began making wide rings
and rings of radiance;
it keeps nosing for His shape

and it finds it again, in
the white echo of a pigeon
with its wings extended
like a shirt on a clothesline,
like a white shirt on Monday
dripping from a clothesline,
like the greeting of a scarecrow
or a man yawning
at the end of a field.

THE FORTUNATE TRAVELLER

for Susan Sontag

And I heard a voice in the midst of the four beasts say,
A measure of wheat for a penny,
and three measures of barley for a penny;
and see thou hurt not the oil and the wine.

Revelation 6:6

I

It was in winter. Steeples, spires
congealed like holy candles. Rotting snow
flaked from Europe's ceiling. A compact man,
I crossed the canal in a gray overcoat,
on one lapel a crimson buttonhole
for the cold ecstasy of the assassin.
In the square coffin manacled to my wrist:
small countries pleaded through the mesh of graphs,
in treble-spaced, Xeroxed forms to the World Bank
on which I had scrawled the one word, MERCY;

I sat on a cold bench
under some skeletal lindens.
Two other gentlemen, black skins gone gray
as their identical, belted overcoats,
crossed the white river.
They spoke the stilted French
of their dark river,
whose hooked worm, multiplying its pale sickle,
could thin the harvest of the winter streets.
"Then we can depend on you to get us those tractors?"
"I gave my word."
"May my country ask you why you are doing this, sir?"
Silence.

"You know if you betray us, you cannot hide?"
A tug. Smoke trailing its dark cry.

At the window in Haiti, I remember
a gekko pressed against the hotel glass,
with white palms, concentrating head.
With a child's hands. Mercy, monsieur. Mercy.
Famine sighs like a scythe
across the field of statistics and the desert
is a moving mouth. In the hold of this earth
10,000,000 shoreless souls are drifting.
Somalia: 765,000, their skeletons will go under the tidal sand.
"We'll meet you in Bristol to conclude the agreement?"
Steeples like tribal lances, through congealing fog
the cries of wounded churchbells wrapped in cotton,
gray mist enfolding the conspirator
like a sealed envelope next to its heart.

No one will look up now to see the jet
fade like a weevil through a cloud of flour.
One flies first-class, one is so fortunate.
Like a telescope reversed, the traveller's eye
swiftly screws down the individual sorrow
to an oval nest of antic numerals,
and the iris, interlocking with this globe,
condenses it to zero, then a cloud.
Beetle-black taxi from Heathrow to my flat.
We are roaches,
riddling the state cabinets, entering the dark holes
of power, carapaced in topcoats,
scuttling around columns, signaling for taxis,
with frantic antennae, to other huddles with roaches;
we infect with optimism, and when
the cabinets crack, we are the first

to scuttle, radiating separately
back to Geneva, Bonn, Washington, London.

Under the dripping planes of Hampstead Heath,
I read her letter again, watching the drizzle
disfigure its pleading like mascara. Margo,
I cannot bear to watch the nations cry.
Then the phone: "We will pay you in Bristol."
Days in fetid bedclothes swallowing cold tea,
the phone stifled by the pillow. The telly
a blue storm with soundless snow.
I'd light the gas and see a tiger's tongue.
I was rehearsing the ecstasies of starvation
for what I had to do. *And have not charity.*

I found my pity, desperately researching
the origins of history, from reed-built communes
by sacred lakes, turning with the first sprocketed
water-driven wheels. I smelled imagination
among bestial hides by the gleam of fat,
seeking in all races a common ingenuity.
I envisaged an Africa flooded with such light
as alchemized the first fields of emmer wheat and barley,
when we savages dyed our pale dead with ochre,
and bordered our temples
with the ceremonial vulva of the conch
in the gray epoch of the obsidian adze.
I sowed the Sahara with rippling cereals,
my charity fertilized these aridities.

What was my field? Late sixteenth century.
My field was a dank acre. A Sussex don,
I taught the Jacobean anxieties: *The White Devil.*
Flamineo's torch startles the brooding yews.

The drawn sword comes in strides. I loved my Duchess,
the white flame of her soul blown out between
the smoking cypresses. Then I saw children pounce
on green meat with a rat's ferocity.

I called them up and took the train to Bristol,
my blood the Severn's dregs and silver.
On Severn's estuary the pieces flash,
Iscariot's salary, patron saint of spies.
I thought, who cares how many million starve?
Their rising souls will lighten the world's weight
and level its gull-glittering waterline;
we left at sunset down the estuary.

England recedes. The forked white gull
screeches, circling back.
Even the birds are pulled back by their orbit,
even mercy has its magnetic field.
                              Back in the cabin,
I uncap the whiskey, the porthole
mists with glaucoma. By the time I'm pissed,
England, England will be
that pale serrated indigo on the sea-line.
"You are so fortunate, you get to see the world—"
Indeed, indeed, sirs, I have seen the world.
Spray splashes the portholes and vision blurs.

Leaning on the hot rail, watching the hot sea,
I saw them far off, kneeling on hot sand
in the pious genuflections of the locust,
as Ponce's armored knees crush Florida
to the funereal fragrance of white lilies.

Now I have come to where the phantoms live,
I have no fear of phantoms, but of the real.
The sabbath benedictions of the islands.
Treble clef of the snail on the scored leaf,
the Tantum Ergo of black choristers
soars through the organ pipes of coconuts.
Across the dirty beach surpliced with lace,
they pass a brown lagoon behind the priest,
pale and unshaven in his frayed soutane,
into the concrete church at Canaries;
as Albert Schweitzer moves to the harmonium
of morning, and to the pluming chimneys,
the groundswell lifts *Lebensraum, Lebensraum.*

Black faces sprinkled with continual dew—
dew on the speckled croton, dew
on the hard leaf of the knotted plum tree,
dew on the elephant ears of the dasheen.
Through Kurtz's teeth, white skull in elephant grass,
the imperial fiction sings. Sunday
wrinkles downriver from the Heart of Darkness.
The heart of darkness is not Africa.
The heart of darkness is the core of fire
in the white center of the holocaust.
The heart of darkness is the rubber claw
selecting a scalpel in antiseptic light,
the hills of children's shoes outside the chimneys,
the tinkling nickel instruments on the white altar;
Jacob, in his last card, sent me these verses:
"Think of a God who doesn't lose His sleep
if trees burst into tears or glaciers weep.
So, aping His indifference, I write now,
not Anno Domini: After Dachau."

The night maid brings a lamp and draws the blinds.
I stay out on the veranda with the stars.
Breakfast congealed to supper on its plate.

There is no sea as restless as my mind.
The promontories snore. They snore like whales.
Cetus, the whale, was Christ.
The ember dies, the sky smokes like an ash heap.
Reeds wash their hands of guilt and the lagoon
is stained. Louder, since it rained,
a gauze of sand flies hisses from the marsh.

Since God is dead, and these are not His stars,
but man-lit, sulphurous, sanctuary lamps,
it's in the heart of darkness of this earth
that backward tribes keep vigil of His Body,
in deya, lampion, and this bedside lamp.
Keep the news from their blissful ignorance.
Like lice, like lice, the hungry of this earth
swarm to the tree of life. If those who starve
like these rain-flies who shed glazed wings in light
grew from sharp shoulder blades their brittle vans
and soared toward that tree, how it would seethe—
ah, Justice! But fires
drench them like vermin, quotas
prevent them, and they remain
compassionate fodder for the travel book,
its paragraphs like windows from a train,
for everywhere that earth shows its rib cage
and the moon goggles with the eyes of children,
we turn away to read. Rimbaud learned that.
                                    Rimbaud, at dusk,

idling his wrist in water past temples
the plumed dates still protect in Roman file,
knew that we cared less for one human face
than for the scrolls in Alexandria's ashes,
that the bright water could not dye his hand
any more than poetry. The dhow's silhouette
moved through the blinding coinage of the river
that, endlessly, until we pay one debt,
shrouds, every night, an ordinary secret.

IV

The drawn sword comes in strides.
It stretches for the length of the empty beach;
the fishermen's huts shut their eyes tight.
A frisson shakes the palm trees,
and sweats on the traveller's tree.
They've found out my sanctuary. Philippe, last night:
"It had two gentlemen in the village yesterday, sir,
asking for you while you was in town.
I tell them you was in town. They send to tell you,
there is no hurry. They will be coming back."

In loaves of cloud, *and have not charity*,
the weevil will make a sahara of Kansas,
the ant shall eat Russia.
Their soft teeth shall make, *and have not charity*,
the harvest's desolation,
and the brown globe crack like a begging bowl,
and though you fire oceans of surplus grain,
and have not charity,

still, through thin stalks,
the smoking stubble, stalks
grasshopper: third horseman,
the leather-helmed locust.

THE SEASON OF PHANTASMAL PEACE

Then all the nations of birds lifted together
the huge net of the shadows of this earth
in multitudinous dialects, twittering tongues,
stitching and crossing it. They lifted up
the shadows of long pines down trackless slopes,
the shadows of glass-faced towers down evening streets,
the shadow of a frail plant on a city sill—
the net rising soundless at night, the birds' cries soundless, until
there was no longer dusk, or season, decline, or weather,
only this passage of phantasmal light
that not the narrowest shadow dared to sever.

And men could not see, looking up, what the wild geese drew,
what the ospreys trailed behind them in silvery ropes
that flashed in the icy sunlight; they could not hear
battalions of starlings waging peaceful cries,
bearing the net higher, covering this world
like the vines of an orchard, or a mother drawing
the trembling gauze over the trembling eyes
of a child fluttering to sleep;
                              it was the light
that you will see at evening on the side of a hill
in yellow October, and no one hearing knew
what change had brought into the raven's cawing,
the killdeer's screech, the ember-circling chough
such an immense, soundless, and high concern
for the fields and cities where the birds belong,
except it was their seasonal passing, Love,
made seasonless, or, from the high privilege of their birth,
something brighter than pity for the wingless ones
below them who shared dark holes in windows and in houses,
and higher they lifted the net with soundless voices

above all change, betrayals of falling suns,
and this season lasted one moment, like the pause
between dusk and darkness, between fury and peace,
but, for such as our earth is now, it lasted long.

FROM

Midsummer

(1984)

I

The jet bores like a silverfish through volumes of cloud—
clouds that will keep no record of where we have passed,
not the sea's mirror, not the coral busy with its own
culture; they aren't doors of dissolving stone,
but pages in a damp culture that come apart.
So a hole in their parchment opens, and suddenly, in a vast
dereliction of sunlight, there's that island known
to the traveller Trollope, and the fellow traveller Froude,
for making nothing. Not even a people. The jet's shadow
ripples over green jungles as steadily as a minnow
through seaweed. Our sunlight is shared by Rome
and your white paper, Joseph. Here, as everywhere else,
it is the same age. In cities, in settlements of mud,
light has never had epochs. Near the rusty harbor
around Port of Spain bright suburbs fade into words—
Maraval, Diego Martin—the highways long as regrets,
and steeples so tiny you couldn't hear their bells,
nor the sharp exclamations of whitewashed minarets
from green villages. The lowering window resounds
over pages of earth, the canefields set in stanzas.
Skimming over an ochre swamp like a fast cloud of egrets
are nouns that find their branches as simply as birds.
It comes too fast, this shelving sense of home—
canes rushing the wing, a fence; a world that still stands as
the trundling tires keep shaking and shaking the heart.

Companion in Rome, whom Rome makes as old as Rome,
old as that peeling fresco whose flaking paint
is the clouds, you are crouched in some ancient pensione
where the only new thing is paper, like young St. Jerome
with his rock vault. Tonsured, you're muttering a line
that your exiled country will soon learn by heart,
to a flaking, sunlit ledge where a pigeon gurgles.
Midsummer's furnace casts everything in bronze.
Traffic flows in slow coils, like the doors of a baptistry,
and even the kitten's eyes blaze with Byzantine icons.
That old woman in black, unwrinkling your sheet with a palm,
her home is Rome, its history is her house.
Every Caesar's life has shrunk to a candle's column
in her saucer. Salt cleans their bloodstained togas.
She stacks up the popes like towels in cathedral drawers;
now in her stone kitchen, under the domes of onions,
she slices a light, as thick as cheese, into epochs.
Her kitchen wall flakes like an atlas where, once,
Ibi dracones was written, where unchristened cannibals
gnawed on the dry heads of coconuts as Ugolino did.
Hell's hearth is as cold as Pompeii's. We're punished by bells
as gentle as lilies. Luck to your Roman elegies
that the honey of time will riddle like those of Ovid.
Corals up to their windows in sand are my sacred domes,
gulls circling a seine are the pigeons of my St. Mark's,
silver legions of mackerel race through our catacombs.

At the Queen's Park Hotel, with its white, high-ceilinged rooms,
I reenter my first local mirror. A skidding roach
in the porcelain basin slides from its path to Parnassus.
Every word I have written took the wrong approach.
I cannot connect these lines with the lines in my face.
The child who died in me has left his print on
the tangled bed linen, and it was his small voice
that whispered from the gargling throat of the basin.
Out on the balcony I remember how morning was:
It was like a granite corner in Piero della Francesca's
"Resurrection," the cold, sleeping foot
prickling like the small palms up by the Hilton.
On the dewy Savannah, gently revolved by their grooms,
snorting, delicate-ankled racehorses exercise,
as delicate-ankled as brown smoke from the bakeries.
Sweat darkens their sides, and dew has frosted the skins
of the big American taxis parked all night on the street.
In black asphalt alleys marked by a ribbon of sunlight,
the closed faces of shacks are touched by that phrase in Traherne:
"The corn was orient and immortal wheat,"
and the canefields of Caroni. With all summer to burn,
a breeze strolls down to the docks, and the sea begins.

This Spanish port, piratical in diverseness,
with its one-eyed lighthouse, this damned sea of noise,
this ochre harbor, mantled by its own scum,
offers, from white wrought-iron balconies,
the nineteenth-century view. You can watch it become
more African hourly—crusted roofs, hot as skillets
peppered with cries; between fast-fry wagons,
floating seraphic Muslims cannot make it hush.
By the pitch of noon, the one thing wanting
is a paddle-wheeler with its rusty parrot's scream,
whistling in to be warped, and Mr. Kurtz on the landing.
Stay on the right bank in the imperial dream—
the Thames, not the Congo. From the small-island masts
of the schooner basin to the plate-glass fronts
of the Holiday Inn is one step, and from need to greed
through the river of clogged, circling traffic is
a few steps more. The world had no time to change
to a doorman's braid from the loincloths of Africa.
So, when the stores draw their blinds, like an empire's ending,
and the banks fade like the peaks of the Hindu Kush,
a cloaked wind, bent like a scavenger, rakes the trash
in the gutters. It is hard not to see the past's
vision of lampposts branching over streets of bush,
the plazas cracked by the jungle's furious seed.

V

The hemispheres lie sweating, flesh to flesh,
on a damp bed. The far ocean grinds in waves
of air-conditioning. The air is scaled like a fish
that leaves dry salt on the hands, and one believes
only in ice, the white zones of refrigerators.
In muslin midsummer along Fourteenth Street, hucksters
with cardboard luggage stacked near the peeling rind
of advertisements have made the Big Apple a mango;
shy as wallflowers at first, the dazed high-rises
rock to reggae and salsa; democracy's price is
two steps forward and three steps back in the Aztec tango
of assimilation, with no bar to the barrio.
On Fridays, an exodus crawls to the Hamptons.
Spit dries on the lips of the curb, and sweat
makes the furniture float away in islands.
Walk the breezy scrub dunes from Montauk to Amagansett,
while the salt of the earth turns into dirt in the cities. The vista
in dusty travel windows blooms with umbrellas
that they cannot go back to. Rats, biting the hands
that fed them. In that drugged dance of dealers,
remote-controlled by a Walkman like he can't stop,
Jesus propositions a seersucker suit, "Hey, mister,
just a sec . . ." The thumb of an Irish cop
rolls his bullets like beads. Glued to his own transistor.

Midsummer stretches beside me with its cat's yawn.
Trees with dust on their lips, cars melting down
in its furnace. Heat staggers the drifting mongrels.
The capitol has been repainted rose, the rails
round Woodford Square the color of rusting blood.
Casa Rosada, the Argentinian mood,
croons from the balcony. Monotonous lurid bushes
brush the damp clouds with the ideograms of buzzards
over the Chinese groceries. The oven alleys stifle.
In Belmont, mournful tailors peer over old machines,
stitching June and July together seamlessly.
And one waits for midsummer lightning as the armed sentry
in boredom waits for the crack of a rifle.
But I feed on its dust, its ordinariness,
on the faith that fills its exiles with horror,
on the hills at dusk with their dusty orange lights,
even on the pilot light in the reeking harbor
that turns like a police car's. The terror
is local, at least. Like the magnolia's whorish whiff.
All night, the barks of a revolution crying wolf.
The moon shines like a lost button.
The yellow sodium lights on the wharf come on.
In streets, dishes clatter behind dim windows.
The night is companionable, the future as fierce as
tomorrow's sun everywhere. I can understand
Borges's blind love for Buenos Aires,
how a man feels the streets of a city swell in his hand.

VII

Our houses are one step from the gutter. Plastic curtains
or cheap prints hide what is dark behind windows—
the pedaled sewing machine, the photos, the paper rose
on its doily. The porch rail is lined with red tins.
A man's passing height is the same size as their doors,
and the doors themselves, usually no wider than coffins,
sometimes have carved in their fretwork little half-moons.
The hills have no echoes. Not the echo of ruins.
Empty lots nod with their palanquins of green.
Any crack in the sidewalk was made by the primal fault
of the first map of the world, its boundaries and powers.
By a pile of red sand, of seeding, abandoned gravel
near a burnt-out lot, a fresh jungle unfurls its green
elephants' ears of wild yams and dasheen.
One step over the low wall, if you should care to,
recaptures a childhood whose vines fasten your foot.
And this is the lot of all wanderers, this is their fate,
that the more they wander, the more the world grows wide.
So, however far you have travelled, your
steps make more holes and the mesh is multiplied—
or why should you suddenly think of Tomas Venclova,
and why should I care about whatever they did to Heberto
when exiles must make their own maps, when this asphalt
takes you far from the action, past hedges of unaligned flowers?

XIII

Today I respect structure, the antithesis of conceit.
The overworked muck of my paintings, my bad plots! But always,
when the air is empty, I hear actors talking,
the resonance of what is both ordinary and wise.
Specters multiply with age, the peopled head
is crossed by impatient characters, the ears clamped shut;
behind them I hear the actors mutter and shout—
the lit stage is empty, the set prepared,
and I cannot find the key to let them out.
O Christ, my craft, and the long time it is taking!
Sometimes the flash is seen, a sudden exultation
of lightning fixing earth in its place; the asphalt's skin
smells freshly of childhood in the drying rain.
Then I believe that it is still possible, the happiness
of truth, and the young poet who stands in the mirror
smiles with a nod. He looks beautiful from this distance.
And I hope I am what he saw, an enduring ruin.

With the frenzy of an old snake shedding its skin,
the speckled road, scored with ruts, smelling of mold,
twisted on itself and reentered the forest
where the dasheen leaves thicken and folk stories begin.
Sunset would threaten us as we climbed closer
to her house up the asphalt hill road, whose yam vines
wrangled over gutters with the dark reek of moss,
the shutters closing like the eyelids of that mimosa
called Ti-Marie; then—lucent as paper lanterns,
lamplight glowed through the ribs, house after house—
there was her own lamp at the black twist of the path.
There's childhood, and there's childhood's aftermath.
She began to remember at the minute of the fireflies,
to the sound of pipe water banging in kerosene tins,
stories she told to my brother and myself.
Her leaves were the libraries of the Caribbean.
The luck that was ours, those fragrant origins!
Her head was magnificent, Sidone. In the gully of her voice
shadows stood up and walked, her voice travels my shelves.
She was the lamplight in the stare of two mesmerized boys
still joined in one shadow, indivisible twins.

I can sense it coming from far, too, Maman, the tide
since day has passed its turn, but I still note
that as a white gull flashes over the sea, its underside
catches the green, and I promise to use it later.
The imagination no longer goes as far as the horizon,
but it keeps coming back. At the edge of the water
it returns clean, scoured things that, like rubbish,
the sea has whitened, chaste. Disparate scenes.
The pink and blue chattel houses in the Virgins
in the trade winds. My name caught in
the kernel of my great-aunt's throat.
A yard, an old brown man with a mustache
like a general's, a boy drawing castor-oil leaves in
great detail, hoping to be another Albrecht Dürer.
I have cherished these better than coherence
as the same tide for us both, Maman, comes nearer—
the vine leaves medaling an old wire fence
and, in the shade-freckled yard, an old man like a colonel
under the green cannonballs of calabash.

XVI

So what shall we do for the dead, to whose conch-bordered
tumuli our lifelong attraction is drawn
as to a magnetic empire, whose cities lie ordered
with streets and rational avenues, exact as the grid
of our vibrating metropolis? In our arrogance, we imagine
that they, too, share the immense, inaudible pulse
of the clock-shaped earth, slower than ours, maybe, but within
our dimension, our simple mathematical formulae.
Any peace so indifferent, where all our differences fuse,
is an insult to imagine; what use is any labor we
accept? They must find our prayers boring, for one prays
that they will keep missing us when they have no urge
to be ever-remembered, they cannot see what we hoard—
photograph, letter, keepsake, muttered or knitted homily—
as we change flags and houses. We still wish them to serve
us, expecting from death what we expect of our prayers—
that their hearts lift like ours with the surge
of the surf and the cupolas of the sunset, that the kingfisher
startles their darkness sometimes. But each one prefers
the silence that was his birthright, and the shore
where the others wait neither to end nor begin.

I pause to hear a racketing triumph of cicadas
setting life's pitch, but to live at their pitch
of joy is unendurable. Turn off
that sound. After the plunge of silence,
the eye gets used to the shapes of furniture, and the mind
to darkness. The cicadas are frantic as my mother's
feet, treading the needles of approaching rain.
Days thick as leaves then, close to each other as hours,
and a sunburnt smell rose up from the drizzled road.
I stitch her lines to mine now with the same machine.
What work lies ahead of us, what sunlight for generations!—
The lemon-rind light in Vermeer, to know it will wait
there for others, the broken eucalyptus
leaf, still sharply smelling of turpentine,
the breadfruit's foliage, rust-edged like van Ruysdael.
The Dutch blood in me is drawn to detail.
I once brushed a drop of water from a Flemish still life
in a book of prints, believing it was real.
It reflected the world in its crystal, quivering with weight.
What joy in that sweat drop, knowing others will persevere!
Let them write, "At fifty he reversed the seasons,
the road of his blood sang with the chattering cicadas,"
as when I took to the road to paint in my eighteenth year.

XIX

GAUGUIN

I

On the quays of Papeete, the dawdling white-ducked colonists
drinking with whores whose skin is the copper of pennies
pretend, watching the wild skins of the light and shade,
that a straight vermouth re-creates the metropolis,
but the sun has scorched those memories from my head—
Cézanne bricking in color, each brick no bigger than a square inch,
the pointillists' dots like a million irises.
I saw in my own cheekbones the mule's head of a Breton,
the placid, implacable strategy of the Mongol,
the mustache like the downturned horns of a helmet;
the chain of my blood pulled me to darker nations,
though I looked like any other sallow, crumpled colon
stepping up to the pier that day from the customs launch.
I am Watteau's wild oats, his illegitimate heir.
Get off your arses, you clerks, and find your fate,
the devil's prayer book is the hymn of patience,
grumbling in the fog. Pack, leave! I left too late.

II

I have never pretended that summer was paradise,
or that these virgins were virginal; on their wooden trays
are the fruits of my knowledge, radiant with disease,
and they offer you this, in their ripe sea-almond eyes,
their clay breasts growing like ingots in a furnace.
No, what I have plated in amber is not an ideal, as
Puvis de Chavannes desired it, but corrupt—

the spot on the ginger lily's vulva, the plantain's phalloi,
the volcano that chafes like a chancre, the lava's smoke
that climbs to the sibilant goddess with its hiss.
I have baked the gold of their bodies in that alloy;
tell the Evangelists paradise smells of sulphur,
that I have felt the beads in my blood erupt
as my brush stroked their backs, the cervix
of a defrocked Jesuit numbering his chaplet.
I placed a blue death mask there in my Book of Hours
that those who dream of an earthly paradise may read it
as men. My frescoes in sackcloth to the goddess Maya.
The mangoes redden like coals in a barbecue pit,
patient as the palms of Atlas, the papaya.

XXI

A long, white, summer cloud, like a cleared linen table,
makes heaven emptier, like after-dinner Sundays
when the Bible begs to be lifted, and the old terrifying verses
raise a sandstorm and bone-white Palestinian rocks
where a ram totters for purchase, bleating like Isaiah.
Dry rage of the desert fathers that scared a child,
the Baptist crying by the cracked river basin, curses
that made the rose an intellectual fire.
Through the skull's stone eyes, the radiant logwood
consumes this August, and a white sun sucks
sweat from the desert. A shadow marks the Word.
I have forgotten a child's hope of the resurrection,
bodies locked up in musting cupboard drawers
among the fish knives and the napery (all the dead earth holds)
to be pulled open at the hour of our birth—
the cloud waits in emptiness for the apostles,
for the fruit, wine amphoras, mutton on groaning trestles,
but only the servant knows heaven is still possible,
some freckled Martha, radiant, dependable,
singing a hymn from your childhood while she folds
her Savior like a white napkin in the earth.

Rest, Christ! from the tireless war. See, it's midsummer,
but what roars in the throat of the oaks is martial man,
the marching hosannas darken the wheat of Russia,
the coiled ram hides in the rocks of Afghanistan.
Crowned hydrants gush, baptizing the street urchins,
the water cannons blot their screams in mist,
but snow does not melt from the furnace brow of Mahomet,
or napkins hemorrhage from the brow of Christ.
Along the island the almonds seethe with anger,
the wind that churns these orchards of white surf
and whistles dervishes up from the hot sand
revolves this globe, this painted O that spins,
reciting as it moves, tribes, frontiers,
dots that are sounds, cities that love their names,
while weather vanes still scrape the sky for omens.
Though they have different sounds for "God" or "hunger,"
the opposing alphabets in city squares
shout with one voice, nation takes on nation,
and, from their fury of pronunciation,
children lie torn on rubble for a noun.

With the stampeding hiss and scurry of green lemmings,
midsummer's leaves race to extinction like the roar
of a Brixton riot tunneled by water hoses;
they seethe toward autumn's fire—it is in their nature,
being men as well as leaves, to die for the sun.
The leaf stems tug at their chains, the branches bending
like Boer cattle under Tory whips that drag every wagon
nearer to apartheid. And, for me, that closes
the child's fairy tale of an antic England—fairy rings,
thatched cottages fenced with dog roses,
a green gale lifting the hair of Warwickshire.
I was there to add some color to the British theater.
"But the blacks can't do Shakespeare, they have no experience."
This was true. Their thick skulls bled with rancor
when the riot police and the skinheads exchanged quips
you could trace to the Sonnets, or the Moor's eclipse.
Praise had bled my lines white of any more anger,
and snow had inducted me into white fellowships,
while Calibans howled down the barred streets of an empire
that began with Caedmon's raceless dew, and is ending
in the alleys of Brixton, burning like Turner's ships.

Something primal in our spine makes the child swing
from the gnarled trapeze of a sea-almond branch.
I have been comparing the sea almond's shapes to the suffering
in van Gogh's orchards. And that, too, is primal. A bunch
of sea grapes hangs over the calm sea. The shadows
I shovel with a dry leaf are as warm as ash, as
noon jerks toward its rigid, inert center.
Sunbathers broil on their grid, the shallows they enter
are so warm that out in the reef the blear grouper lunges
at nothing, teased by self-scaring minnows.
Abruptly remembering its job, a breaker glazes
the sand that dries fast. For hours, without a heave,
the sea suspires through the deep lungs of sponges.
In the thatched beach bar, a clock tests its stiff elbow
every minute and, outside, an even older iguana
climbs hand over claw, as unloved as Quasimodo,
into his belfry of shade, swaying there. When a
cloud darkens, my terror caused it. Lizzie and Anna
lie idling on different rafts, their shadows under them.
The curled swell has the clarity of lime.
In two more days my daughters will go home.
The frame of human happiness is time,
the child's swing slackens to a metronome.
Happiness sparkles on the sea like soda.

Perhaps if I'd nurtured some divine disease,
like Keats in eternal Rome, or Chekhov at Yalta,
something that sharpened the salt fragrance of sweat
with the lancing nib of my pen, my gift would increase,
as the hand of a cloud turning over the sea will alter
the sunlight—clouds smudged like silver plate,
leaves that keep trying to summarize my life.
Under the brain's white coral is a seething anthill.
You had such a deep faith in that green water, once.
The skittering fish were harried by your will—
the stingray halved itself in clear bottom sand,
its tail a whip, its back as broad as a shovel;
the sea horse was fragile as glass, like grass, every tendril
of the wandering medusa: friends and poisons.
But to curse your birthplace is the final evil.
`You could map my limitations four yards up from a beach—
a boat with broken ribs, the logwood that grows only thorns,
a fisherman throwing away fish guts outside his hovel.
What if the lines I cast bulge into a book
that has caught nothing? Wasn't it privilege
to have judged one's work by the glare of greater minds,
though the spool of days that midsummer's reel rewinds
comes bobbling back with its question, its empty hook?

Gold dung and urinous straw from the horse garages,
click-clop of hooves sparking cold cobblestone.
From bricked-in carriage yards, exhaling arches
send the stale air of transcendental Boston—
tasseled black hansoms trotting under elms,
tilting their crops to the shade of Henry James.
I return to the city of my exile down Storrow Drive,
the tunnel with its split seraphs flying *en face*,
with finite sorrow; blocks long as paragraphs
pass in a style to which I'm not accustomed,
since, if I were, I would have been costumed
to drape the cloaks of couples who arrive
for dinner, drawing their chairs from tables where each glass,
catching the transcendental clustered lights,
twirled with perceptions. Style is character—
so my forehead crusts like brick, my sockets char
like a burnt brownstone in the Negro Quarter;
but when a fog obscures the Boston Common
and, up Beacon Hill, the old gas standards stutter
to save their period, I see a black coachman,
with gloves as white as his white-ankled horse,
who counts their laughter, their lamplit good nights,
then jerks the reins of his brass-handled hearse.

Along Cape Cod, salt crannies of white harbors,
white spires, white filling stations, the orthodox
New England offering of clam-and-oyster bars,
like drying barnacles leech harder to their docks
as their day ebbs. Colonies of dark seamen,
whose ears were tuned to their earringed ancestors'
hymn of the Mediterranean's ground bass,
thin out like flocks of some endangered species,
their gutturals, like a parched seal's, on the rocks.
High on the hillsides, the crosstrees of pines
endure the Sabbath with the nerves of aspens.
They hear the Pilgrim's howl changed from the sibyl's,
that there are many nations but one God,
black hat, black-suited with his silver buckle,
damning the rock pool for its naiad's chuckle,
striking this coast with his priapic rod.
A chilling wind blows from my Methodist childhood.
The Fall is all around us—it is New England's
hellfire sermon, and my own voice grows hoarse in
the fog whose bellowing horn is the sea siren's:
a trawler groping from the Port of Boston,
snow, mixed with steam, blurring the thought of islands.

XXXIV

Thalassa! Thalassa! The thud of that echoing blue
on the heart! Going to the Eastern shuttle at LaGuardia,
I mistook a swash of green-painted roof for the sea.
And my ears, that second, were shells that held the roar
of a burnished army scrambling down troughs of sand
in an avalanche of crabs, to the conch's horn in Xenophon.
My eyes flashed a watery green, I felt through each hand,
channel and vein, the startling change in hue
made by the current between Pigeon Point and Store
Bay, my blood royaled by that blue.
I know midsummer is the same thing everywhere—
Aix, Santa Fe, dust powdering the poplars of Arles,
that it swivels like a dog at its shadow by the Charles
when the footpaths swirl with dust, not snow, in eddies—
but my nib, like the beak of the sea-swift heads nowhere else;
to where the legions sprawl like starfish sunning themselves
till the conch's moan calls the slanted spears
of the rain to march on in Anabasis.
The sun has whitened the legions to brittle shells.
Homer, who tired of wars and gods and kings,
had the sea's silence for prologue and epilogue.
That old wave-wanderer with his drowsing gaze is
a pelican rocked on the stern of an empty pirogue,
a salt-grizzled gaffer, shaking rain from his wings.

XXXV

Mud. Clods. The sucking heel of the rain-flinger.
Sometimes the gusts of rain veered like the sails
of dragon-beaked vessels dipping to Avalon
and mist. For hours, driving along
the skittering ridges of Wales, we carried the figure
of Langland's Plowman on the rain-seeded glass,
matching the tires with his striding heels,
while splintered puddles dripped from the roadside grass.
Once, in the drizzle, a crouched, clay-covered ghost
rose in his pivot, and the turning disk of the fields
with their plowed stanzas sang of a freshness lost.
Villages began. We had crossed into England—
the fields, not their names, were the same. We found a caff,
parked in a thin drizzle, then crammed into a pew
of red leatherette. Outside, with thumb and finger,
a careful sun was picking the lint from things.
The sun brightened like a sign, the world was new
while the cairns, the castled hillocks, the stony kings
were scabbarded in sleep, yet what made me think
that the crash of chivalry in a kitchen sink
was my own dispossession? I could sense, from calf
to flinging wrist, my veins ache in a knot.
There was mist on the window. I rubbed it and looked out
at the helmets of wet cars in the parking lot.

The oak inns creak in their joints as light declines
from the ale-colored skies of Warwickshire.
Autumn has blown the froth from the foaming orchards,
so white-haired regulars draw chairs nearer the grate
to spit on logs that crackle into leaves of fire.
But they grow deafer, not sure if what they hear
is the drone of the abbeys from matins to compline,
or the hornet's nest of a chain saw working late
on the knoll up there back of the Norman chapel.
Evening loosens the moth, the owl shifts its weight,
a fish-mouthed moon swims up from wavering elms,
but four old men are out on the garden benches,
talking of the bows they have drawn, their strings of wenches,
their coined eyes shrewdly glittering like the Thames'
estuaries. I heard their old talk carried
through cables laid across the Atlantic bed,
their gossip rustles like an apple orchard's
in my own head, and I can drop their names
like familiars—those bastard grandsires
whose maker granted them a primal pardon—
because the worm that cores the rotting apple
of the world and the hornet's chain saw cannot touch the words
of Shallow or Silence in their fading garden.

XXXVIII

Autumn's music grates. From tuning forks of branches,
small beaks scrape the cold. With trembling feather,
with the squeaking nails of their notes, they pierce me, plus
all the hauntings and evasions of gray weather,
and the river veining with marble despite their pleas.
Lunging to St. Martin's marshes, toward the salt breaks
corrugated by windy sunlight, to reed-whistling islets
the geese chevron, too high for a shadow. Over brown bricks
the soundless white scream of contrails made by jets
remains. Earlier and earlier the brownstones darken.
Now the islands feel farther than something out of the *Georgics*.
Maple and elm close in. But palms require translation,
and their long lines stiffen with dead characters.
Vergilian Brookline! By five, then four, the sun sets;
the lines of passengers at each trolley station,
waiting to go underground, have the faces of actors
when a play must close. Or yours, looking up from a desk,
from a play you hadn't reread for several years.
The look on the face of the sea when the day is finished,
or the seats in an empty theater, each one with its reasons
for what went wrong. They didn't know your language,
the characters were simple, there was no change of seasons
or sets. There was too much poetry. It was the wrong age.

The camps hold their distance—brown chestnuts and gray smoke
that coils like barbed wire. The profit in guilt continues.
Brown pigeons goose-step, squirrels pile up acorns like little shoes,
and moss, voiceless as smoke, hushes the peeled bodies
like abandoned kindling. In the clear pools, fat
trout rising to lures bubble in umlauts.
Forty years gone, in my island childhood, I felt that
the gift of poetry had made me one of the chosen,
that all experience was kindling to the fire of the Muse.
Now I see her in autumn on that pine bench where she sits,
their nut-brown ideal, in gold plaits and *lederhosen*,
the blood drops of poppies embroidered on her white bodice,
the spirit of autumn to every Hans and Fritz
whose gaze raked the stubble fields when the smoky cries
of rooks were nearly human. They placed their cause in
her cornsilk crown, her cornflower iris,
winnower of chaff for whom the swastikas flash
in skeletal harvests. But had I known then
that the fronds of my island were harrows, its sand the ash
of the distant camps, would I have broken my pen
because this century's pastorals were being written
by the chimneys of Dachau, of Auschwitz, of Sachsenhausen?

Chicago's avenues, as white as Poland.
A blizzard of heavenly coke hushes the ghettos.
The scratched sky flickers like a TV set.
Down Michigan Avenue, slow as the glacial prose
of historians, my taxi crawls. The stalled cars are as frozen
as the faces of cloaked queues on a Warsaw street,
or the hands of black derelicts flexing over a fire-
barrel under the El; above, the punctured sky
is needled by rockets that keep both Empires high.
It will be both ice and fire. In the sibyl's crystal
the globe is shaken with ash, with a child's *frisson*.
It'll be like this. A bird cry will sound like a pistol
down the avenues. Cars like dead horses, their muzzles
foaming with ice. From the cab's dashboard, a tinny
dispatcher's voice warns of more snow. A picture
lights up the set—first, indecipherable puzzles;
then, in plain black and white, a snow slope with pines
as shaggy as the manes of barbarian ponies;
then, a Mongol in yak's skin, teeth broken as dice,
grinning at the needles of the silent cities
of the plains below him up in the Himalayas,
who slaps the snow from his sides and turns away as,
in lancelike birches, the horde's ponies whinny.

Raw ochre sea cliffs in the slanting afternoon,
at the bursting end of Balandra, the dry beach's end,
that a shadow's dial wipes out of sight and mind.
White sanderlings race the withdrawing surf to pick,
with wink-quick stabs, shellfish between the pebbles,
ignoring the horizon where a sail goes out
like the love of Prospero for his island kingdom.
A grape leaf shields the sun with veined, orange hand,
but its wick blows out, and the sanderlings are gone.
Go, light, make weightless the burden of our thought,
let our misfortune have no need for magic,
be untranslatable in verse or prose.
Let us darken like stones that have never frowned or known
the need for art or medicine, for Prospero's
snake-knotted staff, or sea-bewildering stick;
erase these ciphers of birds' prints on sand.
Proportion benedict us, as in fables,
that in life's last third, its movements, we accept the
measurement of our acts from one to three,
and boarding this craft, pull till a dark wind
rolls this pen on a desktop, a broken oar, a scepter
swayed by the surf, the scansion of the sea.

I once gave my daughters, separately, two conch shells
that were dived from the reef, or sold on the beach, I forget.
They use them as doorstops or bookends, but their wet
pink palates are the soundless singing of angels.
I once wrote a poem called "The Yellow Cemetery,"
when I was nineteen. Lizzie's age. I'm fifty-three.
These poems I heaved aren't linked to any tradition
like a mossed cairn; each goes down like a stone
to the seabed, settling, but let them, with luck, lie
where stones are deep, in the sea's memory.
Let them be, in water, as my father, who did watercolors,
entered his work. He became one of his shadows,
wavering and faint in the midsummer sunlight.
His name was Warwick Walcott. I sometimes believe
that his father, in love or bitter benediction,
named him for Warwickshire. Ironies
are moving. Now, when I rewrite a line,
or sketch on the fast-drying paper the coconut fronds
that he did so faintly, my daughters' hands move in mine.
Conchs move over the sea floor. I used to move
my father's grave from the blackened Anglican headstones
in Castries to where I could love both at once—
the sea and his absence. Youth is stronger than fiction.

Since all of your work was really an effort to appease
the past, a need to be admitted among your peers,
let the inheritors question the sibyl and the Sphinx,
and learn that a raceless critic is a primate's dream.
You were distressed by your habitat, you shall not find peace
till you and your origins reconcile; your jaw must droop
and your knuckles scrape the ground of your native place.
Squat on a damp rock round which white lilies stiffen,
pricking their ears; count as the syllables drop
like dew from primeval ferns; note how the earth drinks
language as precious, depending upon the race.
Then, on dank ground, using a twig for a pen,
write Genesis and watch the Word begin.
Elephants will mill at their water hole to trumpet a
new style. Mongoose, arrested in rut,
and saucer-eyed mandrills, drinking from the leaves,
will nod as a dew-lapped lizard discourses on "Lives
of the Black Poets," gripping a branch like a lectern for better
delivery. Already, up in that simian Academe,
a chimp in bifocals, his lower lip a jut,
tears misting the lenses, is turning your *Oeuvres Complètes*.

I heard them marching the leaf-wet roads of my head,
the sucked vowels of a syntax trampled to mud,
a division of dictions, one troop black, barefooted,
the other in redcoats bright as their sovereign's blood;
their feet scuffled like rain, the bare soles with the shod.
One fought for a queen, the other was chained in her service,
but both, in bitterness, travelled the same road.
Our occupation and the Army of Occupation
are born enemies, but what mortar can size
the broken stones of the barracks of Brimstone Hill
to the gaping brick of Belfast? Have we changed sides
to the mustached sergeants and the horsy gentry
because we serve English, like a two-headed sentry
guarding its borders? No language is neutral;
the green oak of English is a murmurous cathedral
where some took umbrage, some peace, but every shade, all,
helped widen its shadow. I used to haunt the arches
of the British barracks of Vigie. There were leaves there,
bright, rotting like revers or epaulettes, and the stenches
of history and piss. Leaves piled like the dropped aitches
of soldiers from rival shires, from the brimstone trenches
of Agincourt to the gas of the Somme. On Poppy Day
our schools bought red paper flowers. They were for Flanders.
I saw Hotspur cursing the smoke through which a popinjay
minced from the battle. Those raging commanders
from Thersites to Percy, their rant is our model.
I pinned the poppy to my blazer. It bled like a vowel.

The midsummer sea, the hot pitch road, this grass, these shacks that
    made me,
jungle and razor grass shimmering by the roadside, the edge of art;
wood lice are humming in the sacred wood,
nothing can burn them out, they are in the blood;
their rose mouths, like cherubs, sing of the slow science
of dying—all heads, with, at each ear, a gauzy wing.
Up at Forest Reserve, before branches break into sea,
I looked through the moving, grassed window and thought "pines,"
or conifers of some sort. I thought, they must suffer
in this tropical heat with their child's idea of Russia.
Then suddenly, from their rotting logs, distracting signs
of the faith I betrayed, or the faith that betrayed me—
yellow butterflies rising on the road to Valencia
stuttering "yes" to resurrection; "yes, yes is our answer,"
the gold-robed Nunc Dimittis of their certain choir.
Where's my child's hymnbook, the poems edged in gold leaf,
the heaven I worship with no faith in heaven,
as the Word turned toward poetry in its grief?
Ah, bread of life, that only love can leaven!
Ah, Joseph, though no man ever dies in his own country,
the grateful grass will grow thick from his heart.

FROM

The Arkansas Testament

(1987)

CUL DE SAC VALLEY

A panel of sunrise
on a hillside shop
gave these stanzas
their stilted shape.

If my craft is blest;
if this hand is as
accurate, as honest
as their carpenter's,

every frame, intent
on its angles, would
echo this settlement
of unpainted wood

as consonants scroll
off my shaving plane
in the fragrant Creole
of their native grain;

from a trestle bench
they'd curl at my foot,
C's, R's, with a French
or West African root

from a dialect throng-
ing, its leaves unread
yet light on the tongue
of their native road;

but drawing towards
my pegged-out twine
with beveled boards
of unpainted pine,

like muttering shale
exhaling trees refresh
memory with their smell:
bois canot, bois campêche,

hissing: *What you wish
from us will never be,
your words is English,
is a different tree.*

     II

In the rivulet's gravel
light gutturals begin,
in the valley, a mongrel,
a black vowel barking,

sends up fading ovals;
by a red iron bridge,
menders with shovels
scrape bubbling pitch,

every grating squeak
reaching this height
a tongue they speak
in, but cannot write.

Like the lost idea
of the visible soul

still kindled here
on illiterate soil,

blue smoke climbs far
up, its vein unveering,
from that ochre scar
of a charcoal clearing.

Crusted clouds open
like the pith of loaves
in a charred clay oven
wrapped in fig leaves.

In a rain barrel, water
unwrinkles to glass;
a lime tree's daughter
there studies her face.

The sapling forks into
a girl racing upstairs
from the yard, to enter
this stanza. Now tears

fill her eyes, a mirror's
tears, as her nape knot is
pulled by her mother's
comb; the mother notices,

saying: "In His countenance
are all the valleys made
shining." Her swift hands
plait the rivulet's braid.

Chalk flowers that scribble
the asphalt's black slate

and the hibiscus-bell
tell her she is late,

as surf in the branches
increases like the shoal
of blue-and-white benches
in the government school,

reciting this language
that, on a blackboard,
blinds her like a page
of glare on the road,

so she ambles towards
an inner silence along
a red track the forest
swallows like a tongue.

III

Noon. Dry cicadas whine
like the rusting pedals
of her mother's machine,
then stop. Lime petals

drift like snipt cloth
in the stitched silence;
like pollen, their growth
means her providence.

Noon hems a lime tree
with irregular shade;
from so much symmetry
her back is tired.

The row of Sphinxes
that my eyes rest on
are hills as fixed as
their stony question:

"Can you call each range
by its right name, aloud,
while our features change
between light and cloud?"

But my memory is small
as the sea's thin sound,
what I vaguely recall
is a line of white sand

and lines in the mahogany
of cured faces and stones
muttering under a stony
river, but the questions

dissolving will unravel
their knots—mountain
springs whose gravel
grows hoarse in rain—

as a woodsman relaxes
to hear the sky split
seconds after the axe's
stroke, the names fit

their echo: Mahaut!
Forestière! And far,
the leaf-hoarse echo
of Mabouya! And, ah!

the hill rises and eats
from my hand, the mongrel
yelping happily, repeats
vowel after vowel,

the boughs bow to me,
the dialects applaud
as the sap of memory
races upward.

IV

West of each stanza
that the sunrise made,
banana fields answer
their light; overhead,

a hawk that wheeled,
my heart in its beak,
to the rim of the world
is bringing it back

to the fading bridge,
to the river that turns
in its bed, to the ridge
where the tree returns

from her lessons, late.
Which shack was hers?
Now she climbs straight
up the steps of this verse,

and sits to a supper
of bread and fry-fish

as trees repeat her
darkening English.

Shack windows flare.
Green fireflies arc,
igniting Forestière,
Orléans, Fond St. Jacques,

and the forest runs
sleeping, its eyes shut,
except for one glance
from a lamplit hut;

now, above the closed text
of small shacks that slid
by the headlights: the apex
of a hill like a pyramid.

In the oven-warm night
embers fly. A shop door
flings a panel of light
on the road and an odor

of saltfish. A dry sand
pile scatters in stars.
Catlike, Pigeon Island
pins the sea in its claws.

THE THREE MUSICIANS

for Hunter François

"Once Christmas coming
it have a breeze as
fresh as Bethlehem in
the glorious cedars.

From town to Vieuxfort,
Vieuxfort to Castries,
it does varnish the road
through the villages.

We does put red tins
on the porch for pardon,
we whitewash the stones
from the first garden;

in the sprinkled yard
by the white rose tree
is the soft dent made
by an angel's knee,

whose robes so pure
they does pleat like when
water twists from a ewer
of porcelain;

so for young and old
like refresh. That week,
break a lime leaf, it cold
as an archangel's cheek,

whose shadow, swift
up the hillside grass,
does make cedars lift
so his wings can pass,"

sings Madame Isidor,
her front step scoured
for her first visitor,
Our barefoot Lord.

He was poorer than them,
no place for his bed;
"My parlor is Jerusalem,
my table, Gilead."

Whole week she practice
her bow: "Pleased to meet you;
this one here? That is
Joseph, carpenter too."

And that whole week self,
if one vex, next one laugh;
from the glass case Joseph
sets the silver carafe

by two pillars of gold
Johnnie Walker whiskey,
let old people get old,
not Joseph, he brisk, brisk, he

hugging her like his craft,
he stop going to café,
he only singing: "Half
the Herald Angels"; Saturday

he come in a transport from
the market straight home;
a cannon of linoleum
unfurls in their room.

Now the ham there bubbling
for all it's worth
in a kerosene tin
wrapped tight in gray cloth,

and everywhere the earth
smell of raisins, a black cake
she will cut for the birth
of the child she can't make.

Ah, Christmas, Christmas morning!
They hear on the wind,
the whine and warning
of Ti-Boy's violin;

they feel the Blood
of the Innocents pass
through the Roman blade
of poinsettias,

as the three musicians
passing yard after yard,
where the ginger's fragrance
is spikenard;

the cuatro strumming
to their gravelly carol,
they reach. "Come in, come in,
it have whiskey, sorrel—"

Sorrel with its bloody crown
of thorns, by the fence
where the lace bush kneels down
in penitence—

"Joseph, bring three chairs!"
They bow at her door.
Three felt hats. One says,
"*Bon Noel*, Ma' Isidor,

I am Frank Incense,
Mr. Gold, Mr. Myrrh."
They rest their instruments
with care in a corner.

New hats on their knees,
they nod at how neat
everything is, a breeze
dries their trickling sweat.

One lifts his shot glass
with curled finger, so,
toasting the Mistress,
'cause all of them know

she dream of white lace
on soft ebony skin,
but is somehow God's grace
she cannot make children;

the lifting curtains
brighten the linoleum,
they bring a child's presence
to her varnished room.

They eat in silence
the black cake that she brings,
next to their instruments,
three stiff-backed kings,

who hand back their plates
with a piece on the side
for manners, belt two straights,
then start singing like shite;

in the fiddler's screels
they hunger and thirst
for the child. Joseph feels
that his heart will burst.

SAINT LUCIA'S FIRST COMMUNION

At dusk, on the edge of the asphalt's worn-out ribbon,
in white cotton frock, cotton stockings, a black child stands.
First her, then a small field of her. Ah, it's First Communion!
They hold pink ribboned missals in their hands,

the stiff plaits pinned with their white satin moths.
The caterpillar's accordion, still pumping out the myth
along twigs of cotton from whose parted mouths
the wafer pods in belief without an "if"!

So, all across Saint Lucia thousands of innocents
were arranged on church steps, facing the sun's lens,
erect as candles between squinting parents,
before darkness came on like their blinded saint's.

But if it were possible to pull up on the verge
of the dimming asphalt, before its headlights lance
their eyes, to house each child in my hands,
to lower the window a crack, and delicately urge

the last moth delicately in, I'd let the dark car
enclose their blizzard, and on some black hill,
their pulsing wings undusted, loose them in thousands to stagger
heavenward before it came on: the prejudice, the evil!

From this village, soaked like a gray rag in salt water,
a language came, garnished with conch shells,
with a suspicion of berries in its armpits
and elbows like flexible oars. Every ceremony commenced
in the troughs, in the middens, at the daybreak and the daydark
    funerals
attended by crabs. The odors were fortified
by the sea. The anchor of the islands went deep
but was always clear in the sand. Many a shark,
and often the ray, whose wings are as wide as sails,
rose with insomniac stare from the wavering corals,
and a fisherman held up a catfish like a tendriled head.
And the night with its certain, inextinguishable candles
was like All Souls' Night upside down, the way a bat keeps
its own view of the world. So their eyes looked down, amused,
on us, and found we were walking strangely,
and wondered about our sense of balance, how we slept
as if we were dead, how we confused
dreams with ordinary things like nails, or roses,
how rocks aged quickly with moss,
the sea made furrows that had nothing to do with time,
and the sand started whirlwinds with nothing to do at all,
and the shadows answered to the sun alone.
And sometimes, like the top of an old tire,
the black rim of a porpoise. Elpenor, you
who broke your arse, drunk, tumbling down the bulkhead,
and the steersman who sails, like the ray under the breathing waves,
keep moving, there is nothing here for you.
There are different candles and customs here, the dead
are different. Different shells guard their graves.

There are distinctions beyond the paradise
of our horizon. This is not the grape-purple Aegean.
There is no wine here, no cheese, the almonds are green,
the sea grapes bitter, the language is that of slaves.

for Leo St. Helene

The *gens-gagée* kicks off her wrinkled skin.
Clap her soul in a jar! The half-man wolf
can trot with bending elbows, rise, and grin
in lockjawed lycanthropia. Censers dissolve
the ground fog with its whistling, wandering souls,
the unbaptized, unfinished, and uncursed
by holy fiat. The island's griots love
our mushroom elves, the devil's parasols
who creep like grubs from a trunk's rotten holes,
their mouths a sewn seam, their clubfeet reversed.
Exorcism cannot anachronize
those signs we hear past midnight in a wood
where a pale woman like a blind owl flies
to her forked branch, with scarlet moons for eyes
bubbling with doubt. You heard a silver splash?
It's nothing. If it slid from mossed rocks
dismiss it as a tired crab, a fish,
unless our water-mother with dank locks
is sliding under this page below your pen,
only a simple people think they happen.
Dryads and hamadryads were engrained
in the wood's bark, in papyrus, and this paper;
but when our dry leaves crackled to the deer-
footed, hobbling hunter, Papa Bois,
he's just Pan's clone, one more translated satyr.
The crone who steps from her jute sugar sack
(though you line moonlit lintels with white flour),
the *beau l'homme* creeping towards you, front to back,

the ferny footed, faceless, mouse-eared elves,
these fables of the backward and the poor
marbled by moonlight, will grow white and richer.
Our myths are ignorance, theirs are literature.

Kaya now, got to have kaya now,
Got to have kaya now,
For the rain is falling.

BOB MARLEY

Marley was rocking on the transport's stereo
and the beauty was humming the choruses quietly.
I could see where the lights on the planes of her cheek
streaked and defined them; if this were a portrait
you'd leave the highlights for last, these lights
silkened her black skin; I'd have put in an earring,
something simple, in good gold, for contrast, but she
wore no jewelry. I imagined a powerful and sweet
odor coming from her, as from a still panther,
and the head was nothing else but heraldic.
When she looked at me, then away from me politely
because any staring at strangers is impolite,
it was like a statue, like a black Delacroix's
Liberty Leading the People, the gently bulging
whites of her eyes, the carved ebony mouth,
the heft of the torso solid, and a woman's,
but gradually even that was going in the dusk,
except the line of her profile, and the highlit cheek,
and I thought, O Beauty, you are the light of the world!

It was not the only time I would think of that phrase
in the sixteen-seater transport that hummed between
Gros-Ilet and the Market, with its grit of charcoal
and the litter of vegetables after Saturday's sales,
and the roaring rum shops, outside whose bright doors
you saw drunk women on pavements, the saddest of all things,
winding up their week, winding down their week.

The Market, as it closed on this Saturday night,
remembered a childhood of wandering gas lanterns
hung on poles at street corners, and the old roar
of vendors and traffic, when the lamplighter climbed,
hooked the lantern on its pole and moved on to another,
and the children turned their faces to its moth, their
eyes white as their nighties; the Market
itself was closed in its involved darkness
and the shadows quarreled for bread in the shops,
or quarreled for the formal custom of quarreling
in the electric rum shops. I remember the shadows.

The van was slowly filling in the darkening depot.
I sat in the front seat, I had no need for time.
I looked at two girls, one in a yellow bodice
and yellow shorts, with a flower in her hair,
and lusted in peace, the other less interesting.
That evening I had walked the streets of the town
where I was born and grew up, thinking of my mother
with her white hair tinted by the dyeing dusk,
and the tilting box houses that seemed perverse
in their cramp; I had peered into parlors
with half-closed jalousies, at the dim furniture,
Morris chairs, a center table with wax flowers,
and the lithograph of *Christ of the Sacred Heart*,
vendors still selling to the empty streets—
sweets, nuts, sodden chocolates, nut cakes, mints.

An old woman with a straw hat over her headkerchief
hobbled towards us with a basket; somewhere,
some distance off, was a heavier basket
that she couldn't carry. She was in a panic.
She said to the driver: "*Pas quittez moi à terre*,"
which is, in her patois: "Don't leave me stranded,"
which is, in her history and that of her people:

"Don't leave me on earth," or, by a shift of stress:
"Don't leave me the earth" (for an inheritance);
"*Pas quittez moi à terre*, Heavenly transport,
Don't leave me on earth, I've had enough of it."
The bus filled in the dark with heavy shadows
that would not be left on earth; no, that would be left
on the earth, and would have to make out.
Abandonment was something they had grown used to.

And I had abandoned them, I knew that there
sitting in the transport, in the sea-quiet dusk,
with men hunched in canoes, and the orange lights
from the Vigie headland, black boats on the water;
I, who could never solidify my shadow
to be one of their shadows, had left them their earth,
their white rum quarrels, and their coal bags,
their hatred of corporals, of all authority.
I was deeply in love with the woman by the window.
I wanted to be going home with her this evening.
I wanted her to have the key to our small house
by the beach at Gros-Ilet, I wanted her to change
into a smooth white nightie that would pour like water
over the black rocks of her breasts, to lie
simply beside her by the ring of a brass lamp
with a kerosene wick, and tell her in silence
that her hair was like a hill forest at night,
that a trickle of rivers was in her armpits,
that I would buy her Benin if she wanted it,
and never leave her on earth. But the others, too.

Because I felt a great love that could bring me to tears,
and a pity that prickled my eyes like a nettle,
I was afraid I might suddenly start sobbing
on the public transport with the Marley going,
and a small boy peering over the shoulders

of the driver and me at the lights coming,
at the rush of the road in the country darkness,
with lamps in the houses on the small hills,
and thickets of stars; I had abandoned them,
I had left them on earth, I left them to sing
Marley's songs of a sadness as real as the smell
of rain on dry earth, or the smell of damp sand,
and the bus felt warm with their neighborliness,
their consideration, and the polite partings

in the light of its headlamps. In the blare,
in the thud-sobbing music, the claiming scent
that came from their bodies. I wanted the transport
to continue forever, for no one to descend
and say a good night in the beams of the lamps
and take the crooked path up to the lit door,
guided by fireflies; I wanted her beauty
to come into the warmth of considerate wood,
to the relieved rattling of enamel plates
in the kitchen, and the tree in the yard,
but I came to my stop. Outside the Halcyon Hotel.
The lounge would be full of transients like myself.
Then I would walk with the surf up the beach.
I got off the van without saying good night.
Good night would be full of inexpressible love.
They went on in their transport, they left me on earth.

Then, a few yards ahead, the van stopped. A man
shouted my name from the transport window.
I walked up towards him. He held out something.
A pack of cigarettes had dropped from my pocket.
He gave it to me. I turned, hiding my tears.
There was nothing they wanted, nothing I could give them
but this thing I have called "The Light of the World."

for Robert Lee

What sort of moon will float up through the almonds
like a bobbing marker in the surf of trees?
A quarter-moon, like an Iranian dagger?
A capitol with wide spheres of influence?
One with a birthmark like Gorbachev's head?
A local moon, full of its own importance,
a watchman's flashlight with fresh batteries,
startling the trickle from a kitchen drain,
pinning a crab to the hotel's wire fence,
changing its mind like a cat burglar,
probing locked harbors, rattling the foam's chain.

Calm as a kitchen clock without the hands
high on a cupboard shelf of this beach house,
the moon stares on a plastic tablecloth,
where she reprints the shadow of a mouse
bent like a friar nibbling his rosary's
berries with fingers quicker than his mouth;
then islands were the gems of an Infanta,
and tiny armored ants, in Indian file,
hoisted their banners, singing "Sancta, Sancta
Regina," then scattered in armadas
to the cracked wedding cake of her fixed smile.

Her forehead bound as tightly as a nun's
or a black laundress who has pinned the sails,
forgotten, on a clothesline, she was once
the Virgin Queen whose radiance drew the snails
of her horned galleons with their silvery slime,
pale slugs in sand. Insomniac remorse.
Beyond all that now, and way past her prime

her mind is wandering in another tense;
she hears the cannon's surf, the palm frond's gales,
and sees, through the erasures of her face,
those wrecks she christened: *Invincible, Revenge.*

Oceano Nox. Night whispers to the Ocean.
A watchman in a constable's cloak patrols
the hotel's wire boundary. I answer his good night.
His flashlight swivels through a spume of salt,
it passes over the old hill of skulls
made by husked coconut shells, the original fault
unsettled by the shallows' dark commotion;
he sings a reggae in a moon so bright
you can read palms by it. A steel band rolls
glissandos of surf round the hotel pool's
gazebo, doubling the moon's arc light.

A wave of sound, an echo overhead
(not shaking the moon's oval in the pool),
that pulses in the memory, when, from school
to college, I cherished the theater
of high Marlovian clouds, my heritage
of that great globe herself, and what I read
sank in like surf reopening the wet
pores of sand, and swirls in the cave's head,
till on this beach-house wall, centuries later,
I mutter the sea's lines, and they recede
to the emerald and ruby of a fading jet:

"Black is the beauty of the brightest day,"
black the circumference around her rings
that radiate from black invisibly,
black is the music which her round mouth sings,
black is the backcloth on which diadems shine,
black, night's perfection, which conceals its flaws

except the crack of the horizon's line;
now all is changing but my focus was
once on the full moon, not what surrounds the moon,
upon a watchman's flashlight not the watchman,
the mesmerizing wake of History.

I have rehearsed their beauty all this week,
and her white disk moves like a camera's lens
along the ebony of a high-boned cheek,
I mean Anne Daniels's, Lauretta Etienne's,
their bow-carved mouths, their half-globed eyes serene,
surfaces so polished that their skin would squeak
if you pushed your forefinger up the bone,
their laughter white as breakers in their grin,
too modest to be actresses, each one
wrapped in sea cotton, intact from Benin.

Oceano Nox. The clocks resume their motion,
a laser from the lighthouse skims a wave;
a different age is whispering to the ocean,
the fronds will take the old moon by the hand
and lead her gently into a cloud's grave;
I cross the darkened grass back to the house;
then all her radiance comes back again,
making the frogs sundials on the lawn;
there is a ring around her, meaning rain,
and meaning nothing more, in that blank face,
than History's innocence or its remorse.

So let her light dissolve into the sable
and velvet memory of a collared cloud,
dimming the square tiles on a kitchen table,
dulling the cheers of an applauding crowd
of breakers flinging whitecaps into space
when you close in the door and ram the latch, as

you think of women with their necks as supple
as bowing palms, and watch the mouse scuttle
back to its hole. A palm's nib scratches
the roof's parchment. At a brass lamp's base,
new rainflies, and the masts of wooden matches.

A scribbling plague of rainflies. Go to bed.
After the morning rain, the shuddering almond
will shake the sweat of nightmare from its bent head.
The surf will smooth the sand's page and even
the cumuli change their idea of heaven
as the sun wipes the nib of a palm frond,
and from the wet hills, parishes of birds
test a new tongue, because these are their shores,
while the old moon gapes at a loss for words
like any ghost at cockcrow, as a force
threshes the palms, lifting their hearts and yours.

TO NORLINE

This beach will remain empty
for more slate-colored dawns
of lines the surf continually
erases with its sponge,

and someone else will come
from the still-sleeping house,
a coffee mug warming his palm
as my body once cupped yours,

to memorize this passage
of a salt-sipping tern,
like when some line on a page
is loved, and it's hard to turn.

Are they earlier, these
days without afternoons,
whose lamps like crosiers
ask the same questions?

"Will you laugh on the stair
at my fumbling key?
Will your bedroom mirror
stay all day empty?"

Thunderous traffic
shakes snow from a bridge.
Ice floes crack
from the flaw in marriage.

Wind taps my shoulder
to cross on my sign;
crouched engines shudder
at their starting line.

On the sidewalk's sludge
to our lightless house,
I pass the closed church
and its business hours,

along the burnt aisles
of skeletal trees
with no signs of a cardinal's
fiery surplice;

bursitic fingers
on a white fence contract

and the huge iris goes
gray with cataract,

while before me my wish
runs ahead to each room,
turning switch after switch
on to its own welcome;

one of mufflered shadows
on our street, I walk
past orange windows
where marriages work,

raking a moustache
with a tongue that tastes
not your lips, but ash,
in a cold fireplace,

that sour gray ash
such as birch logs make,
spiking every eyelash
in its neuralgic mask,

as the spreading lichen
multiplies its white cells,
our white block as stricken
as that hospital's,

where our child was lost,
as I watched through glass
the white-sheeted ghosts
of the mothers pass.

Snow climbs higher on
the railings, its drifts

shorten the black iron
spikes into arrowheads;

on Brookline's white prairie,
bent, shaggy forms blow—
heads down, thinning out yearly
like the buffalo

in this second Ice Age
that is promised us
by hot gospelers' rage
or white-smocked scientists,

and, at the last lamp,
before the dun door,
I feel winter's cramp
tighter than before.

Spidery damask
laces the panes; it freezes
until the arching mask
of Tragedy sneezes

on theater façades in our
comic opera, and plastic
flakes fall on the furniture
of shrouded Boston, and faster

than a mine shaft caving in
I can see the black hole
we have made of heaven.
I scrape each boot sole

on the step. Then stamp
at the ice-welded door.

I cannot break through its clamp
to the fire at earth's core.

I am growing more scared of
your queue of dresses
hanging like questions, the love
of a hairpin pierces

me. The key cannot fit.
Either it has swollen
or the brass shrunk. I fight
the lock. Then I lean,

gasping smoke. Despair
can be wide, it can whiten
the Arctic, but it's clear
as I force the door open

that it's not really the end of
this world, but our own,
that I have had enough
of any love with you gone.

The cold light in the oven
grins again at the news,
I tuck our quilt even.
I lie down in my shoes.

By the bed, brown silt
streaks my old coffee cup.
I forgot to buy salt.
I eat standing up.

My faith lost in answers,
apples, firelight, bread,
in windows whose branches
left you cold, and bored.

Look, and you will see that the furniture is fading,
that a wardrobe is as insubstantial as a sunset,

that I can see through you, the tissue of your leaves,
the light behind your veins; why do you keep sobbing?

The days run through the light's fingers like dust
or a child's in a sandpit. When you see the stars

do you burst into tears? When you look at the sea
isn't your heart full? Do you think your shadow

can be as long as the desert? I am a child, listen,
I did not invite or invent angels. It is easy

to be an angel, to speak now beyond my eight years,
to have more vestal authority, and to know,

because I have now entered a wisdom, not a silence.
Why do you miss me? I am not missing you, sisters,

neither Judith, whose hair will banner like the leopard's
in the pride of her young bearing, nor Katryn, not Gem

sitting in a corner of her pain, nor my aunt, the one
with the soft eyes that have soothed the one who writes this,

I would not break your heart, and you should know it;
I would not make you suffer, and you should know it;

and I am not suffering, but it is hard to know it.
I am wiser, I share the secret that is only a silence,

with the tyrants of the earth, with the man who piles rags
in a creaking cart, and goes around a corner

of a square at dusk. You measure my age wrongly,
I am not young now, nor old, not a child, nor a bud

snipped before it flowered, I am part of the muscle
of a galloping lion, or a bird keeping low over

dark canes; and what, in your sorrow, in our faces
howling like statues, you call a goodbye

is—I wish you would listen to me—a different welcome,
which you will share with me, and see that it is true.

All this the child spoke inside me, so I wrote it down.
As if his closing grave were the smile of the earth.

GOD REST YE MERRY, GENTLEMEN: PART II

I saw Jesus in the Project.
RICHARD PRYOR

Every street corner is Christmas Eve
in downtown Newark. The Magi walk
in black overcoats hugging a fifth
of methylated spirits, and hookers hook
nothing from the dark cribs of doorways.
A crazy king breaks a bottle in praise
of Welfare, "I'll kill the motherfucker,"
and for black blocks without work
the sky is full of crystal splinters.

A bus breaks out of the mirage of water,
a hippo in wet streetlights, and grinds on
in smoke; every shadow seems to stagger
under the fiery acids of neon—
wavering like a piss, some l tt rs miss-
ing, extinguished—except for two white
nurses, their vocation made whiter
in darkness. It's two days from elections.

Johannesburg is full of starlit shebeens.
It is anti-American to make such connections.
Think of Newark as Christmas Eve,
when all men are your brothers, even
these; bring peace to us in parcels,
let there be no more broken bottles in heaven
over Newark, let it not shine like spit
on a doorstep, think of the evergreen
apex with the gold star over it
on the Day-Glo bumper sticker a passing car sells.

Daughter of your own Son, Mother and Virgin,
great is the sparkle of the high-rise firmament
in acid puddles, the gold star in store windows,
and the yellow star on the night's moth-eaten sleeve
like the black coat He wore through blade-thin elbows
out of the ghetto into the cattle train
from Warsaw; nowhere is His coming more immanent
than downtown Newark, where three lights believe
the starlit cradle, and the evergreen carols
to the sparrow-child: a black coat-flapping urchin
followed by a white star as a police car patrols.

THE ARKANSAS TESTAMENT

for Michael Harper

I

Over Fayetteville, Arkansas,
a slope of memorial pines
guards the stone slabs of forces
fallen for the Confederacy
at some point in the Civil War.
The young stones, flat on their backs,
their beards curling like mosses,
have no names; an occasional surge
in the pines mutters their roster
while their centennial siege,
their entrenched metamorphosis
into cones and needles, goes on.
Over Arkansas, they can see
between the swaying cracks
in the pines the blue of the Union,
as the trunks get rustier.

II

It was midwinter. The dusk was
yielding in flashes of metal
from a slowly surrendering sun
on the billboards, storefronts, and signs
along Highway 71,
then on the brass-numbered doors
of my $17.50 motel,
and the slab of my cold key.

Jet-lagged and travel-gritty,
I fell back on the double bed
like Saul under neighing horses
on the highway to Damascus,
and lay still, as Saul does,
till my name reentered me,
and felt, through the chained door,
dark entering Arkansas.

III

I stared back at the Celotex
ceiling of room 16,
my coat still on, for minutes
as the key warmed my palm—
TV, telephone, maid service,
and a sense of the parking lot
through cinder blocks—homesick
for islands with fringed shores
like the mustard-gold coverlet.
A roach crossed its oceanic
carpet with scurrying oars
to a South that it knew, calm
shallows of crystalline green.
I studied again how glare
dies on a wall, till a complex
neon scribbled its signature.

IV

At the desk, crouched over Mr. _____
I had felt like changing my name

for one beat at the register.
Instead, I'd kept up the game
of pretending whoever I was,
or am, or will be, are the same:
"How'll you pay for this, sir?
Cash or charge?" I missed the
chance of answering, "In kind,
like my color." But her gaze
was corn-country, her eyes frayed
denim. "American Express."
On a pennant, with snarling tusk,
a razorback charged. A tress
of loose hair lifted like maize
in the lounge's indigo dusk.

            v

I dozed off in the early dark
to a smell of detergent pine
and they faded with me: the rug
with its shag, pine-needled floor,
the without-a-calendar wall
now hung with the neon's sign,
no thin-lipped Gideon Bible,
no bed lamp, no magazine,
no bristle-faced fiddler
sawing at "Little Brown Jug,"
or some brochure with a landmark
by which you know Arkansas,
or a mountain spring's white babble,
nothing on a shelf, no shelves;
just a smudge on a wall, the mark
left by two uncoiling selves.

VI

I crucified my coat on one wire
hanger, undressed for bathing,
then saw that other, full-length,
alarmed in the glass coffin
of the bathroom door. Right there,
I decided to stay unshaven,
unsaved, if I found the strength.
Oh, for a day's dirt, unshowered,
no plug for my groveling razor,
to reek of the natural coward
I am, to make this a place for
disposable shavers as well
as my own disposable people!
On a ridge over Fayetteville,
higher than any steeple,
is a white-hot electric cross.

VII

It burns the back of my mind.
It scorches the skin of night;
as a candle repeats the moment
of being blown out, it remained
when I switched off the ceiling light.
That night I slept like the dead,
or a drunk in the tank, like moss
on a wall, like a lover happier
in the loss of love, like soldiers
under the pines, but, as I dreaded,
rose too early. It was four.
Maybe five. I only guessed
by the watch I always keep

when my own house is at rest.
I opened the motel door.
The hills never turned in their sleep.

VIII

Pajamas crammed in my jacket,
the bottoms stuffed into trousers
that sagged, I needed my fix—
my 5 a.m. caffeine addiction.
No rooster crew brassily back at
the white-neon crucifix,
and Arkansas smelt as sweet
as a barn door opening. Like horses
in their starlit, metallic sweat,
parked cars grazed in their stalls.
Dawn was fading the houses
to an even Confederate gray.
On the far side of the highway,
a breeze turned the leaves of an aspen
to the First Epistle of Paul's
to the Corinthians.

IX

The asphalt, quiet as a Sabbath,
by municipal sprinklers anointed,
shot its straight and narrow path
in the white, converging arrows
of Highway 71. They pointed
to Florida, as if tired warriors
dropped them on the Trail of Tears,
but nothing stirred in response

except two rabbinical willows
with nicotine beards, and a plaid
jacket Frisbeeing papers
from a bike to silvery lawns,
tires hissing the peace that passeth
understanding under the black elms,
and morning in Nazareth
was Fayetteville's and Jerusalem's.

    x

Hugging walls in my tippler's hop—
the jive of shuffling bums,
a beat that comes from the chain—
I waited for a while by the grass
of a urinous wall to let
the revolving red eye on top
of a cruising police car pass.
In an all-night garage I saw
the gums of a toothless sybil
in garage tires, and she said:
STAY BLACK AND INVISIBLE
TO THE SIRENS OF ARKANSAS.
The snakes coiled on the pumps
hissed with their metal mouth:
Your shadow still hurts the South,
like Lee's slowly reversing sword.

    XI

There's nothing to understand
in hunger. I watched the shell
of a white sun tapping its yolk

on the dark crust of Fayetteville,
and hurried up in my walk
past warming brick to the smell
of hash browns. Abounding light
raced towards me like a mongrel
hoping that it would be caressed
by my cold, roughening hand,
and I prayed that all could be blest
down Highway 71, the gray calm
of the lanes where a lion
lies down on its traffic island,
a post chevroning into a palm.
The world warmed to its work.

XII

But two doors down, a cafeteria
reminded me of my race.
A soak cursed his vinyl table
steadily, not looking up.
A tall black cook setting glazed
pies, a beehive-blond waitress,
lips like a burst strawberry,
and her "Mornin'" like maple syrup.
Four DEERE caps talking deer hunting.
I looked for my own area.
The muttering black decanter
had all I needed; it could sign for
Sherman's smoking march to Atlanta
or the march to Montgomery.
I was still nothing. A cipher
in its bubbling black zeros, here.

XIII

The self-contempt that it takes
to find my place card among any
of the faces reflected in lakes
of lacquered mahogany
comes easily now. I have laughed
loudest until silence kills
the shoptalk. A fork clicks
on its plate; a cough's rifle shot
shivers the chandeliered room.
A bright arm shakes its manacles.
Every candle-struck face stares into
the ethnic abyss. In the oval
of a silver spoon, the window
bent in a wineglass, the offal
of flattery fed to my craft,
I watch the bright clatter resume.

XIV

I bagged the hot Styrofoam coffee
to the recently repealed law
that any black man out after curfew
could be shot dead in Arkansas.
Liberty turns its face; the doctrine
of Aryan light is upheld
as sunrise stirs the lion-
colored grasses of the veld.
Its seam glints in the mind
of the golden Witwatersrand,
whose clouds froth like a beer stein
in the Boer's sunburnt hand;
the world is flushed with fever.

In some plaid-flannel wood
a buck is roped to a fender—
it is something in their blood.

XV

In a world I saw without end as
one highway with signs, low brown
motels, burger haciendas,
a neat, evangelical town
now pointed through decorous oaks
its calendar comfort—scary
with its simple, God-fearing folks.
Evil was as ordinary
here as good. I kept my word.
This, after all, was the South,
whose plow was still the sword,
its red earth dust in the mouth,
whose gray divisions and dates
swirl in the pine-scented air—
wherever the heart hesitates
that is its true frontier.

XVI

On front porches every weak lamp
went out; on the frame windows
day broadened into the prose
of an average mid-American town.
My meter dropped its limp.
Sunlight flooded Arkansas.
Cold sunshine. I had to draw
my coat tight from the cold, or

suffer the nips of arthritis,
the small arrows that come with age;
the sun began to massage
the needles in the hill's shoulder
with its balsam, but hairs
fall on my collar as I write this
in shorter days, darker years,
more hatred, more racial rage.

XVII

The light, being amber, ignored
the red and green traffic stops,
and, since it had never met me,
went past me without a nod.
It sauntered past the shops,
peered into AUTOMOBILE SALES,
where a serenely revolving Saab
sneered at it. At INDIAN CRAFTS
it regilded the Southern Gothic
sign, climbed one of the trails,
touching leaves as it sent
shadows squirreling. Its shafts,
like the lasers of angels, went
through the pines guarding each slab
of the Confederate Cemetery,
piercing the dead with the quick.

XVIII

Perhaps in these same pines runs,
with cross ties of bleeding thorns,
the track of the Underground Rail-

road way up into Canada,
and what links the Appalachians
is the tinkle of ankle chains
running north, where history is harder
to bear: the hypocrisy
of clouds with Puritan collars.
Wounds from the Indian wars
cut into the soft plank tables
by the picnic lake, and birches
peel like canoes, and the maple's
leaves tumble like Hessians;
hills froth into dogwood, churches
arrow into the Shawmut sky.

XIX

O lakes of pines and still water,
where the wincing muzzles of deer
make rings that widen the idea
of the state past the calendar!
Does this aging Democracy
remember its log-cabin dream,
the way that a man past fifty
imagines a mountain stream?
The pines huddle in quotas
on the lake's calm water line
that draws across them straight as
the stroke of a fountain pen.
My shadow's scribbled question
on the margin of the street
asks, Will I be a citizen
or an afterthought of the state?

XX

Can I bring a palm to my heart
and sing, with eyes on the pole
whose manuscript banner boasts
of the Union with thirteen stars
crossed out, but is borne by the ghosts
of sheeted hunters who ride
to the fire-white cross of the South?
Can I swear to uphold my art
that I share with them too, or worse,
pretend all is past and curse
from the picket lines of my verse
the concept of Apartheid?
The shadow bends to the will
as our oaths of allegiance bend
to the state. What we know of evil
is that it will never end.

XXI

The original sin is our seed,
and that acorn fans into an oak;
the umbrella of Africa's shade,
despite this democracy's mandates,
still sprouts from a Southern street
that holds gray black men in a stoop,
their flintlock red eyes. We have shared
our passbook's open secret
in the hooded eyes of a cop,
the passerby's unuttered aside,
the gesture involuntary, signs,
the excessively polite remark
that turns an idea to acid

in the gut, and here I felt its
poison infecting the hill pines,
all the way to the top.

XXII

Sir, you urge us to divest
ourselves of all earthly things,
like these camphor cabinets
with their fake-pine coffins;
to empty the drawer of the chest
and look far beyond the hurt
on which a cross looks down,
as light floods this asphalt
car park, like the rush Tower
where Raleigh brushes his shirt
and Villon and his brothers cower
at the shadow of the still knot.
There are things that my craft cannot
wield, and one is power;
and though only old age earns the
right to an abstract noun

XXIII

this, Sir, is my Office,
my Arkansas Testament,
my two cupfuls of Cowardice,
my sure, unshaven Salvation,
my people's predicament.
Bless the increasing bliss
of truck tires over asphalt,
and these stains I cannot remove

from the self-soiled heart. This
noon, some broad-backed maid,
half-Indian perhaps, will smooth
this wheat-colored double bed,
and afternoon sun will reprint
the bars of a flag whose cloth—
over motel, steeple, and precinct—
must heal the stripes and the scars.

XXIV

I turned on the TV set.
A light, without any noise,
in amber successive stills,
stirred the waves off Narragansett
and the wheat-islanded towns.
I watched its gold bars explode
on the wagon axles of Mormons,
their brows and hunched shoulders set
toward Zion, their wide oxen road
raising dust in the gopher's nostrils;
then a gravelly announcer's voice
was embalming the Black Hills—
it bade the Mojave rejoice,
it switched off the neon rose
of Vegas, and its shafts came to
the huge organ pipes of sequoias,
the Pacific, and *Today*'s news.

FROM

The Bounty

(1997)

THE BOUNTY

for Alix Walcott

I

Between the vision of the Tourist Board and the true
Paradise lies the desert where Isaiah's elations
force a rose from the sand. The thirty-third canto

cores the dawn clouds with concentric radiance,
the breadfruit opens its palms in praise of the bounty,
bois-pain, tree of bread, slave food, the bliss of John Clare,

torn, wandering Tom, stoat-stroker in his county
of reeds and stalk-crickets, fiddling the dank air,
lacing his boots with vines, steering glazed beetles

with the tenderest prods, knight of the cockchafer,
wrapped in the mists of shires, their snail-horned steeples
palms opening to the cupped pool—but his soul safer

than ours, though iron streams fetter his ankles.
Frost whitening his stubble, he stands in the ford
of a brook like the Baptist lifting his branches to bless

cathedrals and snails, the breaking of this new day,
and the shadows of the beach road near which my mother lies,
with the traffic of insects going to work anyway.

The lizard on the white wall fixed on the hieroglyph
of its stone shadow, the palms' rustling archery,
the souls and sails of circling gulls rhyme with:

"*In la sua volontà è nostra pace,*"
In His will is our peace. Peace in white harbors,
in marinas whose masts agree, in crescent melons

left all night in the fridge, in the Egyptian labors
of ants moving boulders of sugar, words in this sentence,
shadow and light, who live next door like neighbors,

and in sardines with pepper sauce. My mother lies
near the white beach stones, John Clare near the sea-almonds,
yet the bounty returns each daybreak, to my surprise,

to my surprise and betrayal, yes, both at once.
I am moved like you, mad Tom, by a line of ants;
I behold their industry and they are giants.

II

There on the beach, in the desert, lies the dark well
where the rose of my life was lowered, near the shaken plants,
near a pool of fresh tears, tolled by the golden bell

of allamanda, thorns of the bougainvillea, and that is
their bounty! They shine with defiance from weed and flower,
even those that flourish elsewhere, vetch, ivy, clematis,

on whom the sun now rises with all its power,
not for the Tourist Board or for Dante Alighieri,
but because there is no other path for its wheel to take

except to make the ruts of the beach road an allegory
of this poem's career, of yours, that she died for the sake
of a crowning wreath of false laurel; so, John Clare, forgive me,

for this morning's sake, forgive me, coffee, and pardon me,
milk with two packets of artificial sugar,
as I watch these lines grow and the art of poetry harden me

into sorrow as measured as this, to draw the veiled figure
of Mamma entering the standard elegiac.
No, there is grief, there will always be, but it must not madden,

like Clare, who wept for a beetle's loss, for the weight
of the world in a bead of dew on clematis or vetch,
and the fire in these tinder-dry lines of this poem I hate

as much as I love her, poor rain-beaten wretch,
redeemer of mice, earl of the doomed protectorate
of cavalry under your cloak; come on now, enough!

III

Bounty!
        In the bells of tree-frogs with their steady clamor
in the indigo-dark before dawn, the fading morse
of fireflies and crickets, then light on the beetle's armor,

and the toad's too-late presages, nettles of remorse
that shall spring from her grave from the spade's heartbreak.
And yet not to have loved her enough is to love more,

if I confess it, and I confess it. The trickle of underground
springs, the babble of swollen gulches under drenched ferns,
loosening the grip of their roots, till their hairy clods

like unclenching fists swirl wherever the gulch turns
them, and the shuddering aftermath bends the rods
of wild cane. Bounty in the ant's waking fury,

in the snail's chapel stirring under wild yams,
praise in decay and process, awe in the ordinary
in wind that reads the lines of the breadfruit's palms

in the sun contained in a globe of the crystal dew,
bounty in the ants' continuing a line of raw flour,
mercy on the mongoose scuttling past my door,

in the light's parallelogram laid on the kitchen floor,
for Thine is the Kingdom, the Glory, and the Power,
the bells of Saint Clement's in the marigolds on the altar,

in the bougainvillea's thorns, in the imperial lilac
and the feathery palms that nodded at the entry
into Jerusalem, the weight of the world on the back

of an ass; dismounting, He left His cross there for sentry
and sneering centurion; then I believed in His Word,
in a widow's immaculate husband, in pews of brown wood,

when the cattle-bell of the chapel summoned our herd
into the varnished stalls, in whose rustling hymnals I heard
the fresh Jacobean springs, the murmur Clare heard

of bounty abiding, the clear language she taught us,
"as the hart panteth," at this, her keen ears pronged
while her three fawns nibbled the soul-freshening waters,

"as the hart panteth for the water-brooks" that belonged
to the language in which I mourn her now, or when
I showed her my first elegy, her husband's, and then her own.

But can she or can she not read this? Can you read this,
Mamma, or hear it? If I took the pulpit, lay-preacher
like tender Clare, like poor Tom, so that look, Miss!

the ants come to you like children, their beloved teacher
Alix, but unlike the silent recitation of the infants,
the choir that Clare and Tom heard in their rainy county,

we have no solace but utterance, hence this wild cry.
Snails move into harbor, the breadfruit plants on the *Bounty*
will be heaved aboard, and the white God is Captain Bligh.

Across white feathery grave-grass the shadow of the soul
passes, the canvas cracks open on the cross-trees of the *Bounty*,
and the Trades lift the shrouds of the resurrected sail.

All move in their passage to the same mother-country,
the dirt-clawing weasel, the blank owl or sunning seal.
Faith grows mutinous. The ribbed body with its cargo

stalls in its doldrums, the God-captain is cast adrift
by a mutinous Christian, in the wake of the turning *Argo*
plants bob in the ocean's furrows, their shoots dip and lift,

and the soul's Australia is like the New Testament
after the Old World, the code of an eye for an eye;
the horizon spins slowly and Authority's argument

diminishes in power, in the longboat with Captain Bligh.
This was one of your earliest lessons, how the Christ-Son
questions the Father, to settle on another island, haunted by Him,

by the speck of a raging deity on the ruled horizon,
diminishing in meaning and distance, growing more dim:
all these predictable passages that we first disobey

before we become what we challenged; but you never altered
your voice, either sighing or sewing, you would pray
to your husband aloud, pedaling the hymns we all heard

in the varnished pew: "There Is a Green Hill Far Away,"
"Jerusalem the Golden." Your melody faltered
but never your faith in the bounty which is His Word.

v

All of these waves crepitate from the culture of Ovid,
its sibilants and consonants; a universal meter
piles up these signatures like inscriptions of seaweed

that dry in the pungent sun, lines ruled by miter
and laurel, or spray swiftly garlanding the forehead
of an outcrop (and I hope this settles the matter

of presences). No soul was ever invented,
yet every presence is transparent; if I met her
(in her nightdress ankling barefoot, crooning to the shallows),

should I call her shadow that of a pattern invented
by Greco-Roman design, columns of shadows
cast by the Forum, Augustan perspectives—

poplars, casuarina-colonnades, the in-and-out light of almonds
made from original Latin, no leaf but the olive's?
Questions of pitch. Faced with seraphic radiance

(don't interrupt!), mortals rub their skeptical eyes
that hell is a beach-fire at night where embers dance,
with temporal fireflies like thoughts of Paradise;

but there are inexplicable instincts that keep recurring
not from hope or fear only, that are real as stones,
the faces of the dead we wait for as ants are transferring

their cities, though we no longer believe in the shining ones.
I half-expect to see you no longer, then more than half,
almost never, or never then—there I have said it—

but felt something less than final at the edge of your grave,
some other something somewhere, equally dreaded,
since the fear of the infinite is the same as death,

unendurable brightness, the substantial dreading
its own substance, dissolving to gases and vapors,
like our dread of distance; we need a horizon,

a dividing line that turns the stars into neighbors
though infinity separates them, we can think of only one sun:
all I am saying is that the dread of death is in the faces

we love, the dread of our dying, or theirs;
therefore we see in the glint of immeasurable spaces
not stars or falling embers, not meteors, but tears.

VI

The mango trees serenely rust when they are in flower,
nobody knows the name for that voluble cedar
whose bell-flowers fall, the pomme-arac purples its floor.

The blue hills in late afternoon always look sadder.
The country night waiting to come in outside the door;
the firefly keeps striking matches, and the hillside fumes

with a bluish signal of charcoal, then the smoke burns
into a larger question, one that forms and unforms,
then loses itself in a cloud, till the question returns.

Buckets clatter under pipes, villages begin at corners.
A man and his trotting dog come back from their garden.
The sea blazes beyond the rust roofs, dark is on us

before we know it. The earth smells of what's done,
small yards brighten, day dies and its mourners
begin, the first wreath of gnats; this was when we sat down

on bright verandas watching the hills die. Nothing is trite
once the beloved have vanished; empty clothes in a row,
but perhaps our sadness tires them who cherished delight;

not only are they relieved of our customary sorrow,
they are without hunger, without any appetite,
but are part of earth's vegetal fury; their veins grow

with the wild mammy-apple, the open-handed breadfruit,
their heart in the open pomegranate, in the sliced avocado;
ground-doves pick from their palms; ants carry the freight

of their sweetness, their absence in all that we eat,
their savor that sweetens all of our multiple juices,
their faith that we break and chew in a wedge of cassava,

and here at first is the astonishment: that earth rejoices
in the middle of our agony, earth that will have her
for good: wind shines white stones and the shallows' voices.

VII

In spring, after the bear's self-burial, the stuttering
crocuses open and choir, glaciers shelve and thaw,
frozen ponds crack into maps, green lances spring

from the melting fields, flags of rooks rise and tatter
the pierced light, the crumbling quiet avalanches
of an unsteady sky; the vole uncoils and the otter

worries his sleek head through the verge's branches;
crannies, culverts, and creeks roar with wrist-numbing water.
Deer vault invisible hurdles and sniff the sharp air,

squirrels spring up like questions, berries easily redden,
edges delight in their own shapes (whoever their shaper).
But here there is one season, our viridian Eden

is that of the primal garden that engendered decay,
from the seed of a beetle's shard or a dead hare
white and forgotten as winter with spring on its way.

There is no change now, no cycles of spring, autumn, winter,
nor an island's perpetual summer; she took time with her;
no climate, no calendar except for this bountiful day.

As poor Tom fed his last crust to trembling birds,
as by reeds and cold pools John Clare blest these thin musicians,
let the ants teach me again with the long lines of words,

my business and duty, the lesson you taught your sons,
to write of the light's bounty on familiar things
that stand on the verge of translating themselves into news:

the crab, the frigate that floats on cruciform wings,
and that nailed and thorn-riddled tree that opens its pews
to the blackbird that hasn't forgotten her because it sings.

for Adam Zagajewski

I

Europe fulfilled its silhouette in the nineteenth century
with steaming train-stations, gas-lamps, encyclopedias,
the expanding waists of empires, an appetite for inventory
in the novel as a market roaring with ideas.
Bound volumes echoed city-blocks of paragraphs
with ornate parenthetical doorways, crowds on one margin
waiting to cross to the other page; as pigeons gurgle epigraphs
for the next chapter, in which old cobbles begin
the labyrinth of a twisted plot; quiet heresies
over anarchic coffee in steaming cafés (too cold outdoors).
Opposite the closed doors of the Opera two green bronze horses
guard a locked square like bookends, while odors
of the decaying century drift over the gardens
with the smell of books chained in the National Library.
Cross a small bridge into our time under the pardons
of minor medieval saints and the light grows ordinary.
Look back down a linden boulevard that hazes
into a green mist that muffles its clopping horses,
its silk-hats, carriages, the moral width that was, say, Balzac's;
then return to this century of gutted, ashen houses
to the smoke that plumes from distant chimney stacks.

II

Far from streets seething like novels with the century's sorrow,
from charcoal sketches by Kollwitz, the émigré's pain
is feeling his language translated, the synthetic aura
of an alien syntax, an altered construction that will drain

the specific of detail, of damp: creaks of sunlight
on a window-ledge, under a barn door in the hay country
of boyhood, the linen of cafés in an academic light—
in short, the fiction of Europe that turns into theater.
In this dry place without ruins, there is only an echo
of what you have read. It is only much later
that print became real: canals, churches, willows, filthy snow.
This is the envy we finally commit; this happens
to us readers, distant devourers, that its pages whiten
our minds like pavements, or fields where a pen's
track furrows a ditch. We become one of those, then,
who convert the scarves of cirrus at dusk to a diva's
adieu from an opera balcony, ceilings of cherubs, cornucopia
disgorging stone fruit, the setting for a believer's
conviction in healing music: then huge clouds pass,
enormous cumuli rumble like trucks with barrels of news-
print and the faith of redemptive art begins to leave us
as we turn back old engravings to the etched views
that are streaked with soot in wet cobbles and eaves.

III

The cobbles huddle like shorn heads, gables are leaning
over a street to whisper, the walls are scraped of signs
condemning David's star. Gray faces are screening
themselves (like the moon drawing thin curtains
to the tramp of jackboots, as shattered glass rains
diamonds on the pavement). A remorseless silence
took the old tenants away; now there are signs
the streets dare not pronounce, far more their meaning,
why they occurred, but today the repetitions;
the fog clouding the cobbles, the ethnic cleaning.
Arc-lamps come on, and with them, the movie-setting,
the swastika shadows, and the gas-lamps punctuating

a street's interminable sentence. Linden leaves
blow past the closed Opera, and soot-eyed extras are waiting
for one line in a breadline. The shot elegiacally grieves
and the sequel moves with the orchestration of conscience
around the Expressionist corners of the Old Town.
Over accurate paraphernalia, the repeated signs
of a sequel, the cantor's echo, until the ancient tongue
that forbade graven images makes indifferent sense.

IV

That cloud was Europe, dissolving past the thorn branches
of the lignum-vitae, the tree of life. A thunderhead remains
over these islands in crests of arrested avalanches,
a blizzard on a screen in snow-speckled campaigns,
the same old news just changing its borders and policies,
beyond which wolves founder, with red berries for eyes,
and their unheard howling trails off in wisps of smoke
like the frozen cloud over bridges. The barge of Poland
is slowly floating downstream with magisterial
scansion, St. Petersburg's minarets a cloud. Then clouds
are forgotten like battles. Like snow in spring. Like evil.
All that seems marmoreal is only a veil.
Play Timon then, and curse all endeavor as vile,
let the combers continue to crest, to no avail.
Your shadow stays with you, startling the quick crabs
that stiffen until you pass. That cloud means spring
to the Babylonian willows of Amsterdam budding again
like crowds in Pissarro along a wet boulevard's branches,
and the drizzle that sweeps its small wires enshrouds
Notre Dame. In the distance the word Cracow
sounds like artillery. Tanks and snow. Crowds.
Walls riddled with bullet-holes that, like cotton-wool, close.

I CHRISTMAS EVE

Can you genuinely claim these, and do they reclaim you
from your possible margin of disdain, of occasional escape:
the dusk in the orange yards of the shacks, the waxen blue-
green of the breadfruit leaves, the first bulb in the kitchens—shape
and shadow so familiar, so worn, like the handles of brooms
in old women's hands? The small river, the crammed shop
and the men outside it, and the stars that nail down their day.
In short, this affection for what is simple and known,
the direct faces, the deprived but resigned ones
whom you have exalted: are they utterly your own
as surely as your shadow is a thing of the sun's?
The sound rushing past the car windows, not the sea but cane,
the night wind in your eyes like a woman's hair, the fresh
fragrances, then the lights on the hills over Port of Spain,
the nocturnal intimacies that stroke the flesh.
Again, the night grows its velvet, the frogs croak
behind fences, the dogs bark at ghosts, and certainties
settle in the sky, the stars that are no longer questions.
Yes, they reclaim you in a way you need not understand:
candles that never gutter and go out in the breeze,
or tears that glint on night's face for every island.

II

Days change, the sunlight goes, then it returns, and wearily,
under intense mental pain, I remember a corner
of brilliant Saddle Road climbing out of the valley
of leaf-quiet Santa Cruz, a passage with a bridge, one the

desperate memory fastens on even as it passes all the
other possible places; why this particular one?
Perhaps because it disembodies, it neutralizes distance
with the shadows of leaves on the road and the bridge in the sun,
proving that it will remain in any of two directions,
leaving life and approaching the calm of extinction
with the blissful indifference with which a small stream
runs alongside the bridge and the flecked hills of Paramín
and the certainties (they were often of goodness)
that outweigh our coarse needs and the continuous amen
of the brown-shallowed river. Because memory is less
than the place which it cherishes, frames itself from nowhere
except to say that even with the shit and the stress
of what we do to each other, the running stream's bliss
contradicts the self-importance of despair
by these glittering simplicities, water, leaves, and air,
that elate dissolution which goes beyond happiness.

III

Remember childhood? Remember a faraway rain?
Yesterday I wrote a letter and tore it up. Clouds carried bits under the
        hills
like gulls through the steam of the valley to Port of Spain;
then my eyes began to brim from all the old ills
as I lay face-up in bed, muffling the thunder
of a clouded heart while the hills dissolved in ruin.
This is how the rain descends into Santa Cruz,
with wet cheeks, with the hills holding on to snatches of sunlight
until they fade, then the far sound of a river, and surging grass,
the mountains loaded as the clouds that have one bright
fissure that closes into smoke, and things returning to fable
and rumor and the way it was once, it was like this once . . .

Remember the small red berries shaped like a bell
by the road bushes, and a church at the end of innocence,
and the sound of *la rivière Dorée*, through the trees to Choiseul,
the scent of hog plums that I have never smelled since,
the long-shadowed emptiness of small roads, when a singed smell
    rose
from the drizzling asphalt, the way rain hazes the chapel
of La Divina Pastora, and a life of incredible errors?

6

It depends on how you look at the cream church on the cliff
with its rusted roof and a stunted bell tower in the garden
off the road edged with white hard lilies. It could seem sad if
you were from another country, and your doubt did not harden
into pity for the priest in boots and muddy clothes who comes
from a county in Ireland you can't remember, where you felt
perhaps the same sadness for a stone chapel and low walls
heavy with time, an iron sea, and the history of the Celt
told as a savagery of bagpipes and drums.
Turn into this Catholic station, a peaked, brown vestry
and a bleating lamb in the grass. So the visitor believes
the wounded trunk in the shade of large almond leaves.
On a Saturday, shut, and a temperate sky, Blanchisseuse
closed and an elsewhere-remembering sea,
you too could succumb to a helpless shrug that says,
"God! the sad magic that is the hope of black people.
All their drumming and dancing, the ceremonies, the chants.
The *chantwell* screeching like a brass cock on a steeple.
The intricate, unlit labyrinth of their ignorance."
But I feel the love in his veined, mottled hands,
his lilt that lengthens "the road" and makes it Ireland's.

I

My country heart, I am not home till Sesenne sings,
a voice with woodsmoke and ground-doves in it, that cracks
like clay on a road whose tints are the dry season's,
whose cuatros tighten my heartstrings. The shac-shacs
rattle like cicadas under the fur-leaved nettles
of childhood, an old fence at noon, *bel-air*, *quadrille*,
la comette, gracious turns, until delight settles.
A voice like rain on a hot road, a smell of cut grass,
its language as small as the cedar's and sweeter than any
wherever I have gone, that makes my right hand Ishmael,
my guide the star-fingered frangipani.
Our kings and our queens march to her floral reign,
wooden swords of the Rose and the Marguerite, their chorus
the lances of feathered reeds, ochre cliffs and soft combers,
and bright as drizzling banjos the coming rain
and the drizzle going back to Guinea, trailing her hem
like a country dancer. Shadows cross the plain
of Vieuxfort with her voice. Small grazing herds
of horses shine from a passing cloud; I see them
in broken sunlight, like singers remembering the words
of a dying language. I watch the bright wires follow
Sesenne's singing, sunlight in fading rain,
and the names of rivers whose bridges I used to know.

II

The blades of the oleander were rattling like green knives,
the palms of the breadfruit shrugged, and a hissing ghost
recoiled in the casuarinas—they are as alien as olives—

the bougainvillea's lips divided, its mouth aghast;
it was on an ochre road I caught the noise of their lives,
how their rage was rooted, shaking with every gust:
their fitful disenchantment with all my turned leaves,
for all of the years while theirs turned to mulch, then dust.
"We offered you language early, an absolute choice;
you preferred the gutturals of low tide sucked by the shoal
on the gray strand of cities, the way Ireland offered Joyce
his own unwritten dirt road outside Choiseul."
"I have tried to serve both," I said, provoking a roar
from the leaves, shaking their heads, defying translation.
"And there's your betrayal," they said. I said I was sure
that all the trees of the world shared a common elation
of tongues, gommier with linden, *bois-campêche* with the elm.
"You lie, your right hand forgot its origin, O Jerusalem,
but kept its profitable cunning. We remain unuttered, undefined,"
and since road and sun were English words, both of them
endured in their silence the dividing wind.

III

When the violin whines its question and the banjo answers,
my pain increases in stabs, my severances
from odors and roots, the homemade *shac-shac* scraping,
the dip and acknowledgment of courteous country dances,
the smoke I would hold in my arms always escaping
like my father's figure, and now my mother's; let me
for invocation's sacred sake, for the lonely hallowing
of leaves and turning corners, come on the breaking sea
around the sharp brown cliffs of Les Cayes, billowing
breaker, the salt Atlantic wind; I hear a language receding,
unwritten by you, and the voices of children reading
your work in one language only when you had both.
I should ask the clouds to stop moving, for the shadows

to pause, because I can feel it dying and the growth
of all that besieges it, the courtly gestures of grace.
My fingers are like thorns and my eyes are wet
like logwood leaves after a drizzle, the kind in which
the sun and the rain contend for the same place
like the two languages I know—one so rich
in its imperial intimacies, its echo of privilege,
the other like the orange words of a hillside in drought—
but my love of both wide as the Atlantic is large.

10

New creatures ease from earth, nostrils nibbling air,
squirrels abound and repeat themselves like questions,
worms keep inquiring till leaves repeat who they are,
but here we have merely a steadiness without seasons,
and no history, which is boredom interrupted by war.
Civilization is impatience, a frenzy of termites
round the anthills of Babel, signaling antennae
and messages; but here the hermit crab cowers when it meets
a shadow and stops even that of the hermit.
A dark fear of my lengthened shadow, to that I admit,
for this crab to write "Europe" is to see that crouching child
by a dirty canal in Rimbaud, chimneys, and butterflies, old bridges
and the dark smudges of resignation around the coal eyes
of children who all look like Kafka. Treblinka and Auschwitz
passing downriver with the smoke of industrial barges
and the prose of a page from which I brush off the ashes,
the tumuli of the crab holes, the sand hourglass of ages
carried over this bay like the dust of the Harmattan
of our blown tribes dispersing over the islands,
and the moon rising in its search like Diogenes' lantern
over the headland's sphinx, for balance and justice.

for José Antonio

I

Near our ochre pastures with real bulls, your clay one
braces the kitchen lintel. How earthen every noun sounds
with red tiles, bell-tower in level light—Rioja, Aragon!
It stands on its four-square shadow with crescent horns
alert for a shaken red leaf, for the rising sounds,
like the shoal, an inlet of intaken breath, then the roar
as it lowers and gallops on feather hooves hooking air
near the cockerel's strut of the spangled man turning away
from a mirror of sand with "Yes, but I am not ready."
The wave-roar of *olés* cresting from the arena
where the earth is cracked and the only things green are
the spiked agave on the cliff bringing the dust of Navarre
across the ocean. I was never warned about this,
that your flame-straight cypresses sway like our casuarinas,
that those who have seen Spain in the oven of August
are scorched in their hearts forever as herds of dust
drift with these bulls whose model is this small clay ghost.
Swallow of my memory, let us fly south to fierce spaces,
arrowing to Granada through monotonous olives,
towards faint blue mountains to a folk fierce and gracious,
along iron gorges whose springs glitter like knives.

II GRANADA

Red earth and raw, the olive clumps olive and silver
in the thud of wind like a cape shaping the car,
the tormented olives smaller than you thought they were,
as a sadness, not incalculable but measured,

its distance diminishing in the humming coil of the road
widens astonishing Granada. This is how to read
Spain, backwards, like memory, like Arabic, mountains
and predicted cypresses confirming that the only tense
is the past, where a sin lies that is all of Spain's.
It writhes in the olive's trunk, it gapes in the ochre
echo of a stone hillside, like a well's dry mouth: "Lorca."
The black olives of his eyes, the bread dipped in its saucer.
A man in a torn white shirt with its wine-stains,
a black suit, and leather soles stumbling on the stones.
You cannot stand outside, apart from it, and the other ones
on the open hill, the staccato of carbine-fire,
of the dancer's heels, the O of the flamenco singer
and the mouth of the guitar; they are there in Goya,
the clown that dies, eyes open, in *The Third of May*
where the heart of Spain is. Why Spain will always suffer.
Why do they return from this distance, this far away
from the cypresses, the mountains, the olives turning silver?

III   READING MACHADO

The barren frangipani branches uncurl their sweet threat
out of the blue. More echoes than blossoms, they stun the senses
like the nocturnal magnolia, white as the pages I read,
with the prose printed on the left bank of the page
and, on the right, the shale-like speckle of stanzas
and the seam, like a stream stitching its own language.
The Spanish genius bristling like thistles. What provoked this?
The pods of a dry season, heat rippling in cadenzas,
black ruffles and the arc of a white throat?
All echoes, all associations and inferences,
the tone of Antonio Machado, even in translation,
the verb in the earth, the nouns in the stones, the walls,
all inference, all echo, all association,

the blue distance of Spain from bougainvillea verandas
when white flowers sprout from the branches of a bull's horns,
the white frangipani's flowers like the white souls of nuns.
Ponies that move under pines in the autumn mountains,
onions, and rope, the silvery bulbs of garlic, the creak
of saddles and fast water quarreling over clear stones,
from our scorched roads in August rise these heat-cracked stanzas,
all inferences, all echoes, associations.

IV

for Esperanza Lerdá

Storks, ravens, cranes, what do these disparate auguries mean?
The sky ripened then dulled, then across the chimneys
the storks, their legs dangling as if broken, found their nests
over the arches of Alcalá, the cobbled city of Cervantes,
arches and punishing bells, on your wrist a thought rests
like a settling crow. Your death is closer than an ant, as
you look to the day ahead, bountiful, abundant.
I look up at the dry hill in the sun, each shadow a thought.
I imagine my absence; the fatigued leaves will
fall one by one into soundless brown grass in drought
and the raw ochre patches where lilac laces the hill
and the shadows returning exactly some May as they ought,
but with the seam of air I inhabited closed.
A gusting of orange petals crosses Santa Cruz
in a bridal breeze; here combers bouquet in white lace,
and I offer these lines with their thorns to whoever can use
them, the scales of my two islands swayed into place.
I bequeath my eyes to whoever admires Paramín,
my ears to the caves of Las Cuevas, when the silver knot is loosed
from nerve-strings and arteries, and cloud-pages close in amen.

I

This is the first fiction: the biblical plague of dragonflies
crossing the plumes of bamboo after the huge rains
that we thought were locusts, they were there; what magnifies
their importance is plot, to believe that the fiction begins
with the lift of astonishing insects from the very first line.
Horses stamp at the lassos of gnats, and the sweet odor
of their dung mixes with the smell of grass drying,
and I watch the mountains streaming from the sunlit door.
There is symmetry in all this, or all fiction is lying.
Pray for a life without plot, a day without narrative,
but the dragonflies drift like a hive of adjectives loosened
from a dictionary, like bees from the hive of the brain,
and as time passes, they pass, their number is lessened
and their meaning no more than that they come after rain.
They come after rain to this valley when the bamboos have calmed
themselves after threshing and plunging like the manes of horses,
they come with the pestilential host of a prophet armed
for the day of the locust. What summoned their force is
nowhere to be seen, yet the frightening hum of their wings
cruising the garden carries echoes of ancient affliction,
revisitants who have come to remind us of our first wrongs,
grenade-eyed and dragonish; neither science nor fiction.

II

He believed the pain of exile would have passed
by now, but he had stopped counting the days and months,
and lately the seasons, given the promise that nothing can last
for a whole life, much less forever, that if we have suffered once

but thoroughly, a particular loss, we would not suffer it again
in the same way, so that what he counted were the years
whose number he did not repeat aloud, but he knew if rain
fell and after rain the wind swept the plazas, his tears
dried as quickly as the fading sheets of concrete
facing the national park and its bicycle paths
and the drizzle-like silver of wheels, that the heat
of summer in one of the kindest cities of Europe was
nothing compared to the inferno of August at home.
He mutters to himself in the old colonial diction
and he heard how he still said home not only to appease
his hope that he would be there soon, but that he would come
to the rail of the liner and see the serrated indigo ridges
that had waited for him, and all the familiar iron
roofs, and even the vultures balancing on the hot ledges
of the Customs House. He wears black, his hair has grown
white, and he has placed his cane on a bench in the park.
There is no such person. I myself am a fiction,
remembering the hills of the island as it gets dark.

III

He carried his tenebrous thoughts in and out of shadows
like a leopard changing its covert, to find a speckled quiet
appropriate to contemplation, as its yellow eyes close
on a needling yawn, replete with nothing, with emptiness, yet
loaded with its pumping, measured peace, like a herd of zebras
carrying the striped shade of grasses to a watering hole
but in the steadiness of heads and hooves, their fetlocks brace
for a sudden sidewise clatter. The leaves and shadows heal;
all lie down benignly in the thorn-trees' satisfaction,
lion and jackal, when noon is the peaceable kingdom;
they stretch, shudder, and are still, the only action
in their slowly swiveling eyes. Here under the fierce dome

of a cloudless August he feels how the languor that climbs
from stomach to slow-lidding eyes and leonine yawn
shudders in his haunches and crawls along his limbs,
a peace that goes as far back as the umbrella thorn-trees
into a quiet close to Eden, before a dark thought like a cloud
raced over the open grass, and his trotting stalker, lioness,
crouched and, shifting her poise, pounced! Then a small crowd
of hopping, opening vultures and the speckled hyenas.

IV

He endured a purgatorial November, but one
without fire, whose smoke was only the loaded mist
that steamed through the charred woods, where a round sun
peered dimly as it travelled and where shadows were amazed
at any brightness on sidewalk and on ochre wall,
but which the law of seasons faded and slowly erased
as an error. He moved through its crowds like a criminal,
summoning what grace he could find in the lightest
gesture, the casual phrase, holding a cup, eating
without hanging his head, and on those, the brightest
hours that sometimes lanced the gray light, repeating
to himself that this was not his climate or people, no season
as depleting as this, and beyond this there was the sea
and the unrelenting mercy of light, a window in the prison
his mind had become; that suffering was easy
if, beyond it, there was the truth of another sky
and different trees that fitted his nature, his hand
that for all of its sixty-five years had tried not to lie
any more than a crab could travelling its page of sand.
The days would darken with cold, more leaves would die
behind fences, the fog thicken, but beyond them was the good island.

V

He could hear the dogs in the distance, and their baying
led him towards the chapel that rose off the road,
but he did not enter it. This was beneath praying,
and the black dogs were only his thoughts from nights of dread
through the rigid and guerdoning forests of Santa Cruz;
his heart hobbles, bubbling blood like berries on its trail,
three or four palms crest there, and the crazed parrot-cries
are like the clatter of testimony from an obscene trial,
but they cross the rose sky and fade, and a solace returns.
In the hot, hollow afternoon a shout crosses the valley,
a hawk glides, and behind the flame of the immortelle a hill burns
with a flute of blue smoke; this is all there is of value.
O leaves, multiply the days of my absence and subtract them
from the humiliation of punishment, the ambush of disgrace
for what they are: excrement not worthy of any theme,
not the burl and stance of a cedar or the pliant grass,
only the scorn of indifference, of weathering out abuse
like the lissome plunge of branches tossing with the grace
of endurance, bowing under the way that bamboo obeys
the horizontal gusts of the rain, not as martyrdom
but as natural compliance; below him was a house
where without a wound he was more than welcome,
and kind dogs came to the gate jostling for his voice.

VI   MANET IN MARTINIQUE

The teak plant was as stiff as rubber near the iron railing
of the pink veranda at whose center was an arch
that entered a tenebrous, overstuffed salon with the usual sailing
ship in full course through wooden waves, shrouds stiff with starch,
and around, in dolefully tinted cosmetic photos,
a French family: bearded grandpapa and black-bunned *grandmère*

pillows with tassels, porcelains, souvenirs like prose
that had lost its bouquet, Lafcadio Hearn, the usual Flaubert,
more travel memoirs, a Japanese vase, one white rose
of immortal wax. My host left to make a phone-call.
I felt an immeasurable sadness for the ship's sails,
for the stagnant silence of objects, the mute past they carry,
for the glimpse of Fort-de-France harbor through lattices,
"*Notre âme est un trois-mâts cherchant son Icarie*"—
Baudelaire on the wandering soul. This was in the false métropole
of Martinique. A fan stirred one of Maupassant's tales.
Where was the spirit of the house? Some cliché with kohl-
lined eyes, lips like Manet's bougainvillea petals.
I sensed the salon, windows closed, was trying to recall
all it could of Paris; I turned from the wall, and there,
hollow with longing as the wall's gilt-framed clipper,
near stiff rubber leaves in the charged afternoon air,
unsheathed from her marble foot, a red satin slipper.

I am considering a syntax the color of slate,
with glints of quartz for occasional perceptions and
winking mica for wit. I am not weary of the elate,
but gray days are useful, without reflection, like the drained sand
just after twilight. I am considering the avoidance of
an excitable vobabulary or a melodramatic pause like death,
or the remorse of loss or not; there is no loss without love,
but this too must be muted, like the metronome of breath
close to the even heart. Pause. Resume. Pause. Once more.
A gray horse, riderless, grazes where the grass is gone,
a slate-colored horse wrenching tufts on a cold shore,
and the last lurid gash going, the sun closing its house
for the night, and everything near extinction. Even remorse.
Especially remorse and regret and longing and noise,
except the waves in the dark that strangely console
with their steadiness. They are bringing the same old news,
not only the death-rattle of surf on the gargling shoal,
but something further than the last wave, the smell
of pungent weed, of dead crabs whose casings whiten,
and further than the stars that have always looked too small
for those infinite spaces (Pascal) that used to frighten.
I am considering a world without stars and opposites. When?

23

I saw stones that shone with stoniness, I saw thorns
steady in their inimical patience. Now I see nothing after
the lizard has scuttled; I create each response
when there is no balance, neither tears nor laughter
nor life nor death, nor the sequence of tenses;
that is, I can see no past and foresee no future,
for the stones shine in their stoniness, and the logwood thorns
are waiting for nothing, not to be plaited into a crown,
or the lizard to throb on the side of the road as the frog would
till I passed. I see this also as beyond declension,
and not a commemoration of the invincible IS
that changes itself as it proceeds, the past's extension,
or the afternoon-long shadows that are the future's.
Therefore, I foresee myself as blessedly invisible,
anonymous and transparent as the wind, a leaf-light traveller
between branches and stones, the clear, the unsayable
voice that moves over the uncut grass and the yellow
bell of an allamanda by the wall. All of this will soon
be true, but without sorrow, the way stones allow
everything to happen, the way the sea shines in the sun,
silver and bountiful in the slow afternoon.

The sublime always begins with the chord "And then I saw,"
following which apocalyptic cumuli curl and divide
and the light with its silently widening voice might say:
"From that whirling rose that broadens its rings in the void
here come my horsemen: Famine, Plague, Death, and War."
Then the clouds are an avalanche of skulls torrentially rolling
over a still, leaden sea. And here beginneth the season
when the storm-birds panic differently and a bell starts tolling
in the mind from the rocking sea-wash (there is no such sound),
but that is the sway of things, which has the necks of the coconuts
bending like grazing giraffes. I stood on the dark sand
and then I saw that darkness which I gradually accepted
grow startling in its joy, its promised anonymity
in its galloping breakers, in time and the space that kept it
immortal and changing without the least thought of me,
the serrated turret of a rock and the white horse that leapt it,
that spumed and vaulted with the elation of its horsemen,
a swallowing of turmoil of a vertiginous chaos,
the delight of a leaf in a sudden gust of force when
between gray channels the islands are slowly erased
and one dare not ask of the thunder what is its cause.
Let it be written: The dark days also I have praised.

28

Awaking to gratitude in this generous Eden,
far from frenzy and violence in the discretion of distance,
my debt, in Yeats's phrase, to "the bounty of Sweden"
that has built this house facing white combers that stands
for hot, rutted lanes far from the disease of power,
spreads like that copper-beech tree whose roots are Ireland's,
with a foam-haired man pacing around a square tower
muttering to a gray lake stirred by settling swans,
in the glare of reputation; whose declining hour
is exultation and fury both at once.
There is no wood whose branches bear gules of amber
that scream when they are broken, no balsam cure,
nothing beyond those waves I care to remember,
but a few friends gone, and that is a different care
in this headland without distinction, where December
is as green as May and the waves soothe in their unrest.
I heard the brass leaves of the roaring copper-beech,
saw the swans white as winter, names carved on the breast
of the tree trunk in the light and lilt of great speech,
and the prayer of a clock's hands at noon that come to rest
over Ireland's torment. No bounty is greater
than walking to the edge of the rocks where the headland's
detonations exult in their natural meter,
like white wings at Coole, the beat of his clapping swans.

for Sigrid

The sea should have settled him, but its noise is no help.
I am talking about a man whose doors invite a sail
to cross a kitchen-sill at sunrise, to whom the reek of kelp
drying in the sunlit wind on the chattering shoal
or the veils of a drizzle hazing a narrow cave
are a phantom passion; who hears in the feathering lances
of grass a soundless siege, who, when a bird skips a wave,
feels an arrow shoot from his heart and his wrist dances.
He sees the full moon in daylight, the sky's waning rose,
the gray wind, his nurse trawling her shawl of white lace;
whose wounds were sprinkled with salt but who turns over their
    horrors
with each crinkling carapace. I am talking about small odysseys
that, with the rhythm of a galley, launch his waking house
in the thinning indigo hour, as he mutters thanks over
the answer of a freckled, forgiving back in creased linen,
its salt neck and damp hair, and, rising from cover,
to the soundless pad of a leopard or a mewing kitten,
unscrews the coffee-jar and measures two and a half spoons,
and pauses, paralyzed by a sail crossing blue windows,
then dresses in the half-dark, dawn-drawn by the full moon's
magnet, until her light-heaving back is a widow's.
She drags the tides and she hauls the heart by hawsers
stronger than any devotion, and she creates monsters
that have pulled god-settled heroes from their houses
and shawled women watching the fading of the stars.

for Joseph Brodsky

I

On the bright road to Rome, beyond Mantua,
there were reeds of rice, and I heard, in the wind's elation,
the brown dogs of Latin panting alongside the car,
their shadows sliding on the verge in smooth translation,
past fields fenced by poplars, stone farms in character,
nouns from a schoolboy's text, Vergilian, Horatian,
phrases from Ovid passing in a green blur,
heading towards perspectives of noseless busts,
open-mouthed ruins and roofless corridors
of Caesars whose second mantle is now the dust's,
and this voice that rustles out of the reeds is yours.
To every line there is a time and a season.
You refreshed forms and stanzas; these cropped fields are
your stubble grating my cheeks with departure,
gray irises, your corn-wisps of hair blowing away.
Say you haven't vanished, you're still in Italy.
Yeah. Very still. God. Still as the turning fields
of Lombardy, still as the white wastes of that prison
like pages erased by a regime. Though his landscape heals
the exile you shared with Naso, poetry is still treason
because it is truth. Your poplars spin in the sun.

II

Whir of a pigeon's wings outside a wooden window,
the flutter of a fresh soul discarding the exhausted heart.
Sun touches the bell-towers. Clangor of the *cinquecento*,
at wave-slapped landings vaporettos warp and depart

leaving the traveller's shadow on the swaying stage
who looks at the glints of water that his ferry makes
like a comb through blond hair that plaits after its passage,
or book covers enclosing the foam of their final page,
or whatever the whiteness that blinds me with its flakes
erasing pines and conifers. Joseph, why am I writing this
when you cannot read it? The windows of a book spine open
on a courtyard where every cupola is a practice
for your soul encircling the coined water of Venice
like a slate pigeon and the light hurts like rain.
Sunday. The bells of the campaniles' deranged tolling
for you who felt this stone-laced city healed our sins,
like the lion whose iron paw keeps our orb from rolling
under guardian wings. Craft with the necks of violins
and girls with the necks of gondolas were your province.
How ordained, on your birthday, to talk of you to Venice.
These days, in bookstores I drift towards Biography,
my hand gliding over names with a pigeon's opening claws.
The cupolas enclose their parentheses over the sea
beyond the lagoon. Off the ferry, your shade turns the corners
of a book and stands at the end of perspective, waiting for me.

III

In this landscape of vines and hills you carried a theme
that travels across your raked stanzas, sweating the grapes
and blurring their provinces: the slow northern anthem
of fog, the country without borders, clouds whose shapes
change angrily when we begin to associate them
with substantial echoes, holes where eternity gapes
in a small blue door. All solid things await them,
the tree into kindling, the kindling to hearth-smoke,
the dove in the echo of its flight, the rhyme its echo,

the horizon's hyphen that fades, the twigs' handiwork
on a blank page and what smothers their cyrillics: snow,
the white field that a raven crosses with its black caw,
they are a distant geography and not only now,
you were always in them, the fog whose pliant paw
obscures the globe; you were always happier
with the cold and uncertain edges, not blinding sunlight
on water, in this ferry sidling up to the pier
when a traveller puts out the last spark of a cigarette
under his heel, and whose loved face will disappear
into a coin that the fog's fingers rub together.

IV

The foam out on the sparkling strait muttering Montale
in gray salt, a slate sea, and beyond it flecked lilac
and indigo hills, then the sight of cactus in Italy
and palms, names glittering on the edge of the Tyrrhenian.
Your echo comes between the rocks, chuckling in fissures
when the high surf vanishes and is never seen again!
These lines flung for sprats or a catch of rainbow fishes,
the scarlet snapper, the parrot fish, argentine mullet,
and the universal rank smell of poetry, cobalt sea,
and self-surprised palms at the airport; I smell it,
weeds like hair swaying in water, mica in Sicily,
a smell older and fresher than the Norman cathedrals,
or restored aqueducts, the raw hands of fishermen
their anchor of dialect, and phrases drying on walls
based in moss. These are its origins, verse, they remain
with the repeated lines of waves and their crests, oars
and scansion, flocks and one horizon, boats with keels
wedged into sand, your own island or Quasimodo's
or Montale's lines wriggling like a basket of eels.

I am going down to the shallow edge to begin again,
Joseph, with a first line, with an old net, the same expedition.
I will study the opening horizon, the scansion's strokes of the rain,
to dissolve in a fiction greater than our lives, the sea, the sun.

v

My colonnade of cedars between whose arches the ocean
drones the pages of its missal, each trunk a letter
embroidered like a breviary with fruits and vines,
down which I continue to hear an echoing architecture
of stanzas with St. Petersburg's profile, the lines
of an amplified cantor, his tonsured devotion.
Prose is the squire of conduct, poetry the knight
who leans into the flaming dragon with a pen's lance,
is almost unhorsed like a picador, but tilts straight
in the saddle. Crouched over paper with the same stance,
a cloud in its conduct repeats your hair-thinning shape.
A conduct whose meter and poise were modeled on Wystan's,
a poetry whose profile was Roman and open, the bust
of a minor Caesar preferring a province of distance
to the roar of arenas, a duty obscured by dust.
I am lifted above the surf's missal, the columned cedars,
to look down on my digit of sorrow, your stone, I have drifted
over books of cemeteries to the Atlantic whose shores
shrivel, I am an eagle bearing you towards Russia,
holding in my claws the acorn of your heart that restores
you past the Black Sea of Publius Naso
to the roots of a beech-tree; I am lifted with grief and praise, so
that your speck widens with elation, a dot that soars.

Now evening after evening after evening,
August will rustle from the conifers, an orange light
will seep through the stones of the causeway, shadows
lie parallel as oars across the long hull of asphalt,
the heads of burnished horses shake in parched meadows
and prose hesitates on the verge of meter. The vault
increases, its ceiling crossed by bats or swallows,
the heart climbs lilac hills in the light's declension,
and grace dims the eyes of a man nearing his own house.
The trees close their doors, and the surf demands attention.
Evening is an engraving, a silhouette's medallion
darkens loved ones in their profile, like yours,
whose poetry transforms reader into poet. The lion
of the headland darkens like St. Mark's, metaphors
breed and flit in the cave of the mind, and one hears
in the waves' incantation and the August conifers,
and reads the ornate cyrillics of gesturing fronds
as the silent council of cumuli begins convening
over an Atlantic whose light is as calm as a pond's
and lamps bud like fruit in the village, above roofs, and the hive
of constellations appears, evening after evening,
your voice, through the dark reeds of lines that shine with life.

She returns to her role as a seagull. The wind
flaps the shredded wings of the open-air theater
which a different role, in life, made her leave behind.
The lake shines with vanished voices. Nina, years later,
who was a small white body trembling for balance,
has calmed her fright, when one of her first tasks
was learning to control the small storm of her hands.
She wrings your heart like a gull's neck when she asks:
"Remember how it was, Kostia?" Yes. Like this cottage
on a wet day with its salt-rusted bolts, its plants
trying to peer through the windows, its black cortege,
some with umbrella petals of funeral ants
for the child, cyrillics on the thin, translucent page
that she once held to the light; remembered lines
like the shallows, the laughable speech she learns
with joy in their future. The stage with its buried sound
of the lake's polite applause. A seagull returns
like a tilted, balancing N for something it remembers.
She remembers the laughter as his demon burns
behind the wings with its eyes like growing embers,
meaning the evil to come. Perhaps the hills were greener
then, and the trees turned excited pages. Remember, Kostia?
Wind rattles the cottage door and his hands open
it and he stares at her, unchanging, and whispers, "Nina?"
as a flock of white papers rises from a desk dustier
than the years when she spread her wings wide for his pen.

At the end of this line there is an opening door
that gives on a blue balcony where a gull will settle
with hooked fingers, then, like an image leaving an idea,
beat in slow scansion across the hammered metal
of the afternoon sea, a sheet that my right hand steers
a small sail making for Martinique or Sicily.
In the lilac-flecked distance, the same headlands rust
with flecks of houses blown from the spume of the trough,
and the echo of a gull where a gull's shadow raced
between sunlit seas. No cry is exultant enough
for my thanks, for my heart that flings open its hinges
and slants my ribs with light. At the end, a shadow
slower than a gull's over water lengthens, by inches,
and covers the lawn. There is the same high ardor
of rhetorical sunsets in Sicily as over Martinique,
and the same horizon underlines their bright absence,
the long-loved shining there who, perhaps, do not speak
from unutterable delight, since speech is for mortals,
since at the end of each sentence there is a grave
or the sky's blue door or, once, the widening portals
of our disenfranchised sublime. The one light we have
still shines on a spire or a conch-shell as it falls
and folds this page over with a whitening wave.

After the plague, the city-wall caked with flies, the smoke's amnesia,
learn, wanderer, to go nowhere like the stones since
your nose and eyes are now your daughter's hand;
go where the repetition of the breakers grows easier
to bear, no father to kill, no citizens to convince,
and no longer force your memory to understand
whether the dead elect their own government
under the jurisdiction of the sea-almonds;
certain provisions of conduct seal them to a silence
none dare break, and one noun made them transparent,
where they live beyond the conjugations of tense
in their own white city. How easily they disown us,
and everything else here that undermines our toil.
Sit on your plinth in the last light of Colonus,
let your knuckled toes root deep in their own soil.
A butterfly quietly alights on a tyrant's knee;
sit among the sea-eaten boulders and
let the night wind sweep the terraces of the sea.
This is the right light, this pewter shine on the water,
not the carnage of clouds, not the expected wonder
of self-igniting truth and oracular rains,
but these shallows as gentle as the voice of your daughter,
while the gods fade like thunder in the rattling mountains.

FROM

*Tiepolo's
Hound*

(2000)

I

I

They stroll on Sundays down Dronningens Street,
passing the bank and the small island shops

quiet as drawings, keeping from the heat
through Danish arches until the street stops

at the blue, gusting harbor, where like commas
in a shop ledger gulls tick the lined waves.

Sea-light on the cod barrels writes: *St. Thomas*,
the salt breeze brings the sound of Mission slaves

chanting deliverance from all their sins
in tidal couplets of lament and answer,

the horizon underlines their origins—
Pissarros from the ghetto of Braganza

who fled the white hoods of the Inquisition
for the bay's whitecaps, for the folding cross

of a white herring gull over the Mission
droning its passages from Exodus.

Before the family warehouse, near the Customs,
his uncle jerks the locks, rattling their chains,

and lifts his beard to where morning comes
across wide water to the Gentile mountains.

Out of the cobalt bay, her blunt bow cleaving
the rising swell that racing bitterns skip,

the mail boat moans. They feel their bodies leaving
the gliding island, not the blowing ship.

A mongrel follows them, black as its shadow,
nosing their shadows, scuttling when the bells

exult with pardon. Young Camille Pissarro
studies the schooners in their stagnant smells.

He and his starched Sephardic family,
followed from a nervous distance by the hound,

retrace their stroll through Charlotte Amalie
in silence as its Christian bells resound,

sprinkling the cobbles of Dronningens Gade,
the shops whose jalousies in blessing close,

through repetitions of the oval shade
of Danish arches to their high wooden house.

The Synagogue of Blessing and Peace and Loving Deeds
is shut for this Sabbath. The mongrel cowers

through a park's railing. The bells recede.
The afternoon is marked by cedar flowers.

Their street of letters fades, this page of print
in the bleached light of last century recalls

with the sharp memory of a mezzotint:
days of cane carts, the palms' high parasols.

2

My wooden window frames the Sunday street
which a black dog crosses into Woodford Square.

From a stone church, tribal voices repeat
the tidal couplets of lament and prayer.

Behind the rusted lances of a railing
stands the green ribbed fan of a Traveller's Tree;

an iron gate, its croton hedge availing
itself of every hue, screeches on entry.

Walk down the path, enter the yawning stone,
its walls as bare as any synagogue

of painted images. The black congregation
frown in the sun at the sepulchral dog.

There was a shul in old-time Port of Spain,
but where its site precisely was is lost

in the sunlit net of maps whose lanes contain
a spectral faith, white as the mongrel's ghost.

Stiller the palms on Sunday, fiercer the grass,
blacker the shade under the boiling trees,

sharper the shadows, quieter the grace
of afternoon, the city's emptiness.

And over the low hills there is the haze
of heat and a smell of rain in the noise

of trees lightly thrashing where one drop has
singed the scorched asphalt as more petals rise.

A silent city, blest with emptiness
like an engraving. Ornate fretwork eaves,

and the heat rising from the pitch in wires,
from empty backyards with calm breadfruit leaves,

their walls plastered with silence, the same streets
with the same sharp shadows, laced verandas closed

in torpor, until afternoon repeats
the long light with its croton-colored crowds

in the Savannah, not the Tuileries, but
still the Rock Gardens' brush-point cypresses

like a Pissarro canvas, past the shut
gate of the President's Palace, flecked dresses

with gull cries, white flowers and cricketers,
coconut carts, a frilled child with the hoop

of the last century, and, just as it was
in Charlotte Amalie, a slowly creaking sloop.

Laventille's speckled roofs, just as it was
in Cazabon's day, the great Savannah cedars,

the silent lanes at sunrise, parked cars
quiet at their culverts, trainers, owners, breeders

before they moved the paddocks, the low roofs
under the low hills, the sun-sleeved Savannah

under the elegance of grass-muffled hooves,
the cantering snort, the necks reined in; a

joy that was all smell, fresh dung; the jokes
of the Indian grooms, that civilizing

culture of horses, the *fin de siècle* spokes
of trotting carriages, and egrets rising,

as across olive hills a flock of pigeons,
keeping its wide ellipse over dark trees

to the Five Islands, soundlessly joins
its white flecks to the sails on quiet seas.

The white line of chalk birds draws on an Asia
of white-lime walls, prayer flags, and minarets,

blackbirds bring Guinea to thorns of acacia,
and in the saffron of Tiepolo sunsets,

the turbulent paradise of bright rotundas
over aisles of cane, and censer-carried mists,

then, blazing from the ridges of Maracas—
the croton hues of the Impressionists.

3

On my first trip to the Modern I turned a corner,
rooted before the ridged linen of a Cézanne.

A still life. I thought how clean his brushes were!
Across that distance light was my first lesson.

I remember stairs in couplets. The Metropolitan's
marble authority, I remember being

stunned as I studied the exact expanse
of a Renaissance feast, the art of seeing.

Then I caught a slash of pink on the inner thigh
of a white hound entering the cave of a table,

so exact in its lucency at *The Feast of Levi*,
I felt my heart halt. Nothing, not the babble

of the unheard roar that rose from the rich
pearl-lights embroidered on ballooning sleeves,

sharp beards, and gaping goblets, matched the bitch
nosing a forest of hose. So a miracle leaves

its frame, and one epiphanic detail
illuminates an entire epoch:

a medal by Holbein, a Vermeer earring, every scale
of a walking mackerel by Bosch, their sacred shock.

Between me and Venice the thigh of a hound;
my awe of the ordinary, because even as I write,

paused on a step of this couplet, I have never found
its image again, a hound in astounding light.

Everything blurs. Even its painter. Veronese
or Tiepolo in a turmoil of gesturing flesh,

drapery, columns, arches, a crowded terrace,
a balustrade with leaning figures. In the mesh

of Venetian light on its pillared arches
Paolo Veronese's *Feast in the House of Levi*

opens on a soundless page, but no shaft catches
my memory: one stroke for a dog's thigh!

4

But isn't that the exact perspective of loss,
that the loved one's features blur, in dimming detail,

the smile with its dimpled corners, her teasing voice
rasping with affection, as Time draws its veil,

until all you remember are her young knees
gleaming from an olive dress, her way of walking,

as if on a page of self-arranging trees,
hair a gold knot, rose petals silently talking?

I catch an emerald sleeve, light knits her hair,
in a garland of sculpted braids, her burnt cheeks;

catch her sweet breath, be the blest one near her
at that Lucullan table, lean when she speaks,

as clouds of centuries pass over the brilliant ground
of the fresco's meats and linen, while her wrist

in my forced memory caresses an arched hound,
as all its figures melt in the fresco's mist.

I

What should be true of the remembered life
is a freshness of detail: this is how it was—

the almond's smell from a torn almond leaf,
the spray glazing your face from the bursting waves.

And I, walking like him around the wharf's
barrels and schooners, felt a steady love

growing in me, plaited with the strong weaves
of a fish pot, watching its black hands move,

saw in the shadows in which it believes,
in ruined lanes, and rusted roofs above

the lanes, a language, light, and the dark lives
in sour doorways, an alighting dove.

Our street of smoke and fences, gutters gorged
with weed and reeking, scorching iron grooves

of rusted galvanize, a dialect forged
from burning asphalt, and a sky that moves

with thunderhead cumuli grumbling with rain,
and mongrels staggering to cross the pitch

under the olive Morne that held the ruin
of the barracks, yet all was privilege;

especially if, across the harbor, noon
struck its ring of waves, and the ochre walls

of the old cantonment in the still lagoon
reflected their Italian parallels.

Hill towns in rock light, Giotto, Giorgione,
and later the edges of Cézanne's L'Estaque,

not for these things alone, and yet only
for what they were, themselves, my joy comes back.

2

From my father's cabinet I trace his predecessors
in a small blue book: *The English Topographical Draughtsmen,*

his pencil studies, delicately firm as theirs,
the lyrical, light precision of these craftsmen—

Girtin, Sandby, and Cotman, Peter De Wint,
meadows with needle spires in monochrome,

locks and canals with enormous clouds that went
rolling over England, postcards from home,

his namesake's county, Warwickshire. His own
work was a double portrait, a cherished oval

of his wife in oil, his own face, with a soft frown
that seemed to clarify the gentle evil

of an early death. A fine sketch of a cow,
a copy of Millet's *The Gleaners*, Turner's

The Fighting Téméraire, the gathering blow
of a storm with tossing gulls, more than a learner's

skill in them, more than mimicry, a gift.
But a ticking clerk in a colonial government,

his time stopped at the wharf where seagulls lift
and pick at a liner's wake in argument.

There nodding schooners confirmed their names
in oily water, in their Sabbath mooring,

but just as real were etchings of the Thames
by Whistler, coal docks and gulls soaring.

Cross-hatching strokes, and Battersea dividing,
and joining by division, the smoky Thames,

the same bronze stallion, its ringleted king riding,
the barges sliding where the broken water flames.

3

Without ever knowing my father it seems to me now
(I thought I saw him pause in the parenthesis

of our stairs once), from the blank unfurrowed brow
of his self-portrait, that he embodied the tenderness

of water, his preferred medium, its English reticence
but also its fragile delight, like a prediction

of his own passing, its tinted mist and essence,
and the verse that made him my precocious fiction.

The precise furrows of a landscape from which a lark arrows
while, under her parted hood, a blind girl listens,

some sunlit shire behind her, all with a rainbow's
benediction, the light that brims and glistens

like tears in Millais's work were like my mother's
belief in triumph over affliction. A peasant sows

his seeds with a scything motion, the lark's good news
is beyond his hearing, striding these humped furrows

a clod trampling clods in sabots, his wooden shoes
riding the troughs of plowed soil, these boots

my father drew from Millet. These distant landscapes
which his devotion copied, did they despise the roots

and roofs of his island as inferior shapes
in the ministry of apprenticeship? Learning

did not betray his race if he copied a warship's
final berth, a cinder in a Turner sunset burning,

any more than the clouds that hid the lark's *trill-trill*,
or whatever its sound, behind creamy cumuli

over Pontoise, over the flecked Morne or gray hill
above Pontoise, or the stroke in a hound's thigh,

the stroke, the syllable, planted in the furrows
of page and canvas, in varnished pews whose doors

let in the surf of trees, carrying the echoes
of another light, of Venice, of Pontoise.

4

How little we had to go by! At the library window,
I remember one picture, *A Silvery Day near the Needles*,

bright wind on water, one I wanted to do
for its salt, fast clouds, sharp rocks were "the Needles."

Fragile little booklets, reproductions in monochrome,
RENOIR, DÜRER, several Renaissance masters

were our mobile museum, the backyards of home
were the squares of Italy, its piazzas our thick pastures.

Burnt hills that plunged the pilgrim into Umbria,
Giotto's grottoes, cliffs dotted with trees,

cities like colors, Siena; we could see the
Madonna's blue mantle in the sea around Canaries.

All that was radiant, complete, and lovely
was shared in secular ecstasy between us,

the apostolic succession of the
reproductions; Botticelli's Venus,

the stone arches winged like the kneeling
angel in Fra Angelico's *Annunciation*,

astonishing mastery, details revealing
themselves to rapturous examination.

A hill town in Mantegna, afternoon light
across Les Cayes, and dusks of golden wheat,

as pupils we needed both worlds for the sight:
of Troumassee's shallows at the Baptist's feet.

Paintings so far from life fermenting around us!
The skeletal, scabrous mongrels foraging garbage,

the moss-choked canals, backyards with contending odors
purifying in smoke, then to turn a sepia page

from the canals of Guardi, from a formal battle with banners,
the carnival lances of Uccello's pawing horses,

to the chivalric panoply of tossing green bananas
and the prongs of the ginger lily. No metamorphosis

was required by the faiths that made all one:
rock quarries with lions and crouched saints,

or raindrop and dewdrop in measured incantation
on the palm of a yam leaf, the communion of paints.

Whenever a conflagration of sea-almonds
and fat-pork bushes caught the brittle drought

and their copper leaves clattered over the Morne's
redoubts or Vigie barracks, my joy would shout

to the stained air, my body's weight through it
lighter than a spinning leaf, my young head

chattering with birdsong, a bird-pecked fruit;
I saw how the dove's wings were eyed and spotted

and how brief its flight was, but not how long
I would keep such lightness until my sins

crippled and caged me. I felt I would belong
to the dirt road forever, my palette's province,

an irrepressible April with its orange,
yellow, tan, rust, red, and vermilion note

on the bars of dry branches in a language
cooing one vowel from the shell of the dove's throat.

III

I

Flattered by any masterful representation
of things we knew, from Rubens's black faces

devoutly drawn, to the fountaining elation
of feathery palms in an engraving's stasis,

we caught in old prints their sadness, an acceptance
of vacancy in bent cotton figures

through monochrome markets, a distant tense
for a distant life, still, in some ways, ours.

The St. Thomas drawings have it, the taint
of complicit time, the torpor of ex-slaves

and benign planters, suffering made quaint
as a Danish harbor with its wooden waves.

And what of the world, burning outside the library,
the harbor's cobalt, every hot iron roof,

and its mongrel streets? That ordinary
alchemical indifference of youth

transformed by a page's altar, even then,
loved the false pastorals of Puvis de Chavannes,

until the light of redemption came with Gauguin,
our creole painter of *anses*, *mornes*, and *savannes*,

of olive hills, immortelles. He made us seek
what we knew and loved: the burnished skins

of pawpaws and women, a hill in Martinique.
Our martyr. Unique. He died for our sins.

He, Saint Paul, saw the color of his Muse
as a glowing ingot, her breasts were bronze

under the palm of a breadfruit's fleur-de-lys,
his red road to Damascus through our mountains.

Saint Paul, Saint Vincent, in the hallowed toil
of crowning a wave, as green as our *savannes*

shining with wind; pouring linseed oil
and turpentine in cruses with scared hands.

Precious, expensive in its metal cruse,
and poured like secular, sacramental wine,

I smell linseed oil in the wild views
of villages and the tang of turpentine.

This was the edge of manhood, this a boy's
precocious vow, sworn over the capped tubes

like a braced regiment, as his hand deploys
them to assault a barrack's arching cubes.

Where did we get the money from to paint?
Out in the roaring sun, each road was news,

and the cheap muscatel, bought by the pint?
Salt wind encouraged us, and the surf's white noise.

The turgid masonry of the village churches,
in scale provincial cathedrals, loomed over tin

fences and salt-bleached streets, their verges'
stagnant gutters. Rounding a mountain

road they held their station by a sea
of processional crests, saying their Rosaries

to the brown lace altars of Micoud and Dennery,
then, to leeward, softly, at Anse La Raye, Canaries,

Soufrière, Choiseul, Laborie, Vieuxfort, that were
given echoes drawn from the map of France,

its dukedoms pronounced in the verdant patois
of bamboo letters, a palm's sibilance.

There is a D'Ennery in the private maps
Pissarro did of his province, its apostrophe

poised like a gull over these furrowing whitecaps,
these distant breakers with their soundless spray.

Vernacular shallows muttered under bridges
on whose banks cane lances fluttered as the sail

of a wading egret rose towards the ridges
of mountain ferns until the roof grew small.

The coastal road giddied down precipices
to the sweep of Dennery, two sea-gnawed islets

shielding its bay as they endured the size
of shawling Atlantic combers. Their sunsets

were rose as cathedral ceilings with saffron
canyons of cumuli. The chronology of clouds

contained the curled charts of navigation,
battles with smoke and pennants, shrouds

of settling canvas, as afternoon descended
past the cobalt wall of the sea to a faint

vermilion and orange, and the sky overhead
ripened to a Tiepolo ceiling. All was paint

and the light in paint, in the dusty olive
of Cézanne's trees, from Impressionist prints

the clumps of mangoes, from brush and palette knife,
Canaries framed in the cubes of Aix-en-Provence.

Fond St. Jacques, D'elles Soeurs, La Fargue, Moule à Chique
trees from Courbet and Corot, Bal en Bouche,

our landscapes emerging in French though we speak
English as we work. My pen replaced a brush.

3

I matched the first paragraph of *The Red and the Black*
in translation to a promontory on the sky of the page

resting on the harbor line with the recumbent arc
of the Vigie peninsula, across the sea from the college.

Even in translation a crispness in the Stendhal
shone from the barrack's gamboge arches, a prose

bracing in its width; so every village cathedral,
with its rusted zinc roofs through clumps of almonds, rose

in inheritance from Stendhal or Cézanne's L'Estaque,
the impasto indigo bay, the ochre walls of Provence,

organic examples from a veranda, the barrack
arches were Stendhal's brick consonants.

I resolved, from example, that nothing matched the vow,
not even a line of verse like a street with shacks,

a blue sea at the end of the line, that could show
the texture of grass in light, its little shocks.

4

Despite their middens' excremental stench,
their pristine rivulets so clogged with garbage,

the villages clung to a false pride, their French
namesakes; in faith, in carpentry, in language,

so that the harbor with its flour-bag sails,
the rusted vermilion of the market's roofs

made every wharf a miniature Marseilles
when, slow as a cloud, a high cruise ship arrives.

We saw it through guarded gates that shrank our stature,
it loomed as close as paradise and as forbidden;

it was a separate city, with its own legislature
of perfection, its braided ruler hidden.

Its immaculate officers lined up at the rails,
like settling gulls; then, with a long moan at dusk,

its cabin lights budded high over the lateen sails
of tree canoes, it blocked the sun's orange disc

and left us to empty streets and the lapping wharves
and the remembering bollards where it had moored,

to the astonished gossip of small waves,
and the light of cities in the word "abroad."

XX

I

Over the years the feast's details grew fainter,
less urgent, and with it this: I could not recall

my first love's features; memory was my painter,
but her gold-haired figure rose and left its wall.

She had become as spectral as the hound,
a paint-thin phantom of real flesh and voice

on a flaking wall; but time has always found
ways to erase the outlines of our joys.

Paint would preserve her white wax hand that fed
the hound, the light on her rich sleeve, but she,

whom my young adoration once compared
to the fresco's replica, had moved away from me.

The dying light will alchemize the harbor,
whiten the schooners' hulls, and the immense

clouds change their ceiling on bright water.
She lives in paint that cannot change its tense.

Was the name Tiepolo there for euphony?
No skill in the depiction of the beast

ageless, perfection, any one of the
two names might have done it; who painted it best

was not at issue, mastery grew easy,
but where I first beheld the spectral hound.

I would say Veronese for Ver-o-nes-e,
I heard the echo and took it for the sound.

Over the years the arc of the lost hound
faded further; its phantom had appeared

when I, mounting the stairs of these couplets, found
the frame of memory again, but its rust never cleared.

It faded like a pattern Time unstitched
from a hunting tapestry, like a daylight owl.

Was the white beast old age or only a long-wished-
for death, or simply the transparent soul?

2

I ravaged a volume on Tiepolo later.
I was searching for myself now, and I found

The Meeting of Antony and Cleopatra,
I was that gray Moor clutching a wolfhound,

tan and excitable the dog frets at her,
the Queen gliding in jewels and her train.

Venice is dimming, her diadems in eclipse,
her fleet foundering at Actium, once again

the pages turn their sails, this time: *The Banquet
of Antony and Cleopatra.* Here the Queen

poises a pearl over a goblet; in the quiet,
a Moor in a doublet and brown hound frame the scene.

This was something I had not seen before,
since every figure lent the light perfection,

that every hound had its attendant Moor
restraining it with dutiful affection.

I riffled through the derisive catalogue
determined that the fact was not a vision.

(The dog, the dog, where was the goddamned dog?)
Their postures wrong. Nothing confirmed my version.

The prints confirmed his debt to Veronese,
his distant master; tiringly inspired,

he learnt from him to keep his gestures busy
and the light clear; by now he has acquired

the weight and flourish of a public syntax
Veron-easy with colloquial scholarship,

the repetition of deep-fissured backs
and saffron clouds bearing their Virgin up.

Enormous banners gusting in the wind,
golden clouds lift the apostolic host,

their postures born from Veronese's mind,
he is their shaper, their instructive ghost.

Bright-bellied stallions neigh, and chariots
stir tinted smoke, not dust, their pawing hooves

trample the light, the bright rotunda riots
with fury that is motionless but moves.

O turbulence, astounding in its stasis;
O bright and paradisal wind conveying

the swirl of robes, the light-uplifted faces
to the clouds' core, ascending and yet staying

with their bare soles as if their legion spun
like leaves in an autumn gust, but noiselessly,

a saffron glow, not from our mortal sun
that sets and rises, shadowless ecstasy

ordained, we understand that orthodox
depiction, but joy carries it away

to weightless grace, the way a pilgrim walks
on cloud-paths to the Holy Family.

3

They evolve via Veronese, his
bodies that tumble in bright buoyancy

and lift above cloud-chasmed crevices,
their robes in a vertiginous argosy,

his *putti*, light and smooth as bubbles blown
by a saffron wind; it is always late

afternoon in his paradise, in the blest stone
bay of a ceiling busy with its freight;

Venice inverted, hectic with the sails
of crossing saints and, above them, the Star

of the coined water, weighed in her scales
commerce and faith, money and mystery.

Dante in paint, but not quite paradise; yet
there is a fixed sublime in Tiepolo,

whose light is always a little before sunset,
a sweet dissolving like high summer snow,

a vision so acclimatized to faith
and orthodoxy that when we look on her

we see a breathless beauty without breath,
the Infant-cradling, cloud-enthroned Madonna.

4

I had followed in the footprints of the hound,
and not the hound my shadow, the hound was white,

if that were all, then nothing had been found.
It stands as still as when he painted it.

I still believe its phantom and the event
that, from apprenticeship, led me so far,

when the bright startling thigh before me went
like its own candle, separate, secular.

Where it had led me, the desperate, tenuous claim,
the thread that kept its labyrinthine course

through the brocaded channels whose jewels flame
when sunrise strikes the water with such force?

To History, a bellowing Minotaur
pursued and slain, following, as termites do,

these furrowing tunnels, couplets to where
this mixed obscenity made by the two

coupling worlds, a beast in the shaft
of light, trampled its filth, a beast

that was my fear, my self, my craft,
not the white elegant wolfhound at the feast.

If recognition was the grace I needed
to elevate my race from its foul lair

by prayer, by poetry, by couplets repeated
over its carcass, I was both slain and slayer.

Time swung its pendulum's axe through any weather,
it swayed inside my heart. I heard it where

the dial stared, then brought its palms together
at noon and midnight in a steepled prayer.

XXI

I

Blessed Mary of the Derelicts. The church in Venice,
painted at nineteen, confirms the arch he spanned,

the hound's progenitor, the young Veronese;
a fresco's page arrests my halting hand

but none holds in its frame the arching dog
that has become spectral, a vision

loosened from its epoch; the rustling catalogue
whispers Veronese, but here, as contradiction,

is another print! *Apelles Painting Campaspe*
is this allegory Tiepolo has painted himself,

painting his costumed models, on the floor, what must be
his mascot: a white lapdog revels in the wealth

of Venetian light. Alexander sprawls in a chair.
An admiring African peers from the canvas's edge

where a bare-shouldered model, Campaspe with gold hair,
sees her myth evolve. The Moor silent with privilege.

If the frame is Time, with the usual saffron burning
of his ceilings over which robed figures glide,

we presume from the African's posture that I too am learning
both skill and conversion watching from the painting's side.

Santa Maria del Rosario, Sant'Alvise,
Santa Maria della Visitazione, formal research

recites his ceilings in Italy, as faith raises the
scaffold of Giambattista Tiepolo in an island church,

his figure receding in the lifted devotion
of fishermen who cross themselves with salted eyes

as he climbs to his crow's nest above the muttering ocean
of vespers to chart the geography of paradise.

Each rusting village acknowledged her dominion,
Star of the Sea, from its dark, echoing nave,

her canoes genuflecting for Communion
before the lace-fringed altar of a wave.

Each reproduction, even in monochrome,
fresco or ceiling in a pale ochre wash,

made the world through its window one with Rome,
her scepter a cane stalk, her orb a calabash.

The cult and elevation of the Virgin
through roiling, soundless cloud was not my own

upbringing, far less his, and yet conversion
of a kind came with the echoing stone

cupolas, frescoes, banners, and ceilings, the same
ceremonies of Communion, the Mass in Latin,

even in hovels with their struggling flame
to the Madonna, and the throne she sat in.

And the beads of islands, bedded like the seeds
of a sugar apple in their pith of foam,

from the Synagogue of Blessing and Peace and Loving Deeds
to the black chapels where our songs came from.

Volumes of turning cloud in a conch-shell sky,
a floating Madonna, putti with ears like wings,

over tin and blackened shingles the squat belfry
of Anse La Raye divides us when it rings,

and a sky in rose and gold confirms the harmony
of a single faith, trucks with broad breadfruit leaves

to the scrolled palm pillars of the Scuola dei Carmini,
the watery light pearled on the Virgin's sleeves,

the bright stroke on a mongrel scavenging sand
before dark on the fading beach of Canaries,

the light in the dog's thigh made by the sun's hand,
as it turns and fills its outline in a masterpiece.

3

Garnet-eyed and gazing towards Zion,
a settlement of Abyssinian apostles,

bearded as smoke, have founded a religion
based on the horizon, while the old one jostles

for space in the old cathedral. Garbage in drains,
the furnace that rules the village by its stasis.

They have designed themselves so that what remains
is the Coptic fantasy in their stoned faces.

They have designed their faith, with leonine
locks, some shaggy with rust, till, in repose,

banners and beards are one in their design,
figures not Veronese's or Tiepolo's.

They have not seen Dürer's panels: Four Apostles,
not the Moorish princes of the Renaissance,

they echo a blue altarpiece in their postures,
one turbaned soldier with a bamboo lance.

On the beach a young tourist with her head inclined
towards an infant she cradles in her arms

is a Fra Angelico in a blue wraparound, as the wind
begins the incantations of pliable palms;

everywhere a craft confirming images,
from a nosing mongrel to a challenging ceiling

of cloud. The mind raised on mirages
sees my father's copy of storm gulls wheeling.

4

Vessel, apprentice and interpreter,
my own delight, before the frames of Time,

was innocent, ignorant and corruptible,
monodic as our climate in its sublime

indifference to seasonal modulations,
to schools, to epochs; I had read them, yes,

but art was not an index of elations;
it ignored error, it trusted its own eyes.

The hound's thigh blurred the smoky dyes around it,
it mixed the schools of distinct centuries,

fixed in its stance it stays where I had found it,
painted by both, Tiepolo, Veronese;

since what is crucial was not true ascription
to either hand—rather the consequence

of my astonishment, which has blent this fiction
to what is true without a change of tense.

Not that Time in a larger frame might have shown the gift
I believed in, and something more astonishing might

have resulted in paint, when on a cloud's wall swift
birds dart over it like a brush's flight

over a causeway with feathery branches, as azaleas
blaze in a vase like that canvas with its zinc glare

in my first Cézanne. He too was crazed by failures,
you can see the gleam of a madman in his stare.

My father's bones in my wrist, in the white Easter
linen of a crucified canvas nailed for his sons—

Lucien, son of Camille, Domenico of Giambattista,
from hand to veined hand the gift, from example, inheritance.

Ah, the hyphen of unfinished things, the unachieved—
like that shaft of light in the fading sky, the lance

of a brush crossing the canvas! O loss, that believed
in Time and its talent! The racing shadows advance.

XXII

I

One dawn I woke up to the gradual terror
that all I had written of the hound was false.

I had pursued a melody of error,
my craft seduced by the twin siren calls

of Memory changing to Imagination,
of Reason into Rhyme. I knew I stood

before the uproar of a feast. Its station
was Venice, unvisited. Its poles were my dark wood,

from which the hound, now a chained Cerberus, growled
and lunged its treble heads at Accuracy,

a simple fact made myth, and the myth fouled
by its demonic piss. Tiepolo, Veronese,

the image I had cherished made no sense,
my memory's transference of their frescoes

meant that I never learnt the difference
between Veronese's gift and Tiepolo's.

And yet I hold my ground and hold it till
I trace the evasive hound beyond my fear

that it never existed, that exhaustion will
claim action as illusion, from despair.

Because if both Venetians painted frescoes,
then what I thought I saw had to be panels

or canvas seamed, but still the image grows
with more conviction there and nowhere else.

Then how could I be standing in two places,
first, in a Venice I had never seen,

despite its sharpness of prong-bearded faces,
then at the Metropolitan? What did the dog mean?

2

Over the years I abandoned the claim
of a passion which, if it existed, naturally faded

from my island Pissarro, rooted in his fame,
a smoke wisp on the Seine, his exile dictated

by a fiction that sought from him discipleship
in light and affection for our shacks and ridges

touched by crepuscular orange. No black steamship
roiled in its wake a pain that was ever his;

no loss of St. Thomas. Our characters are blent
not by talent but by climate and calling. Cézanne's

signing his work, *Pupil of Pissarro*, all I meant
was only affection's homage, and affection's

envy, benign as dusk arching over Charlotte Amalie,
and night, when centuries vanish, or when dawns rise

on the golden alleys of Paris, Castries, or Italy,
ceilings of Tiepolo or Veronese in changing skies.

A change of Muses, a change of light and customs,
of crooked tracks for avenues of bricks for straw,

change fiddling orchestras for firelit drums,
they were never his people, we were there to draw.

They, and everything else. Our native grace
is still a backward bending, out of fashion

in theaters and galleries, an island race
damned to the provincialities of passion.

My Muses pass, in their earth-rooted stride,
basket-balancing illiterate women, their load,

an earthen vessel, its springs of joy inside,
pliant shadows striding down a mountain road.

In evening light a frangipani's antlers
darken over spume crests and become invisible

even to the full moon, and as dusk always does
for my eyes, and his lights bud on the black hill

to a cobbled brook's tireless recitation
in voluble pebbles as lucent as the ones

under the soles of the Baptist. Morning sun
on the corrugating stream over clean stones.

3

I thoroughly understand all he endures:
that sense of charity to a gifted stranger,

open to their gatherings, these voluble bores,
these brilliant jeerers. Friends are a danger,

proud of the tribal subtleties of their
suffering, its knot of meaning, of blood on the street

for an idea, their pain is privilege, a clear
tradition, proud in triumph, prouder in defeat,

for which they have made a language they share
in intellectual, odorless sweat.

Because they measure evil by the seasons, the clear
death of October, its massacre of leaves,

my monodic climate has no history. I hear
their bright applause for one another's lives.

My fault was ignorance of their History
and my contempt for it, they are my Old Masters,

sunlight and pastures, a tireless sea
with its one tense, one crest where the last was.

No scansions for the seasons, no epochs
for the fast scumbling surf, no dates

or decades for the salt-streaming rocks,
no spires or towers for the sailing frigates.

4

One sunrise I felt an ordinary
width of enlightenment in my motel,

at the Ramada Inn in Albany.
I was bent, writing, he was bent as well,

but in nineteenth-century St. Thomas
my body filled his penciled silhouette

in arched Dronningens Gade, my trousers
rolled to the calves, in a sisal hat at the market

which I now tip in my acknowledgment
to him and Mr. Melbye. I'll be born

a hundred years later, but we're both bent
over this paper; I am being drawn,

anonymous as my own ancestor,
my Africa erased, if not his France,

the cobbled sunlit street with a dirt floor
and a quick sketch my one inheritance.

Then one noon where acacias shade the beach
I saw the parody of Tiepolo's hound

in the short salt grass, requiring no research,
but something still unpainted, on its own ground.

I had seen wolfhounds straining on the leash,
their haunches taut on tapestries of Spring;

now I had found, whose azure was a beach,
this tottering, abandoned, houseless thing.

A starved pup trembling by the hard sea,
far from the backyards of a village street.

She cried out in compassion. This was not the
cosseted lapdog in its satin seat,

not even Goya's mutt peering from a fissure
of that infernal chasm in the Prado,

but one that shook with local terror, unsure
of everything, even its shadow.

Its swollen belly was shivering from the heat
of starvation; she moaned and picked it up,

this was the mongrel's heir, not in a great
fresco, but bastardy, abandonment, and hope

and love enough perhaps to help it live
like all its breed, and charity, and care,

we set it down in the village to survive
like all my ancestry. The hound was here.

XXIII

I

Teaching in St. Thomas, I had never sought it out,
the Synagogue of Blessing and Peace and Loving Deeds;

in the tourist streets I never gave a thought
to the lost shops that were Dronningens Gade's.

Liners whitened the hectic port, as always,
with the exact, vivid banality

of its postcards; its sunlit stone alleys
hid the lost shul of Charlotte Amalie

but along hot shadowed roads frothing with trees
that led to the steep college, you saw

those customary pastorals of the Antilles,
yards and rust fences that he learnt to draw.

I passed, climbing the hot hill to the college,
him and Fitz Melbye sketching in the shade.

I stopped. I heard their charcoals scratch the page
and their light laughter, but not what they said.

I felt a line enclose my lineaments
and those of other shapes around me too,

a bare dirt yard stacked with old implements,
its patterned leaves, cross-hatched, and as the view

grew backwards quickly, I grew back as well,
my clothes were lighter and my stance as frozen

as the penciled branches of an immortelle.
I shrank into the posture they had chosen,

and felt, in barefoot weightlessness, that choice
transparently defined, straw hat, white cotton

fabric, drawn with a withdrawn voice,
knowing that I, not it, would be forgotten,

keeping my position as a model does,
a young slave, mixed and newly manumitted

last century and a half in old St. Thomas,
my figure now emerging, and it said:

"I and my kind move and not move; your drawing
is edged with a kindness my own lines contain,

but yours may just be love of your own calling
and not for us, since sunshine softens pain,

and we seem painless here, or the marketplace
where I discern myself among its figures,

placid adornments, models of the race.
Mission accomplished, exile-humming niggers

by a bay's harp, in pencil-shaded yards,
here for your practice; but do not leave us here,

for cities where our voices have no words."
Our figures muttered, but he could not hear,

and to this day they still receive no answer,
even while I scolded his fast-shadowed hand.

"We lost our roots as yours were far Braganza,
but this is our new world, of reeds and sand."

2

Both kept on drawing, and the sketch each made
that leafy afternoon was left unsigned,

holding my body while my spirit strayed
in catalogues, where I can never find

its exact apparition, as I have not found,
though I am sure I saw it, Tiepolo's

or Paolo Veronese's spectral hound,
I hide in white among white cotton Negroes.

I said, "You could have been our pioneer.
Treacherous Gauguin judged you a second-rater.

Yours could have been his archipelago, where
hues are primal, red trees, green shade, blue water."

He said, "My history veins backwards
to the black soil of my birthplace, whose trees

are a hallowed forest; its leaf-words
uttering the language of my ancestors,

then, for ringed centuries, a helpless dimming
of distance made both bark and language fade

to an alphabet of bats and swallows skimming
the twilight gables of Dronningens Gade."

The ground doves brood and strut, a swallow calls
from crusted eaves, "Adieu, Monsieur Gauguin";

the placid afternoons of his pastorals
once he changed islands; both began again,

one on the Île de Paris's moss-blackened walls
with barges creasing the mud-colored Seine,

the other near Tahiti's waterfalls
and flower-haired women in their foaming basin.

Are all the paintings then falsifications
of his real origins, was his island betrayed?

Instead of linden walks and railway stations,
our palms and windmills? Think what he would have made

(but how could he, what color was his Muse,
and what was there to paint except black skins?)

of flame trees in the fields of Santa Cruz;
others took root and stood the difference,

and some even achieved a gratitude
beyond their dislocation, saw what was given

and seized it with possessed delight, made good
from an infernal, disease-riddled heaven,

and let the ship go, trailing its red banner
out of their harbor, like *The Téméraire*.

St. Thomas stays unpainted, every savannah
trails its flame tree that fades. This is not fair.

3

Out of the open window, the tall palms dream
of Zion, the thick clouds graze like sheep,

"If I forget thee . . ." Children share childhood. See him,
one oven-hot afternoon when parents sleep,

stretched out on a straw carpet, an innocent
studying the freight train of a millipede

before the world into which we are sent
stings with each poisonous and different creed.

He saw frigates veer over a smoky hill,
all that, regenerate, recurs; he would have seen

in flower beds a hummingbird's soundless drill
with electric wings, its emerald machine

that darts as soon as it settles, a windmill's
vanes grind to a halt with slavery, the sign

of the season changing on scorched hills
a rainbow's fury, the rain's trawling seine.

He woke, like us, to dew. He watched voracious
caterpillars of rain nibble the horizon,

the sun-dried tamarinds, rusting acacias
grown brittle as firewood for August's oven,

saw puffs of cloud from the fort's rusted cannon,
regiments of slaughtered flowers at the root

of cedars whose huge shade contracts at noon,
smelled earth's scorched iron in the autumnal drought.

Surely he recalled how the remorseless March
sun scorched the hills, the consoling verandas,

the family afternoons on the fretwork porch
in the infinity of Antillean Sundays,

to the soft bellows of a butterfly's wings,
the folded Bible of a velvet moth,

a swaying canna lily's bell that brings
a hymn of black flies to a tablecloth.

Sea-wires on the ceiling, he watched them once,
from the languor of mosquito nets, lying down,

paralyzed by floating afternoons,
the sea, past scorching roofs, a leaden cauldron.

Seasons and paintings cross, reversible,
Hobbema's, the shade-crossed casuarina walk,

the surf foams in apple orchards, cedars talk
poplar, and autumn claims the hills of April.

Grenade sugar-apples, cannonball calabash,
the first breeze and the cool of coming rain

from moaning ground doves, the burnt smell of bush,
the flecks of sea beyond a sugar mill's ruin,

decrepit doors in backyards blowing smoke,
a black pup nosing puddles by a yam fence,

from a dog to the Doge's Palace, drains that mock,
with gliding leaves and reeds, aureate Venice.

Once, near Dinard, a Roman aqueduct
soaring in sea mist, a rook shipped its oars,

in a homecoming glide, with wings it tucked
like brushes that lie crossed after Pontoise.

4

These couplets climb the pillared sanctum
of invitation to Salon, Academy,

its lectern for the elect. I thank them
for helping me to cross a treacherous sea

to find a marble hound. Mutely pleading
outside is a black mongrel; I examine a small

bas-relief that shows a wolfhound leading
a straining huntress. Well, it is fall,

so the season flares and fades, a reading,
an opening, a lavish catalogue

of homage to Tiepolo, gossip, breeding.
I think of reeking fish and a black dog.

FROM

The Prodigal

(2004)

I

I

In autumn, on the train to Pennsylvania,
he placed his book facedown on the sunlit seat
and it began to move. Meter established,
carried on calm parallels, he preferred to read
the paragraphs, the gliding blocks of stanzas
framed by the widening windows—
Italian light on the factories, October's
motley in Jersey, wild fans of trees, the blue
metallic Hudson, and in the turning aureate afternoon,
dusk on rose brickwork as if it were Siena.

Nothing. Nobody at the small railroad station.
The willows fan open. Here we hung our harps,
as the river slid past to elegiac banjos
and the barge crawled along an ochre canal
past the white spires of autumnal towns
and racketing freight trains all long whoop and echo.
Stations, bridges and tunnels enter their language
and the scribble of brown twigs on a blank sky.

And now the cars began to fill with pilgrims,
while the book slept. With others in the car,
he felt as if he had become a tunnel
through which they entered the idea of America—
familiar mantling through the tunnel's skin.
It was still unfamiliar, the staidness of trains.
And the thoughtful, the separate, gliding in cars
on arrowing rails serenely, each gripped face intent
on the puzzle of distance, as stations pass
without waving, and sad, approaching cities,

announced by the prologue of ramshackle yards
and toothless tunnels, and the foliage rusting
across an old aqueduct, loomed and then dwindled
into their name. There were no stations
or receding platforms in the maps of childhood
nor blizzards of dogwood, no piercing steeples
from buttressed cathedrals, nor statues whose base
held dolphins, blunt browed, repeating themselves.
Look at that man looking from the stalled window—
he contains many absences. He has ridden
over infinite bridges, some with roofs below,
many where the afternoon glittered like mica
on the empty river. There was no time
to fall in love with Florence, to completely understand
Wilmington or the rusty stanchions
that flashed past with their cables
or how the screaming gulls knew
the names of all the women he had lost.
There was sweet meditation on a train
even of certain griefs, a gliding time
on the leveled surface of elegiac earth
more than the immortal motion of a blue bay
next to the stone sails of graves, his growing loss.
Echoing railway stations drew him to fiction,
their web of schedules, incoherent announcements,
the terror of missing his train, and because trains
(their casual accuracy, the joy in their gliding power)
had (there were no trains on the islands
of his young manhood) a child's delight in motion,
the lines and parallels and smoky arches
of unread famous novels would stay the same
for yet another fall with its bright counties,
he knew, through the gliding window, the trees would lift
in lament for all the leaves of the unread books,
Anna Karenina, for the long wail of smoke

across Alpine meadows, for soldiers leaning
out of war-crowded stations, a separate joy
more rooted in landscapes than the flare of battles.

In the middle of the nineteenth century,
somewhere between Balzac and Lautréamont,
a little farther on than Baudelaire Station
where bead-eyed Verlaine sat, my train broke down,
and has been stuck there since. When I got off
I found that I had missed the Twentieth Century.
I studied those small things which besieged the station,
the comical belligerence of dragonflies
and the perpetual astonishment of owls.
It was another country whose time had passed,
with pastoral willows and a belief in drawing.
I saw where Courbet lived; I saw the big quarry
and the lemon light of Jean-Baptiste Camille Corot.
The noise of roaring parliaments, a noise
that sounded like the ocean, whorled in my ear-shell,
was far, and the one sibilance was of the poplars
who once bowed to Hobbema. My joy was stuck.
The small station was empty in the afternoon,
as it had been on the trip to Philadelphia.
I sipped the long delight of a past time
where ambition was too late. My craft was stuck.
My deep delight lay in being dated
like the archaic engine. Peace was immense.
But Time passed differently than it did on water.

II

There is a continent outside my window,
in the Hudson's patient narrative. There's some calm.
But traffic hurtles up the West Side Highway,

and in fall, the embankment blazes, but
even in spring sunlight I have rarely sought
the glittering consolation of the river,
its far-fetched history, the tongues of unknown trees
talk to an old man sitting on a bench.
Along the smoldering autumnal sidewalks,
the secretive coffee-shops, bright flower stalls,
wandering the Village in search of another subject
other than yourself, it is yourself you meet.
An old man remembering white-headed mountains.
And subtly the sense insinuates itself
that frequent exile turns into treachery,
missing the seasons at the table of July
on lower Seventh Avenue when young women glide
like Nereids in their lissome summer dresses,
all those Susannas for a single elder!
In spring the leaves sing round a tireless statue
who will not sit although invited to.

From a fresh- to a salt-water muse. Home to the Hudson.
The bells on a bright Sunday from my bed,
the squares of sunlight on the buildings opposite
the river slate, the sky cloudless, enameled.
Then Sunday brings its summary of the world,
with the serene Hudson and its criss-crossing ferries,
great clouds and a red barge.
Gaze, graze on the numinous grays
of the river, its spectral traffic
and the ghostly bridges, the bouquet of lamps,
along the embankment your name fades into fog.

Clouds, the sag of old towels, sodden in gray windows,
the far shore scumbled by the fog,
ducks bob on the gray river like decoys,
not ducks but the submerged pieces of an old pier,

lights fade from the water, "Such, such were the joys,"
muffled remorse in the December air.

Desire and disease commingling,
commingling, the white hair and the white page
with the fear of white sight, blindness, amputation,
a recurring kidney stone, the plague of AIDS,
shaken in the mirror by that bewildered look,
the truculence, the drooping lip of a spiritual lout.
Look at it any way you like, it's an old man's book
whenever you write it, whenever it comes out,
the age in your armpits in the pleats of your crotch,
the faded perfumes of cherished conversations,
and the toilet gurgling its eclogues, resurrecting names
in its hoarse swiveling into an echo after.
This is the music of memory, water.

On Mondays, Boston classes. Lunch, a Korean corner—
my glasses clouded by a tribal broth,
a soup that tamed shaggy Mongolian horsemen
in steaming tents while their mares stamped the snow.
Asia swirls in a blizzard; winter is rising
on drifts across the pavements, soon every gutter
will be a locked rivulet then it will be time
for rose and orange lights to dot the Prudential,
and sparrows to bulb along the stricken branches.
I missed the fall. It went with a sudden flare
and blew its wick in Gloucester, sank in Salem,
and bleached the salt grass bending off Cape Ann,

flipped seals into the sound, rattled the shades
of a dark house on that headland abandoned
except by Hopper. You know the light I mean.
American light. And the wind is
the sound of an age going out the window,
yellow and red as taxis, the leaves. And then
boring through volumes of cloud, a silverfish—

1

Chasms and fissures of the vertiginous Alps
through the plane window, meadows of snow
on powdery precipices, the cantons of cumuli
grumbling or closing, gasping falls of light
a steady and serene white-knuckled horror
of speckled white serrations, inconceivable
in repetition, spumy avalanches
of forgetting cloud, in the wrong heaven—
a paradise of ice and camouflage
of speeding seraphs' shadows down its slopes
under the metal, featherless wings, the noise
a violation of that pre-primal silence
white and without thought, my fear was white
and my belief obliterated—a black stroke
on a primed canvas, everything was white,
white was the color of nothing, not the night,
my faith was strapped in. It could go no higher.
I doubted that there would be a blest descent
braking like threshing seraph's wings, to spire
and sun-shot field, wide, innocent.

The worst fear widened, to ask of the infinite:
How many more cathedral-spires? How many more
peaks of these ice-seized mountains, and towns
locked in by avalanches with their yellow lights
inside on their brilliant goods, with the clappers
of bells frozen by silence? How many small crows
like commas punctuating the drifts?
Infinite and repetitive as the ridges
patterned like okapi or jaguar, their white forests

are an opposite absolute world, a different life,
but more like a different death. The wanderer's cry
forms an O of terror but muted by the slanted snow
and a fear that is farther than panic. This,
whatever its lesson, is the tacit chorus
of the screaming mountains, the feathering alp,
the frozen ocean of oceanic roofs
above which hangs the white ogling horn—
skeletal tusk of a mastodon above white inns.

II

A small room, brown and dark, its linen
white as the white spur of the Matterhorn
above the balcony and the dark inns in snow,
and, incredibly on the scars of the crevasses,
a train crawling up the mountain. Orange lights
and brighter in the muffled streets of Zermatt,
what element more absolute as itself
than the death-hush of the snow, the voiceless blizzard,
between the brilliant windows of the stores?

He stood outside bright windows filled with music,
faint conversation through the mullioned panes
and crab-clenched chandeliers with pointed flames
above the animate and inanimate faces
of apparitions whose features matched their names,
all gentlemen with some big-buttressed dames,
a fiction in a fiction. The door could open,
he would be more than welcome. The lights were squared
on the lawn's edges. A conspiring pen
had brought him thus far. All that he had dared
lay in elegant ambush whose bright noise
was like the starlit surf whose voice had reared

him. But this was a different climate,
a different country. Now both lives had met
in this achievement. He turned his head
away this time, and walked back towards the road.
The scene was just like something he had read.
Something in boyhood, before he went abroad.
But cowardice called to him. He went back inside;
secure and rigid in their printed places
all of the dancers in that frozen ballroom.

III

As with snow, to feel the air changing,
the heart darken and in the clarity of sunshine—
the clarity of ice, as in the islands,
all spring, all summer, it was the one world
till autumn marshaled its divisions, its flags,
and deer marched with agreeing nodding antlers
into another fiction while we remained
in immortal cobalt, unchanging viridian;
and what was altered was something more profound
than geography, it was the self. It was vocabulary.
Now it was time for the white poem of winter,
when icicles lock the great bronze horse's teeth.
The streets were white. No sidewalks in the streets
and the short snowy distances between the shops
brilliant with winter gear and above the streets
full of skiers with their poles on their shoulders
the chalets, snow-roofed, with peaks like Christmas cards.
From a climate without wolves, what if I dreamt
a white wolf trotted and stood in my path,
there, in the early lights of the busy streets
thickened to silence, coal-eyed, its tongue
a panting flame, snow swarming my eyes.

Then, like a match struck with light! A different glow
than the windows of the hotels, the stores, the inns.
Her hair above the crisp snow of table linen
was like a flare, it led him, stumbling, inane.

He went down early to the lounge. Repeat:
He went down early to the lounge and waited.
The street lights were still on. Then they went out.
Eventually she came and when she came,
she brought the mountain with her into the big room
with her cold cheeks, snow smudged with strawberries,
her body steaming with hues of a banked hearth,
her eyes the blue-green of its dying coals,
and her hair, once it was shaken from its cap
leapt like new fire. Ilse, perhaps, brought in
the muddy tracks between the inns, dark pines,
the unicorn shaft or the priapic horn
of the white mountain, as famous as its stamp,
she brought in echoes of hunted stags folding
from a shot's ricochet through a crevasse
in the warmth of the body which she now unsheathed,
shaking the dust of snow from fur and leather
and hanging her ski-coat on a rack of antlers,
with a glance that pierced him like an icicle,
flashing the blizzard of white teeth, then tousling
the wet hair at the nape of her neck, she stood
for a moment in a blizzard of linen
and the far-lightning flash of cutlery
over the chalets and lodges of Zermatt.

      IV

As far as secular angels go there is always one,
in Venice, in Milan, hardening that horn

of ageing desire and its devastations,
while skiers plunge and slide soundlessly
past crevasses, invisible as thoughts,
like the waitress buttoning her uniform
already pronged by an invisible horn
and lids that sometimes closed as if her form
slept in the white peace after an avalanche.
He looked out through the window at white air,
and there, crawling impossibly like an insect
across the drifts, a train, distinct, impossible.
Now with more promise than he could expect.
Her speech was crisp, and as for the flushed face,
was it a patronizing kindness? Who could tell?
Auf Wiedersehen to the pines and the peaked chalets
to the inns looking like toys behind the car
and the waitresses and Ilse, indifferently
going about their business with the lamps
of the Alpine dusk, and the beds freshly made
as the new snow that blurred the villages
and the lights from the stores on the banked street
and the receding shore of our hotel.
Again, how many farewells and greetings
on cheeks that change their name, how many kisses
near tinkling earrings that fade like carriage bells.

v

On the powdery ridges of the slopes were sheds
where cattle were byred in the winter darkness.
I imagined them blindly gurgitating their fodder,
and beyond them the vertiginous fissures
in the iron cold. There were the absolute,
these peaks, the pitch of temperature and terror,
polar rigidities that magnetized a child

these rocks bearded with icicles, crevasses
from Andersen's "Ice Maiden," Whittier's "Snow-Bound,"
this empire, this infernity of ice.
One afternoon, an eternity ago
in his warm island childhood in a jalousied room
with all the fire of daylight outside
in the bustling, black, barefoot street, his heart
was iced with terror, a frozen pond, in which
glazed faces started behind the glacial prose
of Hans Christian Andersen's "The Ice Maiden"
with its snow-locked horror, and that
afternoon has never left me. I did not know then that
she worked as a blond waitress in Zermatt.

I liked the precocious lamps of the evening.
I had never seen so much snow. It whitened night.
Out of this snow, like weeds that have survived,
came an assiduous fiction, one that the inns,
the gables shelved with white, the muted trails,
and (unavoidable) the sharp horn of the peak,
demanded of the ritual silence, a flare of light,
the flush of a warmed face, some elegy,
some cold enchantress, an ember's memory
of fire, provided since my young manhood
or earlier, of the Ice Maiden. She and the horn
were from the same white magic and when she came,
she lifted her head and the horn hooked my heart,
and the world magnified a greeting into love.

Wide meadows shot with a lemon light under the peaks,
the mineral glint of distant towns, the line of the plain
ending in the exclamation of a belfry!
Entering Lausanne, after the white ridges,
ochre scarps for a long while along the gray lake,
a lake so wide you could not see the other shore,

nor if souls walked along it, arms outstretched.
So many of them now on the other bank!

Then the old gentlemen at lunch in Lausanne
with suits of flawless cut, impeccable manners,
update of Rembrandt's *Syndics of the Drapers' Guild*.
I translated the pink, shaven faces of the Guild
to their dark-paneled and polished ancestry
of John the Baptist heads each borne on a saucer
of white lace, the loaded eyes, the thinning hair
over the white streaks of the foreheads, a syndicate
in which, far back, a negligible ancestor
might have been a member, greeting me
a product of his empire's miscegenation
in old Saint Martin. I could find no trace.
Built in huge gilt frames I sometimes found myself
loitering among the markets and canals;
but in Geneva though I felt hung and mounted
in sepia rooms with a glazed stare.
Immense and gray, with its invisible shore.
The weather sounded like its name: Lausanne.
Thought furred and felt like an alderman's collar,
a chocolate stick for the voracious fog.

Irradiating outwards from that gray lake,
that gray which is the hue of historical peace
Geneva was the color of a statesman's hair,
silvery and elegant and with a statesman's conscience,
banks and furled flags above the banks, and shoes
mirrored and quiet in deep-piled carpets.
The velvet, soft transactions of the world.
Stipple of farmhouse and fields, foothills dissolving
to lilac, violet shadows in the ridged furrows,
a spire slowly spinning away into Italy.

3

Blessed are the small farms conjugating Horace,
and the olive trees as twisted as Ovid's syntax,
Virgilian twilight on the hides of cattle
and the small turreted castles on the Tuscan slopes.
To live in another language with the swallow's wings:
chelidon beating over the rye, shadows on the barley,
between the peeling farms and the rusted poplars,
the bright air full of drunken insects,
the Pervigilium Veneris, Latin words leaping to life
as the train glides into dividing Florence.

Outside Firenze the hill offered itself,
erect-flame cypresses and an ochre castle
sepulchral towards evening, a star's first spark,
over the red-brown tiles of roofs through the olive grove,
dusk delicate as an old gentleman
with mottled hands and watery eyes, our host.
Diabetic, dying, my double.
And here again, a digit in Rome's bustle—
"Rome's bustle," a phrase as casual as a cape
tossed over the shoulder of a dimming pilgrim
in an obscure, anonymous altarpiece.

Those serene soft mountains, those tacit gorges—
that was Abruzzi. I remembered Abruzzi
from *A Farewell to Arms*, with the soft young priest
who invites Frederic Henry there after the war,
and perhaps Frederic Henry got there, whether or not,
here it was now, with small hill towns on the ridges,
where it could be infernally cold. The precise light

defined bright quarries. It looked incorruptible
as the faith of a young priest. Its paint still wet.
It spun past, saying, "You swore not to forget
fighting and the rattle of gunfire in the mountains."
Gone, without echo: Only the tight fine towns,
church tower or spire, the steep rust roofs
revolving slowly past the carriage window.

We drove through the wet sunlight into Pescara.
Wind folded the deckchairs on the esplanade,
slamming them shut. A detached, striped umbrella
somersaulted over the sand. A dishrag sky.
Then the weak sunshine strengthened steadily
and color came back into the sea's face.
The waitress moved among the afternoon tables
setting and straightening the dinner linen;
a girl with jet hair, black as her skirt, red mouth
and cheeks that were brightening now with the sun
and the drying sand. The sky grew Caribbean.
The breakers chumbling in from the Adriatic,
the folded beach umbrellas like a Chinese army
waiting for the drop of their Emperor's sword.
Through the dirty glass of the hotel in Pescara
a mixture of spume and grime, a quiet
like an armistice, the clink, like small weapons, of cutlery,
the rumors darkening like smoke over Albania,
the palms on the sea-front ceaselessly tossing,
the traffic with slow headlights inching through rain.
And O it was lovely coming through the mountains,
castles on the far crests, the flashing olives
and the halted infantry of the pines. All the wars
were over or far away. But the young woman on the bus
past whose beauty the pines, the olives and the small castles swept
in the clarified window, and whose sadness I thought
was like a holiday resort-town in the rain,

the lights of her gray eyes like glistening traffic
whose name, she told me, was a mountain flower's
but one that was quite common in her country,
spoke softly as the drizzle on Pescara's shore-front
of Serbia and its sorrow, of the horrors she had seen
on the sidewalks of Kosovo, and how it was, all war,
the fault of the Jews. Yet she said it with calm eyes.
I learnt this later. I learnt it from the drizzle
and the car lights of Pescara lancing the dark
and the folded umbrellas, quiet as banners
of the long brown hair that bracketed her face.
Leon. Yehuda. Joseph. The war was their fault.
But it was lovely coming through the mountains
that they said were the Apennines when I asked their names.

II

to Luigi Sampietro

The tidal motion of refugees, not the flight of wild geese,
the faces in freight cars, haggard and coal-eyed,
particularly the peaked stare of children,
the huge bundles crossing bridges, axles creaking
as if joints and bones were audible, the dark stain
spreading on maps whose shapes dissolve their frontiers
the way that corpses melt in a lime-pit or
the bright mulch of autumn is trampled into mud,
and the smoke of a cypress signals Sachsenhausen,
those without trains, without mules or horses,
those who have the rocking chair and the sewing machine
heaped on a human cart, a wagon without horses
for horses have long since galloped out of their field
back to the mythology of mercy, back to the cone

of the orange steeple piercing clouds over the lindens
and the stone bells of Sunday over the cobbles,
those who rest their hands on the sides of the carts
as if they were the flanks of mules, and the women
with flint faces, with glazed cheekbones, with eyes
the color of duck-ponds glazed over with ice,
for whom the year has only one season, one sky:
that of the rooks flapping like torn umbrellas,
all have been reduced into a common language,
the homeless, the province-less, to the incredible memory
of apples and clean streams, and the sound of milk
filling the summer churns, where are you from,
what was your district, I know that lake, I know the beer,
and its inns, I believed in its mountains,
now there is a monstrous map that is called Nowhere
and that is where we're all headed, behind it
there is a view called the Province of Mercy,
where the only government is that of the apples
and the only army the wide banners of barley
and its farms are simple, and that is the vision
that narrows in the irises and the dying
and the tired whom we leave in ditches
before they stiffen and their brows go cold
as the stones that have broken our shoes,
as the clouds that grow ashen so quickly after dawn
over palm and poplar, in the deceitful sunrise
of this, your new century.

III

O Serbian sibyl, prophetess
peering between your curtains of brown hair
(or these parentheses), if I were a Jew,
you'd see me shuffling on the cobblestones

of some unpronounceable city, you could watch
my body crumble, like the long, trembling ash
of a cigarette in the hand of a scholar
in a sidewalk restaurant, you beauty
who had the name of a common mountain flower
that hides in a cleft of the rocks
on the white-haired ridges of Albania.

IV

Among ragged palms and pastel balconies,
this miracle also happened in Pescara,
by accident, or by coincident stars.
In the hotel lobby of a forgotten name
as mine will be forgotten by another, I
who was reading a paperback of the life of Nora,
J. Joyce's wife, from which there is now a film,
with a photo of the actress on the cover,
a film at the film festival in that city
with its furrowed bay by a long esplanade,
met the black-haired Irish beauty playing her
and told her that and I showed her the book
to our mutual astonishment, also her friend's
another young Irishwoman with red hair,
her beauty's guardian, I guessed, and I made
of this something more; oracular
and fated, although all it meant
was that we were both here at the festival,
but it was more. Perhaps. I liked to believe
that she was Nora, and not that I was Joyce,
but to be reading the paper with her picture
in the basic, salty furniture of the lobby
while the seaside light made her skin manifest
with Irishness, with none of Nora's fairness

but with her accent, seemed to me a miracle
of which as evidence of that epiphany
while the rain stopped on the shining esplanade,
I have in her warm hand untouched by fame,
like the scrawl of seaweed on unprinted strand,
the lilting whisper of her signature.

4

I

O Genoan, I come as the last line of where you began,
to the port whose wharf holds long shadows and silence,
under the weeds of the prow, nodding and riding with
the wavering map of America. Droplets of oil
conjugate themselves into rainbows, the greased rag
blurs the portholes and the moorings sway
until Genoa glides past, a fog of spires
absorbing the gull's return. Hands close like wings
in the aisles of the cathedral. The palms close
and the psalms and the choir's O
widens and deepens in the wave's trough,
in the interminable metronome, grave and cradle,
until over the crest there is a fresher crest,
against preliminary reefs, the surf's exploding light!
Lice sing in the timber and the sponges open.

Seaside hotels with their salt balconies
whose iron flowers rust with artifice
facing the pompous, cavernous railway station
utilitarian monument of the Fascists;
down the serrated summer coast from Nice
to Genoa, the sea's tinfoil striations
are close to home. The cedar's agitation
repeats the rustling of reversible almonds,
the cheek warmed by a freshly ironed sky;
scent of scorched grass, and, through the limp leaves—
the Mediterranean doing its laundry.
Then somewhere, from the window of your eye,
a flag lifts a corner of the afternoon,
as an iron swarm of Vespas hurtles by

and the Discoverer's statue fades round the turn.
All these remembered women melt into one,
when my small words, like sails, must leave their haven:
the cliffs of shoulders burnt brown by the sun,
and wild jet hair, the banner of the raven.

In Genoa I loved our balcony. Below me,
the white stone statue of the Admiral
kept quiet in the navigating traffic,
the open gate to the Mediterranean, the sea—
with the same swell that heaved the caravel's sigh
at the remorseful future that lay ahead—
in the stone-flagged park close to the railway station.
Conglomerate masonry, shaft-light on brick
in the old Quarter, squeaking pulleys
lifting the sails of laundry across the gulf
of inconsolable alleys, the pigeon's dandruff
powdering the hair and shoulders of creased statues
who forget what they were famous for—
the whitewashed Admiral also. There is no rest for
the insomnia of sculptures, the snow's nightmare,
the smell of history I carry in my clothes
like smoke, the smell of a washed street in Pescara,
the sun-on-stone smell of the hills of Tuscany,
flowers in the weed between the rocks, wild flowers
the train passing their hosannas on the slopes,
and the soul, in exile, sliding into its station—
into History, the Muse of shutters and cabinets,
past the closed cathedral of the gramophone.

II

Envy of statues; this is how it grew:
every day in Milan, en route to class,

I passed my rigid, immortal friend, the General,
on his morose green horse, still there on weekends.
The wars were over but he would not dismount.
Had he died, catapulted in some charge
in some euphonious battle? The bronze charger
was lathered, streaked with sweat, in the summer sun.
We had no such memorials on the island.
Our only cavalry were the charging waves,
pluming with spume, and tossing plunging necks.
Who knows what war he fought in and whose shot
tumbled his whinnying steed? Envy of fountains.
Poor hero on his island in the swirl of traffic,
denied the solace of an umbrageous linden
or chestnut with bright medals through its leaves.
Envy of columns. Calm. Envy of bells.
Peace widened the Sunday avenue in Milan.

Left-handed light at morning on the square,
the Duomo with long shadows where clamoring bells
shake exaltation from blue, virginal air,
squaring off corners, de Chirico parallels—
and where the soundlessly snorting, big-balled horse
whose head, lowered and drooping, means the death
of its rider, holds a far longer breath, longer
than ours in our traffic island.
The widening love of Italy growing stronger
against my will with sunlight in Milan . . .
For we still expect presences, no matter where—
to sit again at a table watching the luminous clatter
of the great mall in Milan; there! was that him,
Joseph in an olive raincoat, like a leaf
on a clear stream with a crowd of leaves
from the edge to the center and sinking into them?

Absence's emblem, the solid specter of your grief,
yes, you can still see his tonsure, his ascetic halo,
till somewhere bars it, a hat or a sign, then
the mall fills with phantoms serenely hurrying
to the same exit the arched doorways of a sunlight
almost celestial, I silently shout their names
but I am inaudible, to them, since they outnumber me,
to them I am the phantom and they are the real ones,
their names still claiming them over the noise
of waiters clearing the tables of their possessions,
of the crumbs of bread and the glasses of recent blood
still clouded with their one breath, the breath
that I too will leave in a water-glass to condense
when I join them following the pale tonsure
of a moon that fades into the glare of the dawn
outside the intricate and immense cathedral
and our terrestrial traffic; the changing light.
Within the circumference of the cathedral
and its immense and bustling piazza
and a long mall of cafés and shops, I saw him,
because I needed to; because a lengthening absence
requires its apparition, lost, then returned again
by the frothing crowd, I was not ready
for the stone-webbed and incantation-hallowed
intricacies of the altars, an architecture
like frozen fury, demanding a surrendering awe.

I wanted to be able to write: "There is nothing like it,
to walk down the Via Veneto before sunrise."
And now, you think: he is going to describe it.

I am going to describe the benediction of June,
the gray cool spring air, its edges at *prima luce*,
too early for coffee from the hotel
and from the locked grids of last night's cafés,
the dew as wet as Pescara's the year before,
and the canvas umbrellas folded in their scabbards,
the reason being the difference in travel-time,
the difference being the night clerk yawning at the end
of his vigil, and the surly, early waiter,
then the long, unechoing empty street
that isn't as quiet as he had imagined,
with traffic building, the spiky palms
outside the American Embassy and two policemen
because of the threat of terrorists, the huge trees
against the pale buildings, the banks and arches
with their dirty flags; the lights still on
in certain buildings as the widening light
palely washed their façades, but the stillness
exactly like Gros Ilet's, the sea and the village,
if not the vermilion buses under the trees
their lights still on, there, here it comes, the light
out of pearl, out of Piero della Francesca,
(you could tell he would mention a painter),
then slowly the whole fresco with the spring's gold
on Ministerio del Lavoro e delle Politiche Sociali
at whose gate a man came out and examined me
as I copied the name down, a bald young man
in an orange windbreaker who scowled
because of my color and the terrorists,
and because my village was unimportantly beautiful
unlike his city and the Via Veneto,
its curved façades gamboge and ochre, gray stone,
the unnamed trees forming a gentle tunnel
over the buses, their lamps now out, vermilion, orange,
and what was missing was the smell of the sea

in the early morning on the small embankment,
but the palms as still in the dawn's docile tissue
Bus No. 63 L 90 Pugliese
whereas no echo in the name Gros Ilet,
no literature, no history, at least until now.
Bus 116, lights on. On the Via Veneto.
Glides, like a fish, softly, or a turning leaf.
I lived in two villages: Greenwich and Gros Ilet,
and loved both almost equally. One had the sea,
gray morning light along the waking water,
the other a great river, and if they asked
what country I was from I'd say, "The light
of that tree-lined sunrise down the Via Veneto."

9

I lay on the bed near the balcony in Guadalajara
and watched the afternoon wind stiffen the leaves.
Later: dusty fields under parched lilac mountains
and clumps of what must have been eucalyptus
by the peeling skin of their barks. I saw your face,
I saw your flesh in theirs, my suffering brother;
jacaranda over the streets, all looking broken,
as if all Mexico had this film of dust,
and between trees dotting the plain, fog,
thick as your clogged breath, shrouding the ranges
of, possibly, Santa de Something. I read this.
March 11. 8:35 a.m. Guadalajara, Saturday.
Roddy. Toronto. Cremated today.
The streets and trees of Mexico covered with ash.
Your soul, my twin, keeps fluttering in my head,
a hummingbird, bewildered by the rafters,
barred by a pane that shows a lucent heaven.
The maid sings behind the house,
with wooden clips in her teeth,
she rips down laundry like an avenging angel
and the hillside surges, sailing. Roddy.
Where are you this bright afternoon? I
am watching a soccer match listlessly
on TV, as you did sunk deep in the socket of the sofa,
your head shrunken, your eyes wet
and every exchange an ordeal.

II

I carry a small white city in my head,
one with its avenues of withered flowers,
with no sound of traffic but the surf,
no lights at dusk on the short street
where my brother and our mother live now
at the one address, so many are their neighbors!
Make room for the accommodation of the dead,
their mounds that multiply by the furrowing sea,
not in the torch-lit catacombs of your head
but by the almond-bright, spume-blown cemetery.
What was our war, veteran of threescore years and ten?
To save the salt light of the island
to protect and exalt its small people
to sit enthroned to a clicking scissors
watching the hot road and the blue flowers across it
and behind the hedge soft blue mountains
and the barber with the face of a boxer
say one who loves his craft more than a victory
not like that arrogantly tilted tailor of Moroni's
assessing you with the eyes of his scissors.

III

The day, with all its pain ahead, is yours.
The ceaseless creasing of the morning sea,
the fluttering gamboge cedar leaves allegro,
the rods of the yawing branches trolling the breeze,
the rusted meadows, the wind-whitened grass,
the coos of the stone-colored ground doves on the road,
the echo of benediction on a house—
its rooms of pain, its veranda of remorse

when joy lanced through its open-hearted doors
like a hummingbird out to the garden and the pool
in which the sky has fallen. These are all yours,
and pain has made them brighter as absence does
after a death, as the light heals the grass.
And the twig-brown lizard scuttles up its branch
like fingers on the struts of a guitar.
I hear the detonations of agave,
the stuttering outbursts of bougainvillea,
I see the acacia's bonfire, the begonia's bayonets,
and the tamarind's thorns and the broadsides of clouds from the
    calabash
and the cedars fluttering their white flags of surrender
and the flame trees' siege of the fort.
I saw black bulls, horns lowered, galloping, goring the mist
that rose, unshrouding the hillocks of Santa Cruz
and the olives of Esperanza,
Andalusian idyll, and answer
and the moon's blank tambourine
and the drizzle's guitars
and the sunlit wires of the rain
the shawls and the used stars
and the ruined fountains.

IV

When we were boys coming home from the beach,
it used to be such a thing! The body would be singing
with salt, the sunlight hummed through the skin
and a fierce thirst made iced water
a gasping benediction, and in the plated heat,
stones scorched the soles, and the cored dove hid
in the heat-limp leaves, and we left the sand
to its mutterings, and the long, cool canoes.

Threescore and ten plus one past our allotment,
in the morning mirror, the disassembled man.
And all the pieces that go to make me up—
the detached front tooth from a lower denture
the thick fog I cannot pierce without my glasses
the shot of pain from a kidney
these piercings of acute mortality.
And your wife, day and night,
assembling your accoutrements
to endure another day on the sofa,
bathrobe, glasses, teeth, because
your hands were leaves in a gust
when the leaves are huge-veined, desiccated,
incapable of protest or applause.
To cedars, to the sea that cannot change its tune,
on rain-washed morning what shall I say then
to the panes reflecting the wet trees and clouds
as if they were storefronts and offices, and
in what voice, since I now hear changing voices?
The change of light on a pink plaster wall
is the change of a culture—how the light is seen,
how it is steady and seasonless in these islands
as opposed to the doomed and mortal sun of midsummer
or in the tightening circle of shadow in the bullring.
This is how a people look at death
and write a literature of gliding transience
as the sun loses its sight, singing of islands.

Sunrise then, the uncontaminated cobalt
of sky and sea. The hours idle, and I,
watching the heaving plumes of the palmistes
in the afternoon wind, I hear the dead sighing
that they are still too cold in the ochre earth
in the sun's sadness, to the caterpillar's accordion
and the ancient courtship of the turtle-doves.

Yellow-billed egret balanced on a black bull
its sheen so ebony rust shines through the coat
as the bamboos translate the threshing of the olives
as the olives the bamboo's calligraphy
a silvery twitter of a flock of fledglings
stuttering for rain, wires of a drizzle,
tinfoil of the afternoon sea and the dove's bassoon.
The house on the hill opposite—
blond beams criss-cross their shadows on gray stone,
finical, full of false confidence, then
a surge of happiness, inexplicable content,
like the light on a golden garden outside Florence,
afternoon wind resilvering the olives
and the sea's doves, white sails
and the fresh elation of dolphins
over the staghorn coral.
Cartagena, Guadalajara,
whose streets, if one eavesdropped,
would speak their demotic Castilian
if dust had not powdered the eucalyptus with silences
on the iron balcony's parenthesis
and the Aztec mask of Mercedes
on the tip of the tongue like a sparrow
dipping into the pool
and flicking its tail like a signature, a name
like the fluttering of wings in a birdbath—
Santiago de Compostela!

v

In a swift receding year, one summer in Spain,
when the lamb-ribs were exquisitely roasted on a pine-fire
your eyes were its coals, your tongue its leaping flame,
my Iberian sibyl, touch-timid Esperanza.

A river roared from its dam, the pines were sprinkled
with its spume that brought boys' cries on the wind
drifting to our picnic and beyond the bank
was the brown spire of the cathedral
as a rose went out in the ashes
and the sunshine cooled and the wind had an edge
when a roar in the pines and the dam would blend
on the Saturday in Spain, in what receding year?

I

The dialect of the scrub in the dry season
withers the flow of English. Things burn for days
without translation, with the heat
of the scorched pastures and their skeletal cows.
Every noun is a stump with its roots showing,
and the creole language rushes like weeds
until the entire island is overrun,
then the rain begins to come in paragraphs
and hazes this page, hazes the gray of islets,
the gray of eyes, the rainstorm's wild-haired beauty.

The first daybreak of rain, the crusted drought
broken in half like bread, the quiet trumpet mouth
of a rainbow and the wiry drizzle fighting
decease, half the year blowing out to sea
in hale, refreshing gusts, the withered lilies
drink with grateful mouths, and the first blackbird
of the new season announces itself on a bough
the hummingbird is reglistened drilling
the pierced hedges, my small shaft to your heart,
my emerald arrow: A crowd crosses a bridge
from Canaries to the Ponte Vecchio, from
Piaille to Pescara, and a volley of blackbirds
fans over Venice or the broken pier of Choiseul,
and love is as wide as the span of my open palm
for frontiers that read like one country,
one map of affection that closes around my pen.
I had forgotten the benediction of rain
edged with sunlight, the prayers of dripping leaves
and the cat testing the edge of the season

with careful paw. And I have nothing more
to write about than gratitude. For *la mer,*
soleil-là, the bow of the *arc-en-ciel*
and the archery of blackbirds from its
radiant bow. The rest of the year is rain.

11

"There was a beautiful rain this morning."
"I was asleep."
         He stroked her forehead.
She smiled at him, then laughed as she kept yawning.
"It was lovely rain." But I thought of the dead
I know. The sun shone through the rain
and it was lovely.
         "I'm sure," she said.
There were so many names the rain recited:
Alan, Joseph and Claude and Charles and Roddy.
The sunlight came through the rain and the drizzle shone
as it had done before for everybody.
For John and Inge, Devindra and Hamilton.
"Blessed are the dead that the rain rains upon,"
wrote Edward Thomas. Her eyes closed in my arms,
but it was sleep. She was asleep again,
while the bright rain moved from Massade to Monchy.

Sometimes I stretch out, or you stretch out your hand,
and we lock palms; our criss-crossed histories join
and two maps fit. Bays, boundaries, rivers, roads,
one country, one warm island. Is that noise rain
on the hot roof, is it sweeping out to sea
by the stones and shells of the almond cemetery?

The road is wet, the leaves wet, but the sun inching,
and always the astonishment: in March?
This blustery, this gray? The waves chopping
and circling and ramming into one another
like sheep in a maddened pen from a whiff of wolf,
or white mares, bug-eyed from the lightning's whip,
and, if they could, whinnying. But the light will win.
The sun fought with the rain in the leaves and won;
then the rain came back and it was finer out to sea.
A drizzle blurred the promontories evenly
and now the manchineels and acacias sparkled
with the new rain and the cows' hides darkened
as the horses dipped their heads and shook their manes,
and over the horizon the faint arc
of an almost imperceptible bow appeared
then dimmed across the channel towards Martinique.
This miracle was usual for the season.
"The sun came out just for you," he said.
And it was true. The light entered her forehead
and blazoned her difference there.
The pastures were beaded, roofs shone on the hills,
a sloop was working its way against huge clouds
as patches of sunlight widened with a new zeal
towards detachment, towards simplicity.
Who said that they were lying side by side,
the cupped spoon of her torso in his own
in the striped shadows of midafternoon?

IV

The doors are open, the house breathes and I feel
a balm so heavy and a benediction

so weightless that the past is just blue air
and cobalt motion lanced with emerald
and sail-flecks and the dove's continuous complaint
about repletion, its swollen note of gratitude—
all incantation is the monody of thanks
to the sky's motionless or moving altars,
even to the faint drone of that silver insect
that is the morning plane over Martinique,
while, take this for what you will, the frangipani
that, for dry months, contorted, crucified
in impotence or barrenness, endured, has come
with pale pink petals and blades of olive leaves,
parable of my loin-longing, my silver age.

From the salt brightness of my balcony
I look across to the abandoned fort;
no History left, just natural history,
as a cloud's shadow subtilizes thought.
On a sloped meadow lifted by the light,
the Hessians spun like blossoms from the immortelle,
the tattered pennons of the sea-almond fluttered
to the spray-white detonations of the lilac
against blue the hue of a grenadier, dried pods
of the flamboyant rattle their sabers
and a mare's whinny across the parched pastures
launches white scuds of sails across the channel,
the race of a schooner launched in a canal.
A gray sky trawls its silver wires of rain;
these are the subtleties of the noon sea:
lime, emerald, lilac, cobalt, ultramarine.

12

1

Prodigal, what were your wanderings about?
The smoke of homecoming, the smoke of departure.
The earth grew music and the tubers sprouted
to Sesenne's singing, rain-water, fresh patois
in a clay carafe, a clear spring in the ferns,
and pure things took root like the sweet-potato vine.
Over the sea at dusk, an arrowing curlew,
as the sun turns into a cipher from a green flash,
clouds crumble like cities, the embers of Carthage;
any man without a history stands in nettles
and no butterflies console him, like surrendering flags,
does he, still a child, long for battles and castles
from the books of his beginning, in a hieratic language
he will never inherit, but one in which he writes
"Over the sea at dusk, an arrowing curlew,"
his whole life a language awaiting translation?

Since I am what I am, how was I made?
To ascribe complexion to the intellect
is not an insult, since it takes its plaid
like the invaluable lizard from its background,
and if our work is piebald mimicry
then virtue lies in its variety
to be adept. On the warm stones of Florence
I subtly alter to a Florentine
till the sun passes, in London
I am pierced by fog, and shaken from reflection
in Venice, a printed page in the sun
on which a cabbage-white unfolds, a bookmark.
To break through veils like spiders' webs,

crack carapaces like a day-moth and achieve
a clarified frenzy and feel the blood settle
like a brown afternoon stream in River Doree
is what I pulsed for in my brain and wrist
for the drifting benediction of a drizzle
drying on this page like asphalt, for peace that passes
like a changing cloud, to a hawk's slow pivot.

II

In the vale of Santa Cruz I look to the hills.
The white flowers have the fury of battle,
they lay siege to the mountains, for war
there is the tumult of the white ravines,
and the cascade's assault; they bow their plumes,
Queen Anne's lace, bougainvillea, orchid and oleander,
and they are as white as arrested avalanches,
angry and Alpine, their petals blur into
a white gust from the Matterhorn or the streets of Zermatt.
Both worlds are welded, they were seamed by delight.
Santa Cruz, in spring. Deep hills with blue clefts.
I have come back for the white egrets
feeding in a flock on the lawn, darting their bills
in that finical stride, gawkily elegant,
then suddenly but leisurely sailing
to settle, but not too far off, like angels.

III

I wake at sunrise to angelic screams.
And time is measuring my grandchildren's cries
and time outpaces the sepia water
of the racing creek, time takes its leisure, cunning

in the blocked hollows of the pool, the elephantine stones
in the leaf-marked lagoon, time sails
with the soundless buzzard over the smoking hills
and the clouds that fray and change
and time waits very quiet between the mountains
and the brown tracks in the valleys of the Northern Range,
a cover of overhanging bamboo, in Maraval
where, if the bed were steeper, a brown stream races
or tries to, pooling in rocks, with great avail
for me at least, or where a range's blues
and indigo over which wide hawks sail
their shadows on the wells of Santa Cruz,
dark benedictions on the brook's muttering shale,
and the horses are slowly plunging their manes
as they climb up from the paved-with-lilies pond,
so much mythology in their unharnessed necks!
These little things take root as I add my praise
to the huge lawn at the back of the house, a field,
a bright, unaltered meadow, a small savannah
for cries and bicycles and joy-crazed dogs
bolting after pedaling boys, the crescent ghost
of the new moon showing and on the thick slopes
this forest like green billowing smoke
pierced by the flame petals of the immortelle.

IV

Petals of the flame tree against ice-cream walls
and the arches across the park with its tacit fountain,
the old idlers on the benches, this is the prose
that spreads like the shade of an immortal banyan
in front of the library, the bulk that darkens
the violin of twilight when traffic has vanished
and nearly over also the colonial regime when the wharves

cradled the rocking schooners of our boyhood to
the echo of vespers in the alien cathedral.
In the hot green silence a dragonfly's drone
crossing the scorched hill to the shade of the cedars
and spiced laurels, the *lauriers canelles*,
the word itself lifting the plurals of its leaves,
from the hot ground, from this page, the singeing smells.
How simple to write this after you have gone,
that your death that afternoon had the same ease
as stopping at the side of the road under the trees
to buy cassava bread that comes in two sorts,
sweet and unsweetened, from the huge cauldron,
on the road between Soufrière and Canaries.
The heat collects in the depths between the ridges
and the high hawks circle in the gathering haze;
like consonants round a vowel, insistent midges
hum round a noun's hexagon, and the hornet's house.
Delve in the hot, still valley of Soufrière,
the black, baking asphalt and its hedges dripping shade
and here is the ultimate nullity despite the moil
of the churning vegetation. The small church
hidden in leaves. In midafternoon, the halt—
then dart of a quizzical lizard across the road.

1

Grass, bleached to straw on the precipice of Les Cayes,
running in the blue and green wind of the Trade,
a small church hidden in a grove past Soufriére,
hot dasheen and purpling pomme arac,
and heavy cattle in a pasture, and the repetition
of patois prayers by the shallows of Troumassee,
and there are still her eyes waiting for the small lights
that bring them to life, in which are reflected
the gold glints of labels in the Folies-Bergère bar
and the rust and orange of an April Glory cedar,
the leaves falling like curses from the *gommier maudit*,
a gull plucking fish from the shallows,
in the distance, the hump of a hazed mountain,
the ochreing meadows and the continuous cresting
of combers coming in, leaves spinning in the breeze
and the spray steadily spuming, the jets of bougainvillea,
all these must mold her cheekbones and a mouth
that says, "I come from Mon Repos," from Saltibus,
from the curve of the road entering Canaries
and from the white nights of an insomniac Atlantic
that toss on the reefs of Praslin, that made me.
O blessed pivot that makes me a palm!
A silent exclamation at the cliff's edge
around whom the horizon silently spins!
What thuds against the hull, butting with such force?
Angels are gliding underneath the keel.

Time, that gnaws at bronze lions and dolphins
that shrivels fountains, had exhausted him;
a cupola in Milan exhaled him like incense,
Abruzzi devoured him, Firenze spat him out,
Rome chewed his arm and flung it over her shoulder
for the rats in the catacombs; Rome took his empty eyes
from the sockets of the Colosseum. Italy ate him.
Its bats at vespers navigated her columns
with an ancient elation, a hand in San Marco's font
aspersed him with foul canal water, then bells
tossed their heads like bulls, and their joy
rattled the campaniles, as innumerable pigeons
settled on the square of his forehead, his kidneys
were served in a modest hotel in Pescara,
a fish mimicked his skeleton in salty Amalfi,
until after a while there was nothing left of him
except this: a name cut on a wall that soon
from the grime of indifference became indecipherable.

III

We were headed steadily into the open sea.
Immeasurable and unplummetable fathoms
too deep for sounding or for any anchor,
the waves quick-running, crests, we were between
the pale blue phantoms of Martinique and Saint Vincent
on the iron rim of the ringing horizon;
the farther we went out, the white bow drumming,
plunging and shearing spray, the wider my fear,
the whiter my spume-shot cowardice, as the peaks
receded, rooted on their separating world,
diminishing in the idea of home, but still the prow

pressed stubbornly through the gulfs and the helmsman
kept nodding in their direction through the glass
between the front deck and the wheel, their direction
meaning what we could not see but he knew was there
from talking on the radio to the other boat
that lay ahead of us towards which we plunged
and droned, a white slip of another smaller cruiser,
convinced by his smiling that we would breach them soon.
"Dolphins," the steersman said. "You will see them playing,"
but this was widening into mania, there were only
the crests that looked to their leaping, no fins,
no arching backs, no sudden frieze, no school today,
but the young captain kept on smiling, I had never
seen such belief in legend, and then, a fin-hint!
not a crest, and then splaying open under the keel
and racing with the bow, the legend broke water
and was reborn, her screams of joy
and my heart drumming harder, and the pale blue islands
were no longer phantom outlines, and the elate spray
slapped our faces with joy, and everything came
back as it was between the other islets, but
those with our own names, sometimes a fin
shot up, sometimes a back arched and reentered
the racily running waves under which they glanced,
I saw their wet brown bodies gunning seaward,
more brown than golden despite the name "dorado,"
but I guess in the wet light their skins shone
too raw, too quiet to be miraculous,
too strange to quiet my fear, the skittering fish
from the first line of the open page, held
and held until the school was lost, the prodigal's home
was the horizon while my own peaks
loomed so inconsolably again, the roads, the roofs
of Soufrière in the wet sunlight. I watched them come.

I had gaped in anticipation of an emblem
carved at a fountain's pediment from another sea
and when the dolphins showed up and I saw them
they arched the way thoughts rise from memory.
They shot out of the glacial swell like skiers
hurtling themselves out of that Alpine surf
with its own crests and plungings, spuming slopes
from which the dolphins seraphically soared
to the harps of ringing wires and humming ropes,
to which my heart clung and those finished hopes
that I would see you again, my twin, "my dolphin."
And yet elation drove the dolphins' course
as if both from and to you, their joy was ours.
And had there been a prophecy that said: "Wait!
On a day of great delight you will see dolphins."
Or, in the ashes and embers of a wrecked sunset
the same voice, falling as quietly as a flag, said,
before the constellations arranged their chaos,
"Those drifting cinders are angels, see how they soar,"
I would not have believed in them, being too old
and skeptical from the fury of one life's
determined benedictions, but they are here.
Angels and dolphins. The second, first.
And always certainly, steadily, on the bright rim
of the world, getting no nearer or nearer, the more
the bow's wedge shuddered towards it, prodigal,
that line of light that shines from the other shore.

FROM

White Egrets

(2010)

I

The chessmen are as rigid on their chessboard
as those life-sized terra-cotta warriors whose vows
to their emperor with bridle, shield and sword
were sworn by a chorus that has lost its voice;
no echo in that astonishing excavation.
Each soldier gave an oath, each gave his word
to die for his emperor, his clan, his nation,
to become a chess piece, breathlessly erect
in shade or crossing sunlight, without hours—
from clay to clay and odorlessly strict.
If vows were visible they might see ours
as changeless chessmen in the changing light
on the lawn outside where bannered breakers toss
and the palms gust with music that is time's
above the chessmen's silence. Motion brings loss.
A sable blackbird twitters in the limes.

Your two cats squat, heraldic sphinxes, with such
desert indifference, such "who-the-hell-are-you?" calm,
they rise and stride away leisurely from your touch,
waiting for you only. To be cradled in one arm,
belly turned upward to be stroked by a brush
tugging burrs from their fur, eyes slitted
in ecstasy. The January sun spreads its balm
on earth's upturned belly, shadows that have always fitted
their shapes, re-fit them. Breakers spread welcome.
Accept it. Watch how spray will burst
like a cat scrambling up the side of a wall,
gripping, sliding, surrendering; how, at first,
its claws hook then slip with a quickening fall
to the lace-rocked foam. That is the heart, coming home,
trying to fasten on everything it moved from,
how salted things only increase its thirst.

3

This was my early war, the bellowing quarrels,
at the pitch of noon, of men moving cargoes
while gulls screeched their monotonous vowels
in complex curses without coming to blows;
muscular men swirling codfish barrels
and heaving rice bags, who had stunted nicknames,
who could, one-handed, hoist phenomenal rolls
of wire, hoist flapping galvanize with both arms
to pitch it into the hold while hooks and winches
swung nearby. At lunch they ate in the shade
of mountainous freight bound with knots and cinches,
ignoring the gulls with their boulders of bread.
Then one would be terribly injured, one lose a leg
to rum and diabetes. You would watch him shrink
into his nickname, not too proud to beg,
who would roar like a lorry revving in the prime of his drink.

I

Cautious of time's light and how often it will allow
the morning shadows to lengthen across the lawn
the stalking egrets to wriggle their beaks and swallow
when you, not they, or you and they, are gone;
for clattering parrots to launch their fleet at sunrise
for April to ignite the African violet
in the drumming world that dampens your tired eyes
behind two clouding lenses, sunrise, sunset,
the quiet ravages of diabetes.
Accept it all with level sentences
with sculpted settlement that sets each stanza,
learn how the bright lawn puts up no defenses
against the egret's stabbing questions and the night's answer.

II

The elegance of those white, orange-billed egrets,
each like a stalking ewer, the thick olive trees,
cedars consoling a stream that roars torrentially
in the wet season; into that peace
beyond desires and beyond regrets,
at which I may arrive eventually,
whose palms droop in the sun like palanquins
with tigerish shadows under them. They shall
be there after my shadow passes with all its sins
into a green thicket of oblivion,
with the rising and setting of a hundred suns
over Santa Cruz Valley when I loved in vain.

III

I watch the huge trees tossing at the edge of the lawn
like a heaving sea without crests, the bamboos plunge
their necks like roped horses as yellow leaves, torn
from the whipping branches, turn to an avalanche;
all this before the rain scarily pours from the burst,
sodden canvas of the sky like a hopeless sail,
gusting in sheets and hazing the hills completely
as if the whole valley were a hull outriding the gale
and the woods were not trees but waves of a running sea.
When light cracks and thunder groans as if cursed
and you are safe in a dark house deep in Santa
Cruz, with the lights out, the current suddenly gone,
you think: "Who'll house the shivering hawk, and the
impeccable egret and the cloud-colored heron,
and the parrots who panic at the false fire of dawn?"

IV

These birds keep modeling for Audubon,
the Snowy Egret or White Heron in a book
that, in my youth, would open like a lawn
in emerald Santa Cruz, knowing how well they look,
strutting perfection. They speckle the islands
on river-bank, in mangrove marsh or cattle pasture,
gliding over ponds, then balancing on the ridge
of a silken heifer, or fleeing disaster
in hurricane weather, and picking ticks
with their electric stab as if it were sheer privilege
to study them in their mythical conceit
that they have beat across the sea from Egypt
with the pharaonic ibis, its orange beak and feet
profiled in quiet to adorn a crypt,

then launch themselves with wings that, beating faster
are certain as a seraph's when they beat.

V

The perpetual ideal is astonishment.
The cool green lawn, the quiet trees, the forest
on the hill there, then, the white gasp of an egret sent
sailing into the frame then teetering to rest
with its gawky stride, erect, an egret-emblem!
Another thought surprises: a hawk on the wrist
of a branch, soundlessly, like a falcon,
shoots into heaven, circling above praise or blame,
with the same high indifference as yours,
now dropping to tear a field mouse with its claws.
The page of the lawn and this open page are the same,
an egret astonishes the page, the high hawk caws
over a dead thing, a love that was pure punishment.

VI

I hadn't seen them for half of the Christmas week,
the egrets, and no one told me why they had gone,
but they are back with the rain now, orange beak,
pink shanks and stabbing head, back on the lawn
where they used to be in the clear, limitless rain
of the Santa Cruz Valley, which, when it rains, falls
steadily against the cedars till it mists the plain.
The egrets are the color of waterfalls,
and of clouds. Some friends, the few I have left,
are dying, but the egrets stalk through the rain
as if nothing mortal can affect them, or they lift
like abrupt angels, sail, then settle again.

Sometimes the hills themselves disappear
like friends, slowly, but I am happier
that they have come back now, like memory, like prayer.

VII

With the leisure of a leaf falling in the forest,
pale yellow spinning against green—my ending.
Soon it will be the dry season, the hills will rust,
the egrets dip their necks undulant, bending,
stabbing at worms and grubs after the rain,
sometimes erect as bowling pins, they stand
as strips of cotton-wool peel from the mountain,
then when they move, gawkily, they move this hand
with their feet's splayed fingers, their darting necks.
We share one instinct, that ravenous feeding
my pen's beak, plucking up wriggling insects
like nouns and gulping them, the nib reading
as it writes, shaking off angrily what its beak rejects,
selection is what the egrets teach
on the wide-open lawn, heads nodding as they read
in purposeful silence, a language beyond speech.

VIII

We were by the pool of a friend's house in St. Croix
and Joseph and I were talking; he stopped the talk,
on this visit I had hoped that he would enjoy
to point out, with a gasp, not still or stalking
but fixed in the great fruit tree, a sight that shook him
"like something out of Bosch," he said. The huge bird was
suddenly there, perhaps the same one that took him,
a sepulchral egret or heron; the unutterable word was

always with us, like Eumaeus, a third companion
and what got him, who loved snow, what brought it on
was that the bird was such a spectral white.
Now when at noon or evening on the lawn
the egrets soar together in noiseless flight
or tack, like a regatta, the sea-green grass,
they are seraphic souls, as Joseph was.

I

You used to be able to drive (though I don't) across
the wide, pool-sheeted pasture below the house
to the hot, empty beach and park in the starved shade
of the acacias that print those tiny yellow flowers
(blank, printless beaches are part of my trade);
then there were men with tapes and theodolites who measured
the wild, uneven ground. I watched the doomed acres
where yet another luxury hotel will be built
with ordinary people fenced out. The new makers
of our history profit without guilt
and are, in fact, prophets of a policy
that will make the island a mall, and the breakers
grin like waiters, like taxi drivers, these new plantations
by the sea; a slavery without chains, with no blood spilt—
just chain-link fences and signs, the new degradations.
I felt such freedom writing under the acacias.

II

Bossman, if you look in those bush there, you'll find
a whole set of passport, wallet, ID, credit card,
that is no use to them, is money on their mind
and is not every time you'll find them afterwards.
You jest leave your bag wif these things on the sand,
and faster than wind they jump out of the bush
while you there swimming and rubbing tanning lotion
and when you find out it is no good to send
the Special Unit, they done reach Massade.
But I not in that, not me, I does make a lickle

change selling and blowing conch shells, is sad
but is true. Dem faster than any vehicle,
and I self never get in any commotion
except with the waves, and soon all that will be lost.
Is too much tourist and too lickle employment.
How about a lickle life there? Thanks, but Boss,
don't let what I say spoil your enjoyment.

III

You see those breakers coming around Pigeon Island
bowing like nuns in a procession? One thing I know,
when you're gone like my other friends, not to Thailand
or Russia, but wherever it is loved friends go
with their different beliefs, who were like a flock
of seagulls leaving the mirror of the sand,
or a bittern passing lonely Barrel of Beef,
or the sails that an egret hoists leaving its rock;
I go down to the same sea by another road
with manchineel shadows and stunted sea grapes
dwarfed by the wind. I carry something to read:
the wind is bright and shadows race like grief,
I open their books and see their distant shapes
approaching and always arriving, their voices heard
in the page of a cloud, like the soft surf in my head.

6

for August Wilson

August, the quarter-moon dangles like a bugle
over the brick cantonments of the Morne
whose barrack apartments have the serial glow
of postage stamps; the clouds' letters are torn,
and your sweet instrument is put away as
your silver cornet lies in its velvet case
with all those riffs and arias whose characters argue
the way that wind elates the acacias
until they wrestle with the roar of torrents,
black, jagged silhouettes ready to do battle
with enormous hands and eyes with the coming day
in the brick thickets of Pittsburgh and Seattle,
in plays that are their own battle cry and anthem,
I unhook the quarter-moon to blow their praises,
you, Horace Pippin, Romare, Jacob Lawrence,
I saw the moon's bugle there and thought of them.

7

for Oliver Jackman

It's what others do, not us, die, even the closest
on a vainglorious, glorious morning, as the song goes,
the yellow or golden palms glorious and all the rest
a sparkling splendor, die. They're practicing calypsos,
they're putting up and pulling down tents, vendors are slicing
the heads of coconuts around the Savannah, men
are leaning on, then leaping into pirogues, a moon will be rising
tonight in the same place over Morne Coco, then
the full grief will hit me and my heart will toss
like a horse's head or a threshing bamboo grove
that even you could be part of the increasing loss
that is the daily dial of the revolving shade. Love
lies underneath it all though, the more surprising
the death, the deeper the love, the tougher the life.
The pain is over, feathers close your eyelids, Oliver.
What a happy friend and what a fine wife!
Your death is like our friendship beginning over.

I

Like a blackbird that shot out of the daylight
into the benign gloom of the studio, butting the glass,
fluttering and darting then thudding it again,
as if it were searching for a cage that calms
like my mind with its pitiful searching for an exit
from itself, and thinking these days of Pavese,
of a flight from you (who would have thought your shadow
could have been so solid?) that I would easily
like the trapped bird keep butting the wall of your forehead
till you let me fly through the window of your gaze
past Pigeon Island to Isola (to sacred Sicily)
from the opening parenthesis of your palms.

II

I am haunted by hedges of pink oleander
along the Sicilian roads, their consonants of gravel
under the tires, by stone piles, by walls whose wonder
is that there was no need to travel
this far, to recognize things I already knew,
except, and now it grows, the odd broken castle
through whose doors peered a Caribbean blue,
and the name Ortigia that rings like crystal
in its fragile balance. In the pine's rustle
and the silver alder's and the olive's, a difference began,
sounds that needed translation. The sea was the same
except for its history. The island was our patron saint's
birthplace. They shared the same name:
Lucia. The heat had the identical innocence

of an island afternoon, but with a difference,
the way the oleanders looked and the olive's green flame.

III

Soothe me, Vittorio, calm me, Quasimodo,
bless me with your clasped palms, cypress, and syllables
of the trimmed orange oleander on Somebody Street.
Screech my pain, starlings, from the stone balcony
that faces the Saracen coast, blind me, Santa Lucia,
patron saint of both isles and eyes, for my lack of vision!
There was a prophecy repeated in her smallest gestures
to the madness of an old man who loved a brown faun
that grazed on his heart even in drought.
All of you, save him! Save his clogged heart
like a tree thick with prayers like the starlings
repeating their verses from the barred windows
of Passeggio Adorno, vowing a new start,
as he watches the transients hunched over the duck pond
that was Arethusa's fountain, tomorrow, tomorrow.
All of those people and their lucky lives.
I know what I've done, I cannot look beyond.
I treated all of them badly, my three wives.

IV

On the cathedral steps sprinkled by the bells' benediction
like water that blissfully stained the scorching street,
you were not among the small crowd in the sun,
so many in black against the Sicilian heat.
I never entered the shaded church with its pews
facing the tortured altar, but I hoped to find you:
Oh, I did, half-heartedly, but by now it was no use.

The bells meant nothing or the swallows they lifted;
still I felt you were ahead and I was right behind you,
and that you would stop on your shadow and turn your head,
and there in Sicily turn into salt, into fiction.
I don't know the cathedral's name. It's in Syracuse.
I bought a paper in a language I cannot read.
There was nothing in the paper about this. It wasn't news.

v

We never know what memory will do—
my body humming with so much excitement,
I thought my heartbeat sprouted wings and flew
to Syracuse, your harbor, that its flight meant
a return to Sicily and all its sunlit error
where a Greek tanker lay anchored in the blue;
my shadowy treachery, my columned patience
darted through balconies to the gusting area
of the bandstand facing the Bay of the Saracens.
Translucent ghosts, performing without shadows
silhouettes of black actors, shapes on a vase,
their quarrels caught in an oval, while what she does
in those fierce days still beats across my face
like a startled branch or a dove or some other bird's.
My memory's nostrils prick at these odors,
of burnt concrete, or tar, the smell of words
drying like kelp in a rock-pool to a door's
hinges opening like a heart. Gulls rise
like screeching gossips past the hotel windows
as a bosoming wave unbuttons her white bodice.

VI

There never really was a "we" or "ours";
whatever each enjoyed was separate:
a drizzle's drift, the slant of arrowing showers
on a hot road, on roofs, made them elate,
but with a joy defined by separation—
the languor of a glittering afternoon
when a bay's bowl is full of glittering coins,
or a white road is paved by the full moon,
the same delight that separates them joins
without conversion, but close to happiness
in accidental gusts that made the leaves
agree unanimously with one green yes,
yet made a dark division of their lives.
The clouds shone altar-white on moonlit nights;
he was the stubborn, sacrificial victim
of his own hopes, like fireflies whose lights
are like false stars that, with the daylight, dim.

VII

There was no "affair," it was all one-sided.
Bats fretted the treetops then pitched like darts
from the pines. At lunch an invisible presence presided
over the wines and salads as, in fits and starts,
a sinuous organ sobbed to the Bay of the Saracens
flecked with gulls' feathers or the sails of yachts,
yet balance and perfection made no sense.
By the open-air table where I sat alone
a flock of chattering girls passed, premature sirens
fleeing like pipers from the sudden thought of a stone.
Emerald ducks paddled and stabbed their bills
in the cool dark well sacred to Arethusa.

I wondered in the inching sun how it was known
to the ferry's horn, the pines, the Bay's azure hills
and the jeering screaming girls that I would lose her
or an accordion's meandering sob and moan
through the coiled, serpentine alleys of Siracusa.

VIII

How come, despite all this, you never mention old age,
you grizzled satyr with your bristling sea urchin beard,
and a head grown almost as white as this page,
as white cedar flowers shake from the *gommier maudit*,
the cursed cedar, like vowels from your pen? Why?
I'll tell you what they think: you're too old to be
shaken by such a lissom young woman, to need her
in spite of your scarred trunk and trembling hand,
your head rustles with thoughts of her like the cedar
in March, you blaze in her praise like a sea-almond,
the crab scrawls your letters then hides them,
certain that she would never understand.
How boring the love of others is, isn't it, Reader?
This page, touched by the sun's declining arc,
sighs with the same whinge, the Sonnets and Petrarch.

IX

What if all this passion is out of proportion to its subject?
An average beauty, magnified to deific, demonic
stature by the fury of intellect,
a flat-faced girl with slanted eyes and a narrow
waist, and a country lilt to her voice,
that she should infect your day to the very marrow,
to hate the common light and its simple joys?

Where does this sickness come from, because it is
sickness, this conversion of the simplest action
to an ordeal, this hatred of simple delight
in others, of benches in the empty park?
Only her suffering will bring you satisfaction,
old man in the dimming world, only joy is the mark
and silence in the stricken streets where no dogs bark.
I watch them accumulating my errors
steadily repeated as the waves as the sea's
decline, and shadows on the high terrace
facing Syracuse; cafés flare in the dark.

  x

Why does she precede every journey, waiting by
the side of the road, sometimes, sometimes under
a flowering tree, seated on a culvert, stubbornly
wearing the same dress, as close or far as thunder
curling up a mountain? See the mat of sunlight
under that cedar? There she is! Look how the hedges
above Recanati blaze like a line of verse,
or how the palm or the pine tree blazon their edges
above where she waits in the dusk, lifting no arm
in greeting, her gaze looking through you.
How did she know where I was going, so calm
in her unacknowledging patience, the fringe
of her russet locks as her figure recedes
towards our inevitable meeting? She can singe
my memory in advance, so I go where she leads.

XI

So the moths came, responding to invitations
to my beloved's funeral, she whom I had killed
with my caustic jealousy, my commonplace love-hatred,
my pathetic patience, my impotent impatience,
my infatuation or whatever it's called;
and a cortège of caterpillars too gaily dressed for such
a solemn occasion adding some gaiety to it
and the usual fanning lighthearted butterflies who have never
taken any death seriously, then also, an
anachronistic blackbird in a frock coat and Homburg
representing some ministry, undoubtedly Culture,
then a white guy I didn't know, some *l'autre boug*,
then the usual, stooping ecumenical vulture
who pressed his card on me. All of them had known her,
then a patient deputation of worms. All sympathized
but all hoped, like me, that I had outgrown her,
all knew how much her beauty had been prized.

for Paola

I

The day, gray. The mood: slate. Too overcast to swim,
unless a strong sun emerges; which it may.
Our hands, like ants, keep building libraries, storing leaves
and riddling parchment; our books are tombstones, every
    poem a hymn.
And that honey-natured, gifted Italian girl
gone from the leaves of *Poesia*, gone from the wet stones
of Rimini as the ants keep scribbling, the crabs keep
    scuttering, and
the tombstones thicken. She was one of the lovely ones,
lovely in laughter, musical in speech,
so gentle in disposition! Vanished like drying sand,
like the fast shadow of the wind on a sunlit beach,
a crab halts and then continues. Like this ant; this hand.

II

He had seemed negligible but her death
afflicted him with wisdom; now he acquired
authority from pain; you could hear his breath
and the littlest gesture he made was profoundly tired.
Maybe that was what she left him, a strange,
angry diffidence beyond his surrender
and a devotion deeper than his work desired,
for a beauty that had seemed so out of range
of the dull cannon thud that would send her
sprawling on the bedroom carpet; more so
than being merely a widower; they were to be married.

Now she lay white as tousled marble, the classical torso
of a goddess whose brief visit delighted earth.

III

The pine flung its net to snare the evening swallows
back to its branches, their flight was brief as bats',
the yachts lit up and brought Siracusa close,
a broken music drifted from the ferry boats.
At dusk the soul rocks in its homesickness,
in the orange hour its silhouette is a palm
spiky as a sea urchin against the sky
beginning to pulse with stars, the open psalm
of a huge cloud slowly absorbed its dye.
Swifts practiced their archery and the day's fire
roared over Carthage, over Alexandria,
all of the cities were embers in the sun's empire,
and the night in its blindness would choose a
girl with greater vision, Santa Lucia,
patroness of palm and pine tree whose
alphabet was the swallows of Syracuse.

for Giuseppe Cicchelero

IV

Roads shouldered by enclosing walls with narrow
cobbled tracks for streets, those hill towns with their
stamp-sized squares and a sea pinned by the arrow
of a quivering horizon, with names that never wither
for centuries and shadows that are the dial of time. Light
older than wine and a cloud like a tablecloth
spread for lunch under the leaves. I have come this late

to Italy, but better now, perhaps, than in youth
that is never satisfied, whose joys are treacherous,
while my hair rhymes with those far crests, and the bells
of the hilltop towers number my errors,
because we are never where we are, but somewhere else,
even in Italy. This is the bearable truth
of old age; but count your benedictions: those fields
of sunflowers, the torn light on the hills, the haze
of the unheard Adriatic, while the day still hopes
for possibility, cloud shadows racing the slopes.

V

Those hillsides ridged with ramparts and bell towers,
the crests of olives, those wheat-harvested slopes
through glittering aspens, those meadows of sunflower
with luncheon napkins like the miters of popes,
lanes with long shadows, wide-open retreats
guarded by leaping cypresses, shade-splashed ochre
walls, then the towns themselves with streets
as close as chain-mail, named after some mediocre
saint, coiling as one road down to the hazed sea.
All of those little ports, all named for saints,
redeem the sadness that was Sicily
and the stupidity of innocence.
It is like Sicilian light but not the same
sun or my shadow, a bitterness like a loss.
Drink of its bitterness to forget her name,
that is the mercy oblivion allows.

VI

The blue windows, the lemon-colored counterpane,
the knowing that the sea is behind the avenue

with balconies and bicycles, that the gelid traffic
mixes its fumes with coffee-transient interiors,
transient bedsheets, and the transient view
of sea-salted hotels with spiky palms,
in spite of which summer is serious,
since there is inevitably a farewell to arms:
to the storm-haired beauty who will disappear.
The shifted absence of your axis, love
wobbles on your body's pivot, to the carriage's
shudder as it glides past the roofs and beaches
of the Ligurian coast. Things lose their balance
and totter from the small blows of memory.
You wait for revelations, for leaping dolphins,
for nightingales to loosen their knotted throats,
for the bell in the tower to absolve your sins
like the furled sails of the homecoming boats.

VII

As your red hair moved through Leopardi's house,
it was with its modest, flameless fire, Maria.
We toured its rooms in awe of such suffering, whose
stairs constricted its walls, whose climbing aria
was Silvia and solitude; under dark beams,
passing bound volumes in funereal file,
we heard of the great poet's crippled dreams
from our Caravaggio guide and her white smile.
You seemed wrong for the crowd: separate, distinct,
you belonged to the spring-freckled hills outside
Recanati. Your pert, tanned body wrinkled
under its floral print, your look said:
"Why must they feel that love is a great sorrow?
Don't sparrows dart with joy around this house,
though more lugubrious pilgrims come tomorrow?"

Then I looked from the window of his house
and saw, assembled in the little square,
knights ranked to serve the banner of red hair,
their halberds raised, on half a hundred horse.

VIII

Also in Italy I'd never seen anywhere quite
like it—these squares of harvested wheat, panels of
a green crop, maybe corn, tilled hills in rolling light,
dotted with olive and the cypress that I love,
a bleached river-bed and fields of always surprising
sunflowers around Urbino, like nothing I had read,
small hills gently declining then gently rising,
and above the rushing asphalt the window said:
"You have seen Umbria, admired Tuscany,
and gaped at the width of the harbor at Genoa,
now I show you an open secret, do you know any
landscape as lovely as this, do you know a
drive as blest as this one?" I said: "Monterey.
We stopped the car, too, to take in the light,
the breakers, juniper, pine, and the unfolding skies
of the coast. If the grain flung by the sower
in the card brings such astonishment, such a sure
harvest, I have seen them with my own eyes."

IX

Even this far now from that compact, modest hotel,
white walls of summer, tinkle of the ice-cream cart,
baking bicycle path and mineral-water bottle,
another beach postcard stamps itself on my heart;
even this far, weeks later, the itch of sand,

the Adriatic sticks to my back, plating it
with graying salt, bringing irascible mothers and
their rubber-bright children and hating it
at first, the rented chairs, while a hundred
identical iron umbrellas emphasize the size
of the holiday coast and the invincible dread
of families, where each shadow is an oasis,
and vanilla-colored girls rub cream on their thighs
in an advertisement Italy, a plastic happiness
that brought actual content. In the cool lobby,
the elderly idle. I was now one of them.
Studying the slow, humped tourists was my only hobby,
racked now by a whimsical bladder and terrible phlegm.

x

I am astonished at the sunflowers spinning
in huge green meadows above the indigo sea,
amazed at their aureate silence, though they sing
with the inaudible hum of the clocks over Recanati.
Do they turn to face the dusk, just as an army
might obey the last orders of a sinking empire,
their wheels stuck in one rut before the small studs
of stars and the fireflies' meandering fire,
then droop like exhausted meteors in soft thuds
to the earth? In our life elsewhere, sunflowers
come singly but in this coastal province
there can be entire fields of their temporal powers
spread like the cloak of some Renaissance prince,
their banners will wilt, their gold helms fill the void;
they are poems we recite to ourselves, metaphors
of our brief glory, a light we cannot avoid
that was called heaven in Blake's time, but not since.

XI

If all these words were different-colored pebbles,
with little pools that the blue heron might drink from,
a mosaic sheeted and glazed by the vanishing bubbles
of the shallows, and bannered waves marching to the sea's drum
if they were more than black marks on white paper,
and sounds that our eyes make upon their meeting,
they would be all yours, since you are the shaper
of the instant's whim, yours is the steady greeting
of the ground dove in the grove, the net that is hurled
over the wobbling stone bed of the inlet,
and yours is the shell in which an ear is curled
or a praying fetus, prophecy and regret.
Here on the blazing instance of an afternoon, the tiring
heart is happy, the hot sea crinkles like tin,
in the tide pools the black rocks are firing
their usual volleys of mullet in their clear basin;
this is the stillness and heat of a secret place,
where what shapes itself in a rock-pool is a girl's face.

XII

Over and over I will praise the light that ranges
over a terra-cotta wall in Naples, in the ungraspable dusk
that makes every corner flare with the lilacs and oranges
of an amateur painter, praise lurid Venice with its disc
dissolving in the Grand Canal when an inaudible
gunshot scatters the pigeons although Roberta says
that their flocks are now an official nuisance, and no sibyl
or Doge can save them, no statue with her lifted arm,
or will they settle again and a Canaletto calm
return to the shining lagoon, to Santa Maria della Salute,

dusk rippling the water with accordion strokes,
from a god striking his trident? I hear the widening sound
under the rattle of vaporettos past handiworks
of lace that, as you warp nearer, turn into stone:
turn into stone, cherished one, my carved beauty
who makes drowsing lions yawn and bronze stallions frisk.

for Roberta

I

And then there was no more Empire all of a sudden.
Its victories were air, its dominions dirt:
Burma, Canada, Egypt, Africa, India, the Sudan.
The map that had seeped its stain on a schoolboy's shirt
like red ink on a blotter, battles, long sieges.
Dhows and feluccas, hill stations, outposts, flags
fluttering down in the dusk, their golden aegis
went out with the sun, the last gleam on a great crag,
with tiger-eyed turbaned Sikhs, pennons of the Raj
to a sobbing bugle. I see it all come about
again, the tasseled cortège, the clop of the tossing team
with funeral pom-poms, the sergeant major's shout,
the stamp of boots, then the volley; there is no greater theme
than this chasm-deep surrendering of power
the whited eyes and robes of surrendering hordes,
red tunics, and the great names Sind, Turkistan, Cawnpore,
dust-dervishes and the Saharan silence afterwards.

II

A dragonfly's biplane settles and there, on the map,
the archipelago looks as if a continent fell
and scattered into fragments; from Pointe du Cap
to Moule à Chique, *bois-canot, laurier cannelles,*
canoe-wood, spicy laurel, the wind-churned trees
echo the African crests; at night, the stars
are far fishermen's fires, not glittering cities,
Genoa, Milan, London, Madrid, Paris,
but crab-hunters' torches. This small place produces

nothing but beauty, the wind-warped trees, the breakers
on the Dennery cliffs, and the wild light that loosens
a galloping mare on the plain of Vieuxfort make us
merely receiving vessels of each day's grace,
light simplifies us whatever our race or gifts.
I'm content as Kavanagh with his few acres;
for my heart to be torn to shreds like the sea's lace,
to see how its wings catch color when a gull lifts.

I

Down the Conradian docks of the rusted port,
by gnarled sea grapes whose plates are caked with grime,
to a salvo of flame trees from the old English fort,
he waits, the white specter of another time,
or stands, propping the entrance of some hovel
of a rumshop, to slip into the streets
like the bookmark in a nineteenth-century novel,
scuttering from contact as a crab retreats.
He strolls along the waterfront's old stench
to the balcony shade of a store in Soufrière
for the vantage-point of a municipal bench
in the volcanic furnace of its town square.
I just missed him as he darted the other way
in the bobbing crowd disgorging from the ferry
in blue Capri, just as he had fled the bay
of equally blue Campeche and rose-walled Cartagena,
his still elusive silence growing more scary
with every shouted question, because so many were
hurled at him, fleeing last century's crime.

I I

Walking the drenched ramparts, tugging his hat-brim,
maintaining his distance on the deaf page,
he cannot hear the insults hurled at him,
bracing for the sputtering brine. An image
more than a man, this white-drill figure
is smoke from a candle or stick of incense
or a mosquito coil, his fame is bigger

than his empire's now, its slow-burning conscience.
Smoke is the guilt of fire, so where he strolls
in Soufrière, in Sumatra, by any clogged basin
where hulks have foundered and garbage-smoke scrolls
its flag, he travels with its sin,
its collapsed mines, its fortunes sieved through bets.
He crosses a cricket field, overrun with stubble
launching a fleet of white, immaculate egrets.

III

The docks are dark and hooded, the warehouses
locked, and his insomnia rages like the moon
above the zinc roofs and spindly palms; he rouses
himself and dresses slowly in his small room:
he walks to the beach, the hills are brooding whales
against them drift the flambeaux and the lanterns
of the crab fishermen, the yachts have furled their sails,
he goes for this long walk when guilt returns;
indifferent to a constellation's Morse,
his resignation no longer sends
out fleets of power, an echo of that force
like dissipating spume on the night sand.
To the revolving beam of the Cyclopic lighthouse
he hears the suction of his soul's death-rattle,
but his is a history without remorse.
He hears the mocking cannonade of battle
from the charging breakers and sees the pluming hordes
of tribesmen galloping down the hills of sand
and hears the old phrase *"Peccavi. I have Sind."*
Think of the treaties signed by the same one-ringed hand,
think of the width its power could encompass
"one-seventh of the globe," we learnt in class.
Its promontories, docks, its towers and minarets

with the power that vanished as dew does from the grass
in the rising dawn of a sun that never sets.

IV

His fingers sticky with rum around a glass,
he can see the scorched square where a saint presides,
and its dry fountain where lizards shoot through grass
and the cathedral's candlelit insides.
In the sunlit bar the woman draws the blinds,
they look like the slitted lids of a lioness
(the yellow sheaves she hides in are his mind's)
the café is quiet, safe from the street's noise,
what he likes now confirms the aftermath
of great events; a tilted sail, a heron
elaborately picking out its path,
a beetle on its back, such things wear on
his concentrated care since the old scale
has been reduced (as are his circumstances)
on the croton bush by the window the tail
of the cat swishes as a dragonfly dances.
A vast and moral idleness stretching before him,
the café's demotic dialogues at peak hour.
The things he cherishes now are things that bore him,
and how powerlessness contains such power.
The costumes that he wore, and the roles that wore him.

In the mute roar of autumn, in the shrill
treble of the aspens, the basso of the holm-oaks,
in the silvery wandering aria of the Schuylkill,
the poplars choiring with a quillion strokes,
find love for what is not your land, a blazing country
in eastern Pennsylvania with the DVD going
in the rented burgundy Jeep, in the inexhaustible bounty
of fall with the image of Eakins' gentleman rowing
in his slim skiff whenever the trees divide
to reveal a river's serene surprise, flowing
through snow-flecked birches where Indian hunters glide.
The country has caught fire from the single spark
of a prophesying preacher, its embers glowing,
its clouds are smoke in the onrushing dark
a holocaust crackles in this golden oven
in which tribes were consumed, a debt still owing,
while a white country spire insists on heaven.

I

Afternoon. Durrants. Either the lift (elevator),
with shudder and rattle, its parenthesis,
or the brown bar with its glum, punctual waiter
and his whatever accent; biscuits and cheeses
with hot, broadening tea with blessing friends.
Summer London outside, guests, porter, taxis,
the consoling clichés you have come back for,
welcomed, but not absorbed, the little ecstasies
of recognition of home, almost, in the polite roar
of traffic towards dusk; here are all the props,
the elaborate breakfasts, kippers, sporting prints,
the ornate lettering on the smallest shops,
the morning papers and the sense of permanence
under every phrase. This is where it must start:
hereditary in each boy (or chap),
the stain that spreads invisibly from the heart,
like the red of Empire in a schoolroom's map.

II

What have these narrow streets, begrimed with age
and greasy with tradition, their knobbly names,
their pizza joints, their betting shops, that black garage,
the ping and rattle of mesmerizing games
on slot machines, to do with that England on each page
of my fifth-form anthology, now that my mind's
an ageing sea remembering its lines,
the scent and symmetry of Wyatt, Surrey?
Spring grass and roiling clouds dapple a county

with lines like a rutted road stuck in the memory
of a skylark's unheard song, a bounty
pungent as clover, the creak of a country cart
in Constable or John Clare. Words clear the page
like a burst of sparrows over a hedge
"but though from court to cottage he depart,
his saint is sure of his unspotted heart"
and the scent of petrol. Why do these lines
lie like barred sunlight on the lawn to cage
the strutting dove? My passing image in the shops, the signs.

With a change of government the permanent cobalt,
the promises we take with a pinch of salt,
with a change of government the permanent aquamarine,
with a reorganized cabinet the permanent violet,
the permanent lilac over the reef, the permanent flux
of ochre shallows, the torn bunting of the currents
and the receding banners of the breakers.
With a change in government no change in the cricket's
    chirrup,
the low, comical bellow of the bull, or
the astonishing symmetry of tossing horses.
With a change in government the haze of wide rain
which you begin to hear as the ruler hears the crowd
gathering under the balcony, the leader who has promised
the permanent cobalt of a change of government
with the lilac and violet of his cabinet's change.

What? You're going to be Superman at seventy-seven?
Got your weight down? Okay. You've lost seven pounds,
but what you've also lost is belief in heaven
as dear friends die. Still making his rounds,
the postman, the scyther, Basil, whatever you call him—
a cyclist silently exercising on Sunday
down a shade-striped avenue of casuarinas
with bursts of foam on the breakwater's wall. I'm
sure everyone knows it will happen one day,
the yachts, nodding agreement in all the marinas,
the blackbirds in frock coats, the frog's staccato hymn,
seven less pounds and you'll need a slimmer coffin.
You suffer from a furious itch that raises welts
on your neck and forearms, so now you swim
early in the morning to avoid the sun, fear melts
before daylight's beauty, despite all that coughing.

The sorrel rump of a mare in the bush,
her neck stretched out in a shuddering whinny
is straight out of Uccello or Marini,
this salt-promised morning on the road to the beach.
A fine mist carries me to other places—
that haze which means it is raining in Monchy,
and perhaps on the cobbled streets of (here memory pauses).
What was that seafront hotel facing Syracuse?
It will come back like her cheekbones, her face's
aboriginal symmetry, it will all come back,
the obsession that I prayed I would lose,
the voice that stirred like a low-tempered cello,
and the esplanade's name . . . help me, Muse.
Who'd have thought this could happen, the yellow
fading hotel, and now, Christ! her name?
Only the sun on the seafront stays the same
to an old man on a bench for whom the waves are not news.

In my wheelchair in the Virgin lounge at Vieuxfort,
I saw, sitting in her own wheelchair, her beauty
hunched like a crumpled flower, the one whom I thought
as the fire of my young life would do her duty
to be golden and beautiful and young forever
even as I aged. She was treble-chinned, old, her devastating
smile was netted in wrinkles, but I felt the fever
briefly returning as we sat there, crippled, hating
time and the lie of general pleasantries.
Small waves still break against the small stone pier
where a boatman left me in the orange peace
of dusk, a half-century ago, maybe happier
being erect, she like a deer in her shyness, I stalking
an impossible consummation; those who knew us
knew we would never be together, at least, not walking.
Now the silent knives from the intercom went through us.

All day I wish I was at Case-en-Bas,
passing incongruous cactus which grows in the north
in the chasm-deep ruts of the dry season
with the thunderous white horses that dissolve in froth,
and the bush that mimics them with white cotton
to the strengthening smell of kale from the bright
Atlantic, as the road-ruts level and you come upon
a view that dissolves into pure description,
a bay whose arc hints of an infinite
Africa. The trade wind tirelessly frets
the water, combers are long and the swells heave
with weed that smells, a smell nearly rotten
but tolerable soon. Light hurls its nets
over the whitecaps and seagulls grieve
over some common but irreplaceable loss
while a high, disdainful frigate-bird, a *ciseau*,
slides in the clouds then is lost with the forgotten
caravels, privateers, and other frigates
with the changing sails of the sky and a sea so
deep it has lost its stuttering memory of our hates.

32

Be happy now at Cap, for the simplest joys—
for a line of white egrets prompting the last word,
for the sea's recitation reentering my head
with questions it erases, canceling the demonic voice
by which I have recently been possessed; unheard,
it whispers the way the fiend does to a madman
who gibbers to his bloody hands that he was seized
the way the sea swivels in the conch's ear, like the roar
of applause that precedes the actor with increased
doubt to the pitch of paralyzed horror
that his prime is past. If it is true
that my gift has withered, that there's little left of it,
if this man is right then there's nothing else to do
but abandon poetry like a woman because you love it
and would not see her hurt, least of all by me;
so walk to the cliff's edge and soar above it,
the jealousy, the spite, the nastiness with the grace
of a frigate over Barrel of Beef, its rock;
be grateful that you wrote well in this place,
let the torn poems sail from you like a flock
of white egrets in a long last sigh of release.

I

The cruise-boats keep gliding along the brown canal
as quiet as prayer, the leaves are packed with peace,
the elegant house-fronts, repetitive and banal
as the hotel brochure, are still as an altarpiece.
We cruised it with Rufus Collins once, a white macaw
on his piratical shoulder. Rufus is gone.
Canals spread reflection, with calm at the core.
I reflect quietly on how soon I will be going.
I want the year 2009 to be as angled with light
as a Dutch interior or an alley by Vermeer,
to accept my enemy's atrabilious spite,
to paint and write well in what could be my last year.

II

Silly to think of a heritage when there isn't much,
though my mother whose surname was Marlin or Van
      der Mont
took pride in an ancestry she claimed was Dutch.
Now here in Amsterdam, her claim starts to mount.
Legitimate, illegitimate, I want to repaint
these rubicund Flemish faces, even if it's been done
by Frans Hals, by Rubens, by Rembrandt,
the clear gray eyes of Renée, the tree-shade on this side,
the chestnuts that glitter from the breakfast window,
why should I not claim them as fervently as
the pride of Alix Marlin an early widow,

as a creek in the Congo, if her joy was such?
I feel something ending here and something begun
the light strong leaves, the water muttering in Dutch,
the girls going by on bicycles in the sun.

For the crackle and hiss of the word "August,"
like a low bonfire on a beach, for the wriggling
of white masts in the marina on a Wednesday
after work, I would come back and forget the niggling
complaints of what the island lacks, how it is without
the certainties of cities, for a fisherman walking back
to this village with his jigging rod and a good catch
that blazes like rainbows when he shows it to you,
for the ember that goes out suddenly like a match
when the day and all that it brought is finished,
for the lights on the piers and for the first star
for whom my love of the island has never diminished
but will burn steadily when I am gone, wherever you are,
and for the lion's silhouette of Pigeon Island,
and your cat that presumes the posture of
a sphinx and for the long, empty sand
of your absence, for the word "August," like a moaning dove.

43 FORTY ACRES

to Barack Obama

Out of the turmoil emerges one emblem, an engraving—
a young Negro at dawn in straw hat and overalls,
an emblem of impossible prophecy: a crowd
dividing like the furrow which a mule has plowed,
parting for their president; a field of snow-flecked cotton
forty acres wide, of crows with predictable omens
that the young plowman ignores for his unforgotten
cotton-haired ancestors, while lined on one branch are a tense
court of bespectacled owls and, on the field's receding rim
is a gesticulating scarecrow stamping with rage at him
while the small plow continues on this lined page
beyond the moaning ground, the lynching tree, the tornado's
   black vengeance,
and the young plowman feels the change in his veins, heart,
   muscles, tendons,
till the field lies open like a flag as dawn's sure
light streaks the field and furrows wait for the sower.

"So the world is waiting for Obama," my barber said;
and the old fences in the village street and the flowers
brimming over the rusted zinc fences all acquired
a sheen like a visible sigh, and indoors,
in the small barbershop, an election poster
joined another showing all the various hairstyles
available to his young black clients that cost the
same no matter who you were—President of the U.S.—
head smooth as a bowling ball my barber smiles
"Is that a Muslim or African name, Obama?"
benign and gentle with his swift-snipping scissors,
"I wish him luck," and luck waits in each
gable-shadowed street that leads to the beach.
Polo loves politics, once in the glass
there were photos of Malcolm, King, Garvey, Frederick Douglass
frowning in the breadfruit window, also
the yapping dogs, the hoses, the church in Alabama.
Polo is young, black, bald under his baseball cap
but more than a barber he is delicate, adept
and when I leave his throne, shake shorn hair from my lap
I feel changed, like an election promise that is kept.

In the leathery closeness of the car through canefields
burdened with sweetness under the scudding stars,
I reflect on the bliss of failure, how it yields
no secret, no moral or blame while its suffering stays,
how every corner you christen now conceals a crisis.
On a hill the window-lit abbey of Mount Saint Benedict
passes like a ship in the night as a sickle moon rises
from conspiring, nodding cane and lights a hermit
crouched in his fetal cell as I did with my verses.
You drive towards cries and hugs that will comfort you
while the monk denies himself love that can contradict.
You remember those who supported and those who fought you
were stronger than wood or stone, you built a vision,
the lights of London, its bars, theaters, cathedrals,
that with the glass rolled downward like the night wind
in the canes, the treacherous joy with which a star falls,
mean even less now, what you have left behind
is the tacit pity of the heaven over Saint Paul's,
while from that clover-leaf highway rises
the loving city that takes you back as its son.

46

Here's what that bastard calls "the emptiness"—
that blue-green ridge with plunging slopes, the blossoms
like drooping chalices, of the African tulip, the noise
of a smoking torrent—it's his name for when rain comes
down the heights or gusts in sheets across the meadows
of the sea—"the emptiness," the phrase applies
to our pathetic, pompous cities, their fretwork balconies,
their retail stores blasting reggae, either India in the eyes
of uniformed schoolchildren or the emptiness. The image
is from Conrad, of a warship pointlessly firing
into the huge empty jungle; all the endeavors
of our lives are damned to nothing by the tiring
catalogue of a vicious talent that severs
itself from every attachment, a bitterness whose
poison is praised for its virulence. This verse
is part of the emptiness, as is the valley of Santa Cruz,
a genuine benediction as his is a genuine curse.

for Stephanos and Heather

It is coming with the first drops mottling the hot cement,
the patterns budding in the pool, with a horizon
as wide and refreshing as the rain-veiled Georgics,
with the upward swoop of the dove, with the heron
quickening its gawky stride; watch a sail
hide her face in mist and the barred sun shrivel
into gathering cumuli, those huge clouds
trawling gauze skirts of rain as camera-flashes
of lightning record the rattling thunder
and the lances of drizzle start marching.
                        But nothing can equal
the surge of another's presence, the separately beloved
whose reign is the rain's, whose weather is the fragrant darkness
of the parlor, in the kitchen, the lightning's cutlery. But O
when the bursting storm rattles the sky's ceiling
and her body draws closer as a vessel warping
into you, her port, her aisle, and she gently rocks,
her ribs brushing yours, O, on your wedding day
may the worried banners of cirrus fade as the storm moves away.

to Robert Antoni

There was a roar outside like a rocket arching
over the roofs this morning, then, under
the black iron balconies, a brass band, marching,
detonated for some saint or labor union,
defending Catalonia with civic thunder.
You smiled down at them with their banners and sashes;
but all you did in Barcelona was cough,
like one of those veterans with mournful moustaches
left over from the Civil War. That is not enough
for such a great city, but you take time in portions,
one cough at a time, your personal thunder
that turns compassionate heads. What I had waited
for was the name to be a banner over every street,
crucifixions on velvet, candles and purple crêpe
for the crowd in the plaza to leap to its feet
at the flourish and trembling stasis of the matador's cape.
I could never join in the parade; I can't walk fast.
Such is time's ordinance. Lungs that rattle, eyes
that run. Now Barcelona is part of the past.

for Aimé Césaire

I sent you, in Martinique, *maître*,
the unfolding letter of a sail, a letter
beyond the lines of blindingly white breakers,
of lace-laden surplices and congregational shale.
I did not send any letter, though it flailed on the wind,
your island is always in the haze of my mind
with the blown-about sea-birds
in their creole clatter of vowels, *maître* among makers,
whom the reef recites when the copper sea-almonds blaze,
beacons to distant Dakar, and the dolphin's acres.

This page is a cloud between whose fraying edges
a headland with mountains appears brokenly
then is hidden again until what emerges
from the now cloudless blue is the grooved sea
and the whole self-naming island, its ochre verges,
its shadow-plunged valleys and a coiled road
threading the fishing villages, the white, silent surges
of combers along the coast, where a line of gulls has arrowed
into the widening harbor of a town with no noise,
its streets growing closer like print you can now read,
two cruise ships, schooners, a tug, ancestral canoes,
as a cloud slowly covers the page and it goes
white again and the book comes to a close.

D

E

F

G

H

I

M

N

O

P

R

T

Y